On Populist Reason

On Populist Reason

ERNESTO LACLAU

VERSO

London • New York

First published by Verso 2005
This paperback edition published by Verso 2007
© Ernesto Laclau 2005, 2007
All rights reserved

5 7 9 10 8 6 4

Verso
UK: 6 Meard Street, London W1F 0EG
USA: 180 Varick Street, New York, NY 10014-4606
www.versobooks.com

Verso is the imprint of New Left Books

ISBN-13: 978-1-84467-186-1

British Library Cataloguing in Publication Data
A catalogue record for this book is available from the British Library

Library of Congress Cataloging-in-Publication Data
A catalog record for this book is available from the Library of Congress

Printed and bound in the USA by Maple Press

To Chantal,
after 30 years

Contents

Preface

The main issue addressed in this book is the nature and logics of the formation of collective identities. My whole approach has grown out of a basic dissatisfaction with sociological perspectives which either considered the group as the basic unit of social analysis, or tried to transcend that unit by locating it within wider functionalist or structuralist paradigms. The logics that those types of social functioning presuppose are, in my view, too simple and uniform to capture the variety of movements involved in identity construction. Needless to say, methodological individualism in any of its variants – rational choice included – does not provide any alternative to the kind of paradigm that I am trying to put into question.

The route I have tried to follow in order to address these issues is a bifurcated one. The first path is to split the unity of the *group* into smaller unities that we have called *demands*: the unity of the group is, in my view, the result of an articulation of demands. This articulation, however, does not correspond to a stable and positive configuration which could be grasped as a unified whole: on the contrary, since it is in the nature of all demands to present claims to a certain established order, it is in a peculiar relation with that order, being both inside and outside it. As this order cannot fully absorb the demand, it cannot constitute itself as a

coherent totality; the demand, however, requires some kind of totalization if it is going to crystallize in something which is inscribable as a
claim within the 'system'. All these ambiguous and contradictory movements come down to the various forms of articulation between logic of
difference and logic of equivalence, discussed in Chapter 4. As I argue
there, the impossibility of fixing the unity of a social formation in any
conceptually graspable object leads to the centrality of *naming* in constituting that unity, while the need for a social cement to assemble the
heterogeneous elements once their logic of articulation (functionalist or
structuralist) no longer gives this *affect* its centrality in social explanation.
Freud had already clearly understood it: the social bond is a libidinal one.
My study is completed by an expansion of the categories elaborated in
Chapter 4 – logics of difference and equivalence, empty signifiers,
hegemony – to a wider range of political phenomena: thus in Chapter 5
I discuss the notions of floating signifiers and social heterogeneity, and
in Chapter 6 those of representation and democracy.

So why address these issues through a discussion of populism?
Because of the suspicion, which I have had for a long time, that in the
dismissal of populism far more is involved than the relegation of a
peripheral set of phenomena to the margins of social explanation. What
is involved in such a disdainful rejection is, I think, the dismissal of
politics *tout court*, and the assertion that the management of community
is the concern of an administrative power whose source of legitimacy is
a proper knowledge of what a 'good' community is. This has been,
throughout the centuries, the discourse of 'political philosophy', first
instituted by Plato. 'Populism' was always linked to a dangerous excess,
which puts the clear-cut moulds of a rational community into question.
So my task, as I conceived it, was to bring to light the specific logics
inherent in that excess, and to argue that, far from corresponding to
marginal phenomena, they are inscribed in the actual working of *any*
communitarian space. With this is mind, I show how, throughout nineteenth-century discussions on mass psychology, there was a progressive
internalization of those features concerning the 'crowd', which at the
beginning – in the work of Hyppolite Taine, for example – were seen as

an unassimilable excess, but which, as Freud's *Group Psychology* showed, are inherent to any social identity formation. I hope to accomplish this in Part I. Chapter 7 deals with historical cases which illustrate the conditions of emergence of popular identities, while Chapter 8 considers the limits in the constitution of popular identities.

One consequence of this intervention is that the referent of 'populism' becomes blurred, because many phenomena which were not traditionally considered populist come under that umbrella in our analysis. Here there is a potential criticism of my approach, to which I can only respond that the referent of 'populism' in social analysis has always been ambiguous and vague. A brief glance at the literature on populism – discussed in Chapter 1 – suffices to show that it is full of references to the evanescence of the concept and the imprecision of its limits. My attempt has not been to find the *true* referent of populism, but to do the opposite: to show that populism has no referential unity because it is ascribed not to a delimitable phenomenon but to a social logic whose effects cut across many phenomena. Populism is, quite simply, a way of constructing the political.

There are many people who, through their work or through personal conversations over the years, have contributed to shaping my view on these subjects. I will not attempt to list them – any list will always necessarily be incomplete. I have recognized the most important intellectual debts through my quotations in the text. There are a few people, however, who cannot be omitted. There are two contexts within which these ideas have been discussed over the years and which were particularly fruitful for the development of my thought: one is the doctoral seminar on Ideology and Discourse Analysis at the University of Essex, organized by Aletta Norval, David Howarth and Jason Glynos; the other is the graduate seminar on Rhetoric, Psychoanalysis and Politics at the Department of Comparative Literature, State University of New York at Buffalo, which I organized together with my colleague Joan Copjec. My other two main expressions of gratitude go to Chantal Mouffe, whose encouragement and commentaries on my text have been a constant source of stimulus for my work; and to Noreen Harburt, from the Centre for Theoretical Studies, University of Essex, whose technical skills in giving shape to my manuscript have proved – on this occasion, as in numerous others – invaluable. I also want to thank my copy editor, Gillian Beaumont, for her extremely efficient work in improving the English of my manuscript and for her several very useful editorial comments.

Evanston, November 2004

Part I

THE DENIGRATION OF THE MASSES

1

Populism: Ambiguities and Paradoxes

Populism, as a category of political analysis, confronts us with rather idiosyncratic problems. On the one hand it is a recurrent notion, one which is not only in widespread use – being part of the description of a large variety of political movements – but also one which tries to capture something about the latter which is quite central. Midway between the descriptive and the normative, 'populism' intends to grasp something crucially significant about the political and ideological realities to which it refers. The apparent vagueness of the concept is not translated into any doubt concerning the importance of its attributive function. We are far from clear, however, about the *content* of that attribution. A persistent feature of the literature on populism is its reluctance – or difficulty – in giving the concept any precise meaning. Notional clarity – let alone definition – is conspicuously absent from this domain. Most of the time, conceptual apprehension is replaced by appeals to a non-verbalized intuition, or by descriptive enumerations of a variety of 'relevant features' – a relevance which is undermined, in the very gesture which asserts it, by reference to a proliferation of exceptions. Here is a typical example of an intellectual strategy dealing with 'populism' in the existing literature:

Populism itself tends to deny any identification with or classification into the Right/Left dichotomy. It is a multiclass movement, although not all multiclass movements may be considered populist. Populism probably defies any comprehensive definition. Leaving aside this problem for the moment, populism usually includes contrasting components such as a claim for equality of political rights and universal participation for the common people, but fused with some sort of authoritarianism often under charismatic leadership. It also includes socialist demands (or at least a claim for social justice), vigorous defense of small property, strong nationalist components, and denial of the importance of class. It is accompanied with the affirmation of the rights of the common people as against the privileged interest groups, usually considered inimical to the people and the nation. Any of these elements may be stressed according to cultural and social conditions, but they are all present in most populist movements.[1]

The reader will not find any difficulty in extending Germani's list of relevant features or, on the contrary, finding populist movements where several of them are missing. In that case, the only thing we are left with is the impossibility of defining the term – not a very satisfactory situation as far as social analysis is concerned.

I would like, right from the beginning, to advance a hypothesis which will guide our theoretical exploration: that the impasse that Political Theory experiences in relation to populism is far from accidental, for it is rooted in the limitation of the ontological tools currently available to political analysis; that 'populism', as the locus of a theoretical stumbling block, reflects some of the limits inherent in the ways in which Political Theory has approached the question of how social agents 'totalize' the ensemble of their political experience. To develop this hypothesis, I shall start by considering some of the attempts, in the current literature, to deal with the apparent intractability of the question of populism. I shall take as examples the early work of Margaret Canovan,[2] and some of the essays in a well-known book on the subject edited by Ghita Ionescu and Ernest Gellner.[3]

Impasses in the literature on populism

Given the 'vagueness' of the concept of populism and the multiplicity of phenomena which have been subsumed under this label, one would think that a first possible intellectual strategy would be not to try to go beyond the multiplicity itself – that is, to stay within it, to analyse the gamut of empirical cases that it embraces, and to derive whatever conclusions are possible from a limited and descriptive comparison between them. This is what Canovan tries to do in her work, which covers phenomena as disparate as American populism, the Russian *narodniki*, the European agrarian movements of the aftermath of the First World War, Social Credit in Alberta and Peronism in Argentina (among others).

It is important to concentrate for a moment on the way Canovan deals with this diversity (that is, how she tries to master it through a typology) and on the conclusions that she derives from it. Canovan is perfectly aware of the true dimensions of the diversity, which are revealed, to start with, in the plurality of definitions of populism to be found in the literature. This is the list she provides:

1. 'The socialism which [emerges] in backward peasant countries facing the problems of modernisation.'
2. 'Basically the ideology of small rural people threatened by encroaching industrial and financial capital.'
3. 'Basically ... a rural movement seeking to realise traditional values in a changing society.'
4. 'The belief that the majority opinion of the people is checked by an elitist minority.'
5. 'Any creed or movement based on the following major premise: virtue resides in the simple people, who are the overwhelming majority, and in their collective traditions.'
6. 'Populism proclaims that the will of the people as such is supreme over every other standard.'

7. 'A political movement which enjoys the support of the mass of the urban working class and/or peasantry but which does not result from the autonomous organizational power of either of these two sectors.'[4]

Confronted with such a variety, Canovan finds it important to distinguish between an agrarian populism and one which is not necessarily rural but essentially political, and based on the relation between 'the people' and the elites. Taking this distinction as a starting point, she draws the following typology:

Agrarian populisms
1. farmers' radicalism (eg. the US People's Party)
2. peasant movements (eg. The Eastern European Green Rising)
3. intellectual agrarian socialism (eg. the *narodniki*)

Political populisms
4. populist dictatorship (eg. Perón)
5. populist democracy (ie. calls for referendums and 'participation')
6. reactionary populisms (eg. George Wallace and his followers)
7. politicians' populism (ie. broad non ideological coalition-building that draws on the unificatory appeal of 'the people')[5]

The first thing to note is that this typology lacks any coherent criterion around which its distinctions are established. In what sense are agrarian populisms not political? And what is the relationship between the social and political aspects of the 'political' populisms which bring about a model of political mobilization that is different from the agrarian one? Everything happens as if Canovan had simply chosen the impressionistically more visible features of a series of movements taken at random, and moulded her distinctive types on their differences. But this hardly constitutes a typology worth the name. What does guarantee that the categories are exclusive and do not overlap with each other (which, as a matter of fact, is exactly what happens, as Canovan herself recognizes)? It could perhaps be argued that what Canovan is providing is not a typology, in the strong sense of the term, but, rather, a map of the linguistic dispersion that has governed the uses of the term 'populism'. Her allusion to Wittgenstein's 'family resemblances' would seem, to some extent, to point in this direction. But even if this is the case, the logics governing that dispersion require far more precision than Canovan provides. It is not necessary that the features constituting a populist syndrome be reduced to a logically unified model, but at least we should be able to understand what are the family resemblances which, in each case, have governed the circulation of the concept. Canovan, for instance, points out that the populist movement in the USA was not only a farmers' agrarian movement but also had 'a prominent political aspect as a grass-root revolt against the elite or plutocrats, politicians and experts'[6] inspired by Jacksonian democracy. Now, is she not telling us, in that case, that the reason we should call that movement 'populist' is to be found not in its (agrarian) social base but in an inflection of that base by a particular political logic – a political logic which is present in movements which are, socially speaking, quite heterogeneous?

At various points in her analysis, Canovan is on the brink of attributing the specificity of populism to the political logics organizing *any* social content rather than to the contents themselves. Thus, for instance, she asserts that the two features universally present in populism are the appeal to the people and anti-elitism.[7] She goes so far as to remark that neither feature can be permanently ascribed to any particular social or political (ideological) content. This, one would have thought, would open the way to a determination of both features in terms of political logics rather than social contents. Nothing of the kind happens, however, for Canovan finds in that lack of social determinacy a drawback that considerably reduces the usefulness of the categories corresponding to her two universally present features. Thus: 'exaltation of this ambiguous "people" can take a variety of forms. Since it embraces everything from the cynical manipulations of the Peronist rhetoric to the humble self-abasement of the *narodniki*, it does not give much definition to the concept of populism.'[8] And the situation is only marginally better in the case of anti-elitism.[9]

If Canovan's analysis none the less has the merit of not trying to eliminate the multiplicity of forms that populism has historically taken – and,
in this sense, avoids the worst kind of reductionism – most of the literature in the field has not resisted the temptation of ascribing to populism
some particular social content. Donald MacRae, for instance, writes:

> But surely we will automatically and correctly use the term populist when,
> under the threat of some kind of modernization, industrialism, call it what
> you will, a predominantly agricultural segment of society asserts as its charter
> of political action its belief in a community and (usually) a *Volk* as uniquely
> virtuous, it is egalitarian and against all and any élite, looks to a mythical past
> to regenerate the present and confounds usurpation and alien conspiracy,
> refuses to accept any doctrine of social, political or historical inevitability
> and, in consequence, turns to belief in an instant, imminent apocalypse
> mediated by the charisma of heroic leaders and legislators – a kind of new
> Lycurgus. If with all this we find a movement of short-term association
> for political ends to be achieved by state intervention but not a real,
> serious political party, then populism is present in its most typical form.[10]

It comes as no surprise that, after such a detailed description of true
populism, MacRae finds some difficulties in applying his category to
'actually existing' populisms. As a result, he has to accept that contemporary populisms have little in common with his ideal model:

> The populism of the late twentieth century has not, I think, to a very
> important degree been communicated from either Russia or America.
> Rather have items of the European thought world been independently
> spread and re-combined to form various indigenous populisms. In these
> certain of the ambiguities of the older populisms have been compounded
> with both primitivist and progressivist elements. Race (cf. Négritude) and
> religion (especially Islam, but also Buddhism, millenarian Christianity and
> Hinduism) have been added to the mix of archaic virtue and exemplary
> personality. Agrarian primitivism is a diminished force – though in India
> it appears to flourish. Conspiracy and usurpation are conflated in the

various theories about neo-colonialism and the actions of the CIA. The 'asymmetry of civic principles' has become the norm of populist 'direct action'. Spontaneity and integrity are praised, but now they are particularly identified with the young, so that the ideal youth (a familiar figure in myth) has largely replaced the yeoman and the untutored peasant as a cult personality. Modern Marxism in its lurch towards the 'young Marx' has become populistic. There is populism in the consensual concerns and the diffuse a-politicism of the 'New Left'.[11]

The problem with this chaotic enumeration is, of course, that the movements alluded to above have few or none of the features of populism as defined in MacRae's essay. If they are none the less called populist, it is because they are supposed to share something with classical populism, but as to the nature of this something, we are left entirely in the dark.

This is a general characteristic of the literature on populism: the more determinations are included in the general concept, the less that concept is able to hegemonize the concrete analyses. An extreme example is Peter Wiles's essay 'A Syndrome, not a Doctrine'.[12] The concept of populism is elaborated in great detail: twenty-four features which cover a large variety of dimensions, ranging from its not being revolutionary and its opposition to class war, to its adoption of the small co-operative as an economic ideal type, and its being religious, but opposed to the religious establishment. Unsurprisingly, Wiles cannot do otherwise than devote the second part of his essay to the analysis of the exceptions. These are so abundant that one starts to wonder if there is a single political movement which presents all twenty-four features of Wiles's model. He does not even deprive himself of self-contradiction. Thus, we are given notice on page 176 that 'It is also difficult for populism to be proletarian. Traditional thinking is less common among proletarians than artisans. Their work is subject to large-scale discipline, which in fact contradicts the major premise.'

Two pages later, however, we are told that 'Socialism is much more distant than fascism; as can be seen from those quintessential socialists Marx, the Webbs and Stalin. But Lenin admitted a large influx of Narodnik and indeed populism in ideas and manners. He has been followed by other communists, notably Aldo [*sic!*] Gramsci and Mao Tse-Tung.' One wonders what else Lenin and Gramsci were doing but trying to build up a proletarian hegemony.

The sheer absurdity of Wiles's exercise is revealed even more clearly when he tries to list the movements that he considers to be populistic: 'These people and movements, then, are populist, and have much in common: the Levellers; the Diggers; the Chartists (Moral and Physical Force); the Narodniki; the US populists; the Socialist-Revolutionaries; Gandhi; Sinn Fein; the Iron Guard; Social Credit in Alberta; Cárdenas; Haya de la Torre; the CCF in Saskatchewan; Poujade; Belaúnde, Nyerere.'[13] We are not told anything, of course, about that 'much in common' that these leaders and movements are supposed to have – a minimal acquaintance with them is enough to tell us that it cannot, anyway, be the syndrome described at the beginning of Wiles's essay. So his final remark – '(n)o historian can neglect the concept [of populism] as a tool of understanding' – invites the melancholic commentary that in order to neglect a concept, one needs to have it in the first place.

In all the texts considered so far, what is specific about populism – its defining dimension – has been *systematically* avoided. We should start asking ourselves whether the reason for this systematicity does not perhaps lie in some unformulated political prejudices guiding the mind of political analysts. In a moment I shall indicate that the main merit of Peter Worsley's contribution to the debate has been to start moving away from those presuppositions. Before that, however, I should say something about the presuppositions themselves; this I can do by referring to another essay in the Ionescu and Gellner volume: Kenneth Minogue's on 'Populism as a Political Movement'.[14]

There are two distinctions on which Minogue grounds his analysis. The first is the distinction between *rhetoric* and *ideology*: 'We must distinguish carefully between the *rhetoric* used by members of a movement – which may be randomly plagiarized from anywhere according to the needs of the movement and the *ideology* which expresses the deeper current of the movement.'[15] The second is the distinction between a movement and its ideology. Although Minogue is by no means consistent in his use of these distinctions, it is clear that there is, for him, a normative gradation, the lowest level being ascribed to rhetoric and the higher to the movement, with ideology remaining in an uneasy intermediate situation between being part of the institutionalized forms of the movement and degenerating into mere rhetoric. The latter is the manifest destiny of populism, which is an essentially transient political formation. Speaking of American populism, Minogue asserts:

> Here then, we have a movement with two significant characteristics: it disappeared very fast once conditions changed, and its ideology was a patchwork quilt of borrowed elements; indeed, to press hard on the terminology used in section I, it didn't have an ideology in any serious sense, merely a rhetoric. It did not put down deep roots, because there was little to grow at all – merely a hastily constructed rationalisation of difficult times, which could be abandoned once things improved.[16]

And this is what he has to say about Third World ideologies:

> By contrast with established European ideologies, these beliefs have the look of umbrellas hoisted according to the exigencies of the moment but disposable without regret as circumstances change. And this seems entirely sensible as a reaction to the alternation of despair and hope which the peripheral poor of an industrialised world must experience. They cannot afford to be doctrinaire; pragmatism must be the single thread of their behaviour.... I think, then, that we may legitimately rationalise the growing tendency to use the term 'populism' to cover many and various movements as a recognition of this particular character of political ideas in the modern world. Populism is a type of movement found among those aware of belonging to the poor periphery of an industrial system; in this sense, it may be taken as a reaction to industrialism. But it is a reaction of those whose profoundest impulse may often be to industrialise: it is only if you cannot join them (and until you can) that you attack them. And it is this ambivalence which accounts for the intellectual emptiness of populist movements.[17]

Let us concentrate on these distinctions, and on the intellectual strategies which ground them. 'Ideology' can be considered as distinct from the rhetoric involved in political action only if rhetoric is understood as a pure adornment of language which in no way affects the contents transmitted by it. This is the most classical conception of rhetoric, grounded in its differentiation from *logic*. The sociological equivalent of that to which rhetoric is opposed is a notion of social actors as constituted around well-defined interests and rationally negotiating with an external milieu. For such a vision of society, the image of social agents whose identities are constituted around diffuse populist symbols can only be an expression of irrationality. The ethical denigration that Minogue's essay reflects is in fact shared by a great deal of the literature on populism. What happens, however, if the field of logic fails to constitute itself as a closed order, and rhetorical devices are necessary to bring about that closure? In that case, the rhetorical devices themselves – metaphor, metonymy, synecdoche, catachresis – become instruments of an expanded social rationality, and we are no longer able to dismiss an ideological interpellation as *merely* rhetorical. So the imprecision and emptiness of populist political symbols cannot be dismissed so easily: everything depends on the performative act that such an emptiness brings about. About American populists, for instance, Minogue asserts:

> The American populists seem to have been responding, most immediately, to the concrete situation of rural poverty and low prices for what they produced. ... The point is that any movement will select its enemies with an eye to the acquisition of allies; and to proclaim that they were reacting to 'industrial America' gave populists the possibility of alliance with other non-populist groups in American society such as city liberals and urban socialists and anarchists.[18]

But obviously, if through rhetorical operations they managed to constitute broad popular identities which cut across many sectors of the population, *they actually constituted populist subjects*, and there is no point in dismissing this as mere rhetoric. Far from being a parasite of ideology, rhetoric would actually be the anatomy of the ideological world.

The same can be said of the distinction between 'ideology' and 'movement', which is crucial to Minogue's argument – he warns us against the danger, for the student of a movement, of 'surrendering to its ideology'.[19] How, however, do we separate ideology from movement so strictly? The distinction itself evokes only too clearly an old differentiation between ideas in people's heads and actions in which they participate. But this distinction is untenable. Since Wittgenstein, we know that language games comprise both linguistic exchanges and actions in which they are embedded, and speech-act theory has put on a new footing the study of the discursive sequences constituting social institutionalized life. It is in that sense that Chantal Mouffe and I have defined discourses as structured totalities articulating both linguistic and non-linguistic elements.[20] From this point of view, the distinction between a movement and its ideology is not only hopeless, but also irrelevant – what matters is the determination of the discursive sequences through which a social force or movement carries out its overall political performance.

It is evident that my objective in questioning Minogue's distinctions – which are just examples of widespread attitudes in relation to populism – has been, to a large extent, to invert the analytical perspective: instead of starting with a model of political rationality which sees populism in terms of what it lacks – its vagueness, its ideological emptiness, its anti-intellectualism, its transitory character – to enlarge the model or rationality in terms of a generalized rhetoric (what, as we shall see, can be called 'hegemony') so that populism appears as a distinctive and always present possibility of structuration of political life. An approach to populism in terms of abnormality, deviance or manipulation is strictly incompatible with our theoretical strategy.

This is why I find Peter Worsley's essay 'The Concept of Populism'[21] particularly refreshing. Although his intervention stops short of moving from a mainly descriptive exercise to one that attempts to apprehend the specificity of populism *conceptually*, all the incipient noises that he makes in that direction are, I think, fundamentally sound. Three of these moves are particularly promising.

1. He moves from the mere analysis of the content of ideas to the role that they play in a particular cultural context – a role which modifies not only their *uses* but also their very intellectual content.

> It is suggested here, *per contra*, that ideas, in the process of becoming absorbed into successive cultural contexts, different from those in which they were engendered or have hitherto flourished, not only assume a different sociological significance in so far as they will be differently *used* by being incorporated within new frameworks of action, but will be also modified *qua* ideas, since they must necessarily be articulated with other psychic furniture: pre-existing 'interests', cognitive elements and structures, effectual dispositions, etc., which are all part of the receiving *milieu*. The 'original' ideas must intrinsically, therefore, be modified in the process and become *different ideas*.[22]

Now, this is quite important. The task is not so much to compare systems of ideas *qua* ideas as to explore their performative dimensions. Populism's relative ideological simplicity and emptiness, for instance, which is in most cases the prelude to its elitist dismissal, should be approached in terms of what those processes of simplification and emptying attempt to perform – that is to say, the social rationality they express.

2. Worsley sees populism not as a *type* of organization or ideology to be compared with other types such as liberalism, conservatism, communism or socialism, but as a *dimension of political culture* which can be present in movements of quite different ideological sign:

> The populist syndrome ... is much wider than its particular manifestation in the form or context of any particular policy, or of any particular kind of overall ideological system or type of polity: democracy, totalitarianism, etc. This suggests that populism is better regarded as an emphasis, a dimension of political culture in general, not simply as a particular kind of overall ideological system or type of organisation.

Of course, as with all ideal types, it may be very closely approximated to by some political cultures and structures, such as those hitherto labelled 'populist'.[23]

This move is crucial. For if Worsley is correct – as I think he is – then the inanity of the whole exercise of trying to identify the universal contents of populism becomes evident: as we have seen, it has repeatedly led to attempts to identify the social base of populism – only to find out a moment later that one cannot but continue calling 'populist' movements with entirely disparate social bases. But, of course, if one tries to avoid this pitfall by identifying populism with a *dimension* that cuts across ideological and social differences, one is burdened with the task of specifying what that dimension is – something Worsley does not really do, at least in a sufficient and convincing way.

3. These two departures from the classical approach allow Worsley to make a set of other potentially fruitful moves. I shall mention just two. The first is the assertion that, for Third World populisms: 'socio-economic classes are not the crucial social entities that they are in developed countries.... The class struggle is therefore an irrelevant conception.'[24]

Worsley is, of course, referring to Third World ideologies, not giving his own opinion. However, his critical analysis concerning the limits of Lenin's conception of the overlapping, in the Russian peasantry, of socio-economic distinctions and socio-political solidarities suggests that when he discusses the rejection of class struggle by Third World populism he is not just giving an ethnographic account of some form of 'false consciousness', but pointing to a real difficulty in generalizing 'class struggle' as a universal motto of political mobilization.

The second move is his effort to avoid any easy reductionist attempt at seeing a spurious dimension of manipulation as necessarily constitutive of populism. He asserts:

It would be desirable ... to alter part of Shils's definition of populism so that – without eliminating 'pseudo-participation' (demagogy, 'government by television, etc.) – we could also include, and distinguish, genuine and effective popular participation. 'Populism', then, would refer not only to 'direct' relationships between people and leadership (which must, inevitably, in any complex, large-scale society, be predominantly sheer mystification or symbolism), but, more widely, to popular participation in general (including pseudo-participation).[25]

This also is important, for it makes possible the elimination from the analysis of populism of any *necessary* attitude of ethical condemnation – an attitude which, as we have seen, has been at the root of many apparently 'objective' analyses.

Searching for an alternative approach

From this rapid and obviously incomplete exploration of the literature, we can now move on to the search for an alternative perspective which attempts to avoid the blind alleys described above. To do this, we must start by questioning – in some cases inverting – the basic presuppositions of the analysis which has led to them. Two basic points should be taken into account.

1. We have, in the first place, to ask ourselves whether the impossibility (or near impossibility) of defining populism does not result from describing it in such a way that any conceptual apprehension of the kind of rationality inherent to its political logic has been excluded a priori. I think that this is actually the case. If populism is described merely in terms of 'vagueness', 'imprecision', 'intellectual poverty', purely 'transient' as a phenomenon, 'manipulative' in its procedures, and so on, there is no way of determining its *differentia specifica* in positive terms. The whole exercise seems to aim, on the contrary, at separating what is rational and conceptually apprehensible in political action from its dichotomic opposite: a populism conceived as irrational and undefinable. Once this strategic intellectual decision has been taken, it is only natural that the question 'what is populism?' should be replaced by a

different one: 'to what social and ideological reality does populism *apply*?' Having been deprived of all intrinsic rationality, the *explanans* can only be entirely external to the *explanandum*. But, since applying a category is still to assume that there is some kind of external link that justifies the application, the question is usually replaced by a third one: 'of what social reality or situation is populism the *expression*?' At this stage, populism is truly relegated to a mere epiphenomenal level. For this approach, there is nothing in the populist *form* which requires explanation – the question 'why could some political alternatives or aims be expressed only through populist means?' does not even arise. The only thing we are talking about are the social *contents* (class or other sectorial interests) which populism expresses, while we are left in the dark as to why that form of expression is necessary. We are in a similar situation to that described by Marx in relation to the theory of value in classical Political Economy: it was able to show that labour is the *substance* of value, but not to explain why this underlying substance expresses itself under the *form* of an exchange of equivalents. At this point we are usually left with the unpalatable alternatives that we have reviewed: either to restrict populism to one of its historical variants, or to attempt a general definition which will always be too narrow. In the latter case, authors normally turn to the self-defeating exercise referred to above: listing under the label 'populism' a series of quite disparate movements, while not saying anything about what the meaning of that label would be.

2. A first step away from this discursive denigration of populism is not, however, to question the categories used in its description – 'vagueness', 'imprecision', and so on – but to take them at face value while rejecting the prejudices which are at the root of their dismissal. That is: instead of counterposing 'vagueness' to a mature political logic governed by a high degree of precise institutional determination, we should start asking ourselves a different and more basic set of questions: 'is not the "vagueness" of populist discourses the consequence of social reality itself being, in some situations, vague and undetermined?' And in that case, 'wouldn't

populism be, rather than a clumsy political and ideological operation, a performative act endowed with a rationality of its own – that is to say, in some situations, vagueness is a precondition to constructing relevant political meanings?' Finally, 'is populism really a transitional moment derived from the immaturity of social actors and bound to be super-seded at a later stage, or is it, rather, a constant dimension of political action which necessarily arises (in different degrees) in all political dis-courses, subverting and complicating the operations of the so-called "more mature" ideologies?' Let us give an example.

Populism, it is argued, 'simplifies' the political space, replacing a complex set of differences and determinations by a stark dichotomy whose two poles are necessarily imprecise. In 1945, for instance, General Perón took a nationalistic stand and asserted that the Argentinian option was to choose between Braden (the American ambassador) and Perón. And, as is well known, this personalized alternative features in other discourses through dichotomies such as the people versus the oligarchy, toiling masses versus exploiters, and so on. As we can see, there is in these dichotomies, as in those which constitute any politico-ideological frontier, a simplification of the political space (all social singularities tend to group themselves around one or the other of the poles of the dichotomy), and the terms designating both poles have necessarily to be imprecise (otherwise they could not cover all the particularities that they are supposed to regroup). If things are so, however, is not this logic of simplification, and of making some terms imprecise, the very condition of political action? Only in an impossible world in which politics would have been entirely replaced by administration, in which piecemeal engi-neering in dealing with particularized differences would have totally done away with antagonistic dichotomies, would we find that 'imprecision' and 'simplification' would really have been eradicated from the public sphere. In that case, however, the trademark of populism would be just the special emphasis on a political logic which, as such, is a necessary ingredient of politics *tout court*.

Another way of dismissing populism, as we have seen, is to relegate it to 'mere rhetoric'. But, as we have also pointed out, the tropological movement, far from being a mere adornment of a social reality which could be described in non-rhetorical terms, can be seen as the very logic of constitution of political identities. Let us just take the case of metaphor. As we know, metaphor establishes a relation of substitution between terms on the basis of the principle of *analogy*. Now, as I have just said, in any dichotomic structure, a set of particular identities or interests tend to regroup themselves as equivalential differences around one of the poles of the dichotomy. For instance, the wrongs experienced by various sections of 'the people' will be seen as equivalent to each other *vis-à-vis* the 'oligarchy'. But this is simply to say that they are all *analogous* with each other in their confrontation with oligarchic power. And what is this but a metaphorical reaggregation? Needless to say, the breaking of those equivalences in the construction of a more institutionalist discourse would proceed through different but equally rhetorical devices. So far from these devices being *mere* rhetoric, they are inherent in the logics presiding over the constitution and dissolution of *any* political space.

So we can say that progress in understanding populism requires, as a *sine qua non*, rescuing it from its marginal position within the discourse of the social sciences – the latter having confined it to the realm of the non-thinkable, to being the simple opposite of political forms dignified with the status of a full rationality. I should stress that this relegation has been possible only because, from the very beginning, a strong element of ethical condemnation has been present in the consideration of populistic movements. Populism has not only been demoted: it has also been denigrated. Its dismissal has been part of the discursive construction of a certain normality, of an ascetic political universe from which its dangerous logics had to be excluded. In this respect, however, the basic strategies of the anti-populist onslaught are inscribed in another, wider debate, which was the *grande peur* of the nineteenth-century social sciences: the whole discussion concerning 'mass psychology'. This debate, which is paradigmatic for our theme, can to a large extent be seen as the history of the constitution and dissolution of a social frontier separating the normal from the pathological. It was in the course of this discussion that a set of distinctions and oppositions were established that were going to operate as a matrix out of which a whole perspective concerning '*aberrant*' political phenomena – populism included – was organized. The consideration of this matrix will be my starting point. I shall begin with the analysis of a classical text which was at the epicentre of this intellectual history: Gustave Le Bon's *The Crowd*.

2

Le Bon: Suggestion and Distorted Representations

Gustave Le Bon's famous book *The Crowd*[1] is located at an intellectual crossroads. In one sense, it is an extreme version of the way the nineteenth century addressed the new phenomena of mass psychology as belonging to the pathological realm; however, it no longer considers such phenomena as contingent aberrations destined to disappear: they have become permanent features of modern society. As such, they cannot be dismissed and summarily condemned, but have to become the objects of a new technology of power: 'Crowds are somewhat like the sphinx of ancient fable: it is necessary to arrive at a solution of the problems offered by their psychology or to resign ourselves to being devoured by them.'[2] In order to carry out this scientific endeavour, Le Bon drew the most systematic picture of mass psychology which had yet been offered – a picture which met with instantaneous and lasting success, and was admired by many people (Freud among them). The keynote of his analysis was the notion of 'suggestion', to which we will return later. Our point of departure, however, will be the consideration of how suggestion operates, according to Le Bon, in a limited terrain, that of 'images, words and formulas', because here he touches a set of issues which will be crucial to my discussion of populism in Part II of this book.

For Le Bon, the key to the influence that words exercise in the formation of a crowd is to be found in the images that those words evoke *quite independently of their signification.*

> The power of words is bound up with the images they evoke, and is quite independent of their real significance. Words whose sense is the most ill-defined are sometimes those that possess the most influence. Such, for example are the terms democracy, socialism, equality, liberty, etc., whose meaning is so vague that bulky volumes do not suffice to fix it precisely. Yet it is certain that a truly magical power is attached to those short syllables, as if they contained the solution of all problems. They synthesise the most diverse unconscious aspirations and the hope of their realisation.[3]

In contemporary theoretical terms we could say that Le Bon is making allusion here to two well-known phenomena: the unfixity of the relation between signifier and signified (in Le Bon's terms: the relation between words and images) and the process of overdetermination by which a particular word condenses around itself a plurality of meanings. For Le Bon, however, this association of images is not an essential component of language as such, but a perversion of it: words have a true significance which is incompatible with the function of synthesizing a plurality of unconscious aspirations. A strong frontier separating what language truly is from its perversion by the crowd is the unquestioned presupposition of his entire analysis.

Given the arbitrariness of the association between words and images, any rationality is excluded from their mutual articulation:

> Reason and arguments are incapable of combating certain words and formulas. They are uttered with solemnity in the presence of crowds and as soon as they have been pronounced an expression of respect is visible on every countenance, and all heads are bowed. By many they are considered as natural forces, as supernatural powers. They evoke grandiose and vague images in men's minds, but this very vagueness that wraps them in obscurity augments their mysterious power.... All words and all formulas

do not possess the power of evoking images, while there are some which have once had this power, but lost it in the course of use, and cease to waken any response in the mind. They have become vain sounds, whose principal utility is to relieve the person who employs them of the obligation of thinking.[4]

Here we see the limits of the explanation that Le Bon thinks it necessary to provide: his analysis does not try to detect (as Freud's will) the inner logic governing the association between words and images, only to describe its differences from a rationality conceived in terms of a purely denotative signification.

Since the association between words and images is entirely arbitrary, it varies from time to time and from country to country:

> If any particular language be studied, it is seen that the words of which it is composed change rather slowly in the course of the ages, while the images these words evoke or the meaning attached to them change ceaselessly.... [I]t is precisely the words most often employed by the masses which among different peoples possess the most different meanings. Such is the case, for instance, with the words 'democracy' and 'socialism' in such a frequent use nowadays.[5]

And from there Le Bon, as a true new Machiavelli, gives a piece of advice to politicians: 'One of the most essential functions of statesmen consists, then, in baptising with popular or, at any rate, indifferent words things the crowd cannot endure under their old names. The power of words is so great that it suffices to designate in well-chosen terms the most odious things to make them acceptable to the crowds'.[6]

For Le Bon, there is a clear connection between this words/images dialectic and the emergence of illusions, which are the very terrain on which the crowd's discourse is constituted:

> as they [the masses] must have their illusions at all costs, they turn instinctively, as the insect seeks the light, to the rhetoricians who accord them

what they want. No truth, but error has always been the chief factor in the evolution of nations, and the reason why socialism is so powerful today is that it constitutes the last illusion that is still vital.... The masses have never thirsted after truth. They turn aside from evidence that is not to their taste, preferring to deify error, if error seduces them.[7]

The dissociation between the 'true signification' of words and the images they evoke requires some rhetorical devices to make it possible. According to Le Bon, there are three such devices: affirmation, repetition and contagion. 'Affirmation pure and simple, kept free of all reasoning and all proof, is one of the surest means of making an idea enter the mind of the crowds. The conciser an affirmation, the more destitute of every appearance of proof and demonstration, the more weight it carries.'[8] As for repetition, its 'power is due to the fact that the repeated statement is embedded in the long run in those profound regions of our unconscious selves in which the motives of our actions are forged. At the end of a certain time, we have forgotten who is the author of the repeated assertion, and we finish by believing it.'[9] Finally, contagion:

> Ideas, sentiments, emotions and beliefs possess in crowds a contagious power as intense as that of microbes. This phenomenon is very natural, since it is observed even in animals when they are together in number.... In the case of men collected in a crowd all emotions are very rapidly contagious, which explains the suddenness of panics. Brain disorders, like madness, are themselves contagious. The frequency of madness among doctors who are specialists for the mad is notorious. Indeed, forms of madness have recently been cited – agoraphobia, for instance – which are communicable from men to animals.[10]

At this point, we should distinguish the descriptive validity of the features of mass psychology enumerated by Le Bon from the normative judgements with which those features are associated in his discourse. The unfixity of the relationship between words and images is the very precondition of any discursive operation which is politically meaningful. From this point of view, Le Bon's remarks are penetrating and enlightening. What, however, about the distinction between the *true significance* of a term and the images contingently associated with it? That distinction corresponds, broadly speaking, with the distinction between denotation and connotation – one that contemporary semiology has increasingly put into question. In order to have a one-to-one correspondence between signifier and signified, language would need to have the structure of a nomenclature – something which would go against the basic linguistic principle, formulated by Saussure, that in language there are no positive terms, only differences. Language is organized around two poles, the paradigmatic (which Saussure called associative) and the syntagmatic. This means that the associative trends systematically subvert the very possibility of a purely denotative meaning. To take some of the examples given by Saussure: there is in language a tendency towards the regularization of its forms. To the nominative Latin word 'orator' corresponds the genitive 'oratoris', while to the nominative 'honos' corresponds the genitive 'honoris'. But the tendency towards the regularization of linguistic forms makes all words that end with 'r' in the nominative end with 'ris' in the genitive, so that at a more advanced stage in the evolution of Latin, 'honos' is replaced by 'honor'. These associative rules regularizing linguistic forms even create, in some cases, entirely new words. This is the rule that Saussure called the *quatrième proportionelle*: to *réaction* corresponds, as an adjective, *réactionnaire* and, by analogy, *répression* leads to *répressionnaire*, which is a term which did not originally exist in French.[11]

What is most important for our purpose is to stress the fact that this associative process does not operate only at the grammatical level – which was the level primarily studied by Saussure – but also at the semantic one. In actual fact, both levels constantly cross each other, and lead to associations which can advance in a variety of directions. This is the process that psychoanalysis essentially explores. In Freud's study of the Rat Man, for instance, 'rat' becomes associated with 'penis', because rats spread venereal diseases. In this case the association operates primarily at the level of the signified. But in other cases the association results originally from the similitude of words (what Freud called 'verbal bridges'): 'ratten' in German means 'instalments', thus money is brought into the Rat complex; and 'spielratten' means gambling and the father of the Rat Man had incurred gambling debts and was thus also associated with the complex.[12] As we can see, it is a completely secondary matter whether the association starts at the level of the signifier or that of the signified: whichever is the case, the consequences will be felt at both levels and will be translated into a displacement of the relationship signifier/signified.

Since this is the way things are, we cannot simply differentiate the 'true' meaning of a term (which would necessarily be permanent) from a series of images connotatively associated with it, for the associative networks are an integral part of the very structure of language. This assertion certainly does not deprive of their specific characteristics the kind of associations to which Le Bon refers; it implies, however, that this specificity should be located within the context of a larger set of associations, differentiated from each other in terms of their type of performativity. The mistake is to present those associations as perversions of a language whose true meaning would require only syntagmatic combinations.

This is most evident when we consider the three 'rhetorical devices' described by Le Bon as the means of bringing about the dissociation between true signification and evoked meaning. In each case, Le Bon's thesis can be sustained only by considerably simplifying the performative operation that the devices are supposed to carry out. Let us consider them one by one. Affirmation: for Le Bon, this is an illegitimate operation whose only function is to break the link between what is affirmed and any reasoning that would support it. For him, to assert something beyond the possibility of rational proof can only be some form of lying. Is this so, however? Should we conceive of social interaction as a terrain on which there are no affirmations that are not grounded? What if an affirmation is the appeal to recognize something which is present in everybody's experience, but cannot be formalized within the existing dominant social languages? Can such an affirmation – which would be, as in Saint Paul, 'madness for the Greeks and scandal for the Heathen' – be reduced to a lie because it is incommensurable with the existing forms of social rationality? Patently not. To assert something beyond any proof *could be* a first stage in the emergence of a truth which can be affirmed only by breaking with the coherence of the existing discourses. Of course, the case to which Le Bon refers – affirmation without proof as a way of lying – is not an impossible one, but it is only one instance within a series of other possibilities which he does not even consider.

We can say the same about repetition. Some of Le Bon's initial assertions about it can be readily accepted – namely, that it is through repetition that social habits are created, and that these habits are embedded 'in those profound regions of our unconscious selves in which the motives of our actions are forged'. We could say, in that sense, that repetition plays a multiplicity of roles in shaping social relations: through a process of trial and error, it makes possible a community's adjustment to its milieu; a dominated group, through the recognition of the same enemy in a plurality of antagonistic experiences, acquires a sense of its own identity; through the presence of a set of rituals, institutional arrangements, broad images and symbols, a community acquires a sense of its temporal continuity; and so forth. In that sense, repetition is a condition of social and ethical life. As Benjamin Franklin put it: 'I concluded, at length, that the mere speculative conviction that it was in our interest to be completely virtuous, was not sufficient to prevent our slipping; and that the contrary habits must be broken, and good ones acquired and established, before we can have any dependence on a steady, uniform rectitude of conduct.'[13] Le Bon, however, does not explore the plurality of language games that one can play around repetitive practices, and retains from them only one element: their opposition to rational deliberation. Let there be no doubt: what Le Bon is constructing as an exclusive dichotomy is not habit in general versus rationality, but a habit created through manipulation and one which results from the sedimentation of a rational decision. However, since the rationality of the habit is the guarantee of its legitimacy, we are left with no alternative but the categories 'rationality' and 'irrationality'. Thus he asserts:

The inferior reasoning of crowds is based, just as is reasoning of a higher order, on the association of ideas, but between the ideas associated by the crowd there are only apparent bonds of analogy.... The characteristics of the reasoning of crowds are the association of dissimilar things possessing a merely apparent connection between each other, and the immediate generalisation of particular cases.... A chain of logical argumentation is totally incomprehensible to crowds, and for this reason it is permissible to say that they do not reason or that they reason falsely, and are not to be influenced by reasoning.[14]

So it is clear how Le Bon's reasoning is structured: disconnected – that is, purely associative – connotations are opposed to a process of logical argumentation. The result is that there is nothing we can conceive as a specific way of crowd reasoning: its *modus operandi* is treated as the mere negative reverse of rationality conceived in its strict and narrow sense. The possibility that repetition points to something comparable present in a plurality of instances – for example the sense, for a variety of social strata, of sharing a common experience of exploitation – is not taken into consideration at all.

Finally, contagion. For Le Bon, contagion can only be a form of pathological transmission. Its explanation is to be found in the general phenomenon of 'suggestibility' which was, at the time, the *Deus ex machina* omnipresent in the discourse on mass psychology. What, however, explains suggestibility is something to which no attention whatsoever was paid. As Freud put it: 'My resistance took the direction of protesting against the view that suggestion, which explained everything, was itself exempt of explanation.'[15] Also in this case, a set of questions could be formulated which would undermine the dogmatism of Le Bon's view. What, for instance, if contagion were not a disease but the expression of a common feature shared by a group of people, one which is difficult to verbalize in a direct way, and can be expressed only by some form of symbolic representation?

How can we explain Le Bon's systematic simplification of the horizon of possibilities opened by each of the categories he analyses? Why are his explanations so one-sided and biased? It does not take long to realize that it is because his thought is grounded in two crucial assumptions which have dominated much of the early stages of mass psychology. The first, as should be abundantly clear from the passages I have quoted, is that the dividing line between rational forms of social organization and mass phenomena coincides, to a large extent, with the frontier separating the normal from the pathological. This first assumption is, in turn, embedded in another which is certainly present in Le Bon, but also in most of the literature of his time concerning mass behaviour: the distinction between rationality and irrationality would largely overlap with the distinction between the individual and the group. The individual experiences a process of social degradation by becoming part of a group. As he puts it:

> by the mere fact that he forms part of an organised crowd, a man descends several rungs in the ladder of civilisation. Isolated, he may be a cultivated individual; in a crowd, he is a barbarian – that is, a creature acting by instinct. He possesses the spontaneity, the violence, the ferocity, and also the enthusiasm and heroism of primitive beings, whom he further tends to resemble by the facility with which he allows himself to be impressed by words and images – which would be entirely without action on each of the individuals composing the crowds – and to be induced to commit acts contrary to his most obvious interests and his best-known habits.[16]

This fact had been observed long before Le Bon. In the words of Serge Moscovici:

> This phenomenon is universally confirmed by public records. According to Solon, a single Athenian is a wily fox but a group of Athenians is a flock of sheep. Frederick the Great trusted each of his generals as an individual yet he described them as fools when they were gathered together in a council of war. And we are indebted to the Romans for this most apt and universal of proverbs: *Senatores omnes boni viri, senatus romanus mala bestia*, or *senators are all good men, the Roman senate is a noxious beast.*[17]

The intellectual history that I shall sketch in Chapter 3 is largely the history of the progressive abandonment of these two assumptions. This abandonment made possible a different and more nuanced approach to the problems of mass society. I shall begin my story from the zero-degree of this intellectual transformation – that is to say, from the moment in which the two assumptions were formulated in the crudest and most uncompromising way: in the work of Hippolyte Taine. Later, I shall describe how changes in psychiatric theory and a progressive transference of individual 'rationality' to the group opened the way to a new understanding of mass behaviour. (Le Bon himself already represents a certain departure from Tainean dichotomies.) The highest point in this reversal of paradigms is the work of Freud, in which the two assumptions are resolutely abandoned.

3

Suggestion, Imitation, Identification

Mob and social dissolution

Let us take, at random, a couple of quotations from Taine concerning mass mobilization in the course of the French Revolution. (I say at random because there is hardly a page in the *Origines de la France contemporaine* where we could not find an equivalent description.) The first quotation concerns the composition of the participants in a provincial upheaval:

> We have seen how numerous the smugglers, dealers in contraband salt, poachers, vagabonds, beggars, and escaped convicts have become, and how a year of famine increases the number. All are so many recruits for the mobs, and whether in a disturbance or by means of a disturbance each one of them fills his pouch. Around Caux, even to the environs of Rouen, at Roncherolles, Quévrevilly, Préaux, Saint-Jacques and in all the surrounding neighbourhood bands of armed ruffians force their way into the houses, particularly the parsonages, and lay their hands on whatever they please.... The peasants allow themselves to be enticed away by the bandits. Man slips rapidly down the incline of dishonesty; one who is half-honest, and takes part in a riot inadvertently or in spite of himself, repeats the act, allured on by impunity or by gain .... In every important insurrection there are similar evil-doers and vagabonds, enemies of the law, savage, prowling desperados,

who, like wolves, roam about wherever they scent a prey. It is they who serve as the directors and executioners of public or private malice.... Henceforth these constitute the new leaders: for in every mob it is the boldest and least scrupulous who march ahead and set the example in destruction. The example is contagious: the beginning was the craving for bread, the end is murder and incendiarism; the savagery which is unchained adding its unlimited violence to the limited revolt of necessity.[1]

The second quotation refers to the collapse of the mechanisms of authority which make the riots possible:

In the midst of a disintegrated society, under the semblance only of a government, it is manifest that an invasion is under way, an invasion of barbarians which will complete by terror, that which it has begun by violence, and which, like the invasion of the Normans in the tenth and eleventh centuries, ends in the conquest and dispossession of an entire class .... This is the work of Versailles and Paris; and there, at Paris as well as at Versailles, some, through a lack of foresight and infatuation, and others, through blindness and indecision – the latter through weakness and the former through violence – all are labouring to accomplish it.[2]

A few features of this description are immediately visible. Taine does not give us a picture of a clash between social forces whose aims are clearly stated and whose incompatibility would be the source of the ensuing violence. Social aims are certainly present in his description – 'the limited revolt of necessity' – but they are powerless to explain social action. They are overcome by an 'unlimited violence' resulting only from the action of 'vagabonds', 'ruffians' and 'brigands' – that is, by forces which escape every kind of social rationality. In the same way, the government's inability to control the situation has little to do with the objective situation of the monarchy on the eve of the Revolution, but is presented as a result of 'lack of foresight', 'infatuation', 'blindness' and 'indecision' – that is, as a consequence of a *subjective* failure. The whole description of French society that we get from Taine is that of a social organism threatened by the eruption of forces leading to its disintegration. But the important point is that these forces lack any consistency of their own; they are simply the result of freeing instinctual impulses that social norms usually keep under control. How, in that case, do we explain the nature of those impulses?[3]

Let us ask ourselves, to start with, what were the intellectual tools available to a crowd psychologist, in the last third of the nineteenth century, to address this issue. Susanna Barrows summarizes the situation in the following terms: 'From theories on hypnotism, they articulated the mechanism of irritation so characteristic of groups; from popular doctrines of evolution, they constructed a hierarchy of human civilisation; and from medicine, they borrowed the model for abnormal psychology and the most telling metaphors for crowd behaviour: crowds, as described by late-nineteenth-century French men, resembled alcoholics or women'.[4]

In Taine's approach, not all these components have the same weight. Suggestion, which is going to be so central in later crowd theories, does not play any significative role for him. The reasons for this are partly chronological – hypnotism was not yet the central issue that it would become after Charcot adopted it as a valid scientific practice – and partly, as Barrows perceptively points out, deriving from Taine's notion that leaders 'possessed no special skills or charismatic power', as 'only the crazy "dregs" of society could manipulate an assembled multitude'.[5] Apart from that, however, all other dominant features of crowd theory are present in his approach in their crudest form. As a result of the law of mental contagion, mobs are controlled by the most criminal sections of the population. Anarchy is the inevitable result of crowd action, since the latter involves a reversion to a state of nature in which only beastly instincts prevail. This presupposes – in the Darwinian approach – a biological retrogression conceived in terms of what Jackson and Ribot have called the 'mechanism of dissolution'.[6] And alcoholism is closely associated with crowd action. Riots usually end in all manner of alcoholic orgies.[7]

Taine's approach, however, did not limit itself to stressing the irrational nature of crowd behaviour. It was also an attempt to show which strata, within the social body, were particularly prone to degenerate into crowds. The image of French history that Taine presents is one of a progressive decline resulting from the dissolution of the customary institutions which organized the body politic. This decline had started with Absolutism, which, through a relentless centralization, had destroyed all the intermediate bodies which had traditionally structured French social institutions. The process was later accelerated by the Enlightenment, whose utopian plans for social reconstruction had helped to disseminate subversive ideas which undermined any notion of social restraint. So when the revolutionary process started, there was nothing which could contain it within reasonable limits. The third estate could not hegemonize the process, and the leadership fell quite quickly into the hands of the fourth estate – the rabble of the cities which was, for Taine, the real actor in the revolutionary process.

Within this general decline, *any* group could degenerate into a crowd. Taine anticipates what will become the established wisdom among crowd theorists – namely, that rationality belongs to the individual, who loses many of his rational attributes when he participates in a crowd. He likes to compare crowd behaviour to inferior forms of life, like plants or animals, or to primitive forms of social organization.[8] Within contemporary society, the danger of crowd infection is greater in some groups than in others: the aristocracy is less prone to mental contagion than are the popular classes, and women and children are more prone than men. The link between women and crowd behaviour is, in fact, not only Taine's idiosyncratic view; it was a general view at the time.[9] The theory behind such views was that, in the course of biological evolution, men had developed their mental capacities more than women (women's skulls had enlarged less than those of men, and their cerebral strength was also significantly less). This makes them more prone to insanity and less capable of restraining their instinctual impulses. The more the fear of crowds grew towards the end of the nineteenth century, the less flattering the picture of women became: 'In many other descriptions of women written in the nineties, females embodied all that was threatening, debasing and inferior. Like the insane, they revelled in violence; like children, they were incessantly buffeted by instincts; like barbarians, their appetite for blood and sexuality was insatiable.'[10]

At this point in the argument, it should be clear that the whole discourse on crowd behaviour had come to depend so much on drawing a clear line of demarcation between the normal and the pathological that it was in an increasingly ancillary position *vis-à-vis* medical science – especially (but not only) psychiatry. Jaap van Ginneken tells us that the Bibliothèque Nationale in Paris contains several hundred volumes, written at that time, which try to work on this link. Their titles are revealing – one, for instance, published in 1872, is called *Les Hommes et les actes de l'insurrection de Paris devant la psychologie morbide*. The centre of this discussion, which I shall address in the next section, was the debate in France concerning hypnotism and, in Italy, the notion of the 'born criminal' as elaborated by Lombroso and his school.

Hypnosis and criminology [11]

The epicentre of the 'scientific' consideration of crowd psychology was provided by the debate on hypnosis which was raging in French psychiatry in the last decade of the nineteenth century between the Salpêtrière and Nancy schools. This debate, however, took place against the background of a complex intellectual history in which many more options than those finally taken were available to theoreticians of mass behaviour. The very name chosen – crowd – already had pejorative overtones. As Apfelbaum and McGuire assert:

> In truth, the notion of crowd seemed to be essentially a euphemism for violent and destructive behaviour. It should be noted that the term crowd was at that time never used within socialist circles, the socialist being less concerned with mass contagion than with solidarity of collectivism. … Subscription to this destructive conception of crowd behaviour was amply demonstrated by the manner in which those two authors [Tarde and Le Bon] resorted to an overtly value-laden vocabulary in describing the object of their investigations. On the one hand, the descriptions of the

crowd were strangely reminiscent of the anti-Commune polemic literature
of the 1870s.... But at the same time, the reference to the hypnotic suggestion metaphor actually implied a disqualification of those involved in
mass actions, since at this time hypnotic suggestion had developed an
association with psychological pathology.[12]

Mass psychologists had essentially three options if they were going to
appeal to magnetism in the study of crowd behaviour.[13] One was the
spiritualist tradition of Bergasse, Carra and Brissot, whose 'Societies of
Harmony' had constituted some form of semi-mystical anarchism. The
other two were the approaches represented by Charcot at the Salpêtrière
and Liébeault and Bernheim in Nancy, and it is with this debate that we
have to concern ourselves especially. For Charcot, hypnotic phenomena
have a strict physiological basis.

The position of the Charcot school ... is best exemplified by an emphasis
on several major factors, namely: (a) that hypnosis will only occur when
certain physiological conditions are simultaneously met; (b) that hypnotic
somnambulism follows a rigid progression through three distinct stages –
lethargy, catalepsy, and somnambulism; (c) it is irrevocably linked to
neuropathology; and (d) there is a specific organic cause. The link with
pathological disorders was considered so vital to the existence of hypnosis
that it was believed that only an etiological analysis was sufficient to
distinguish between the hypnotic state and the historic condition.[14]

The position of the Nancy school, on the contrary, was more psychological; it refused to accept any necessary link between pathology and
hypnotic suggestion, and maintained that anybody, in a normal state, can
experience the latter.

Now, it is characteristic of the values which governed the theoretical
choices of crowd psychologists that, of the various models of collective
behaviour available to them, they chose the categories of Charcot's
school – precisely those which emphasize the pathological dimension
most. (The terminology they use is frequently that of Bernheim – they

talk about suggestion rather than hypnosis – but the conceptual framework is undoubtedly provided by Charcot's hysterical model. Moreover, as various authors have pointed out, our crowd theorists rarely refer to the debate between the various psychiatric schools, and tend to present the findings of these schools as if they were an undifferentiated whole.) With this operation the fixation of mass behaviour within a pathological framework was complete:

> Therein lies the disqualification of the emergent masses – the choice of a very deliberate model based on pathological disorientation. That this disqualification was intended to be applied to such historical events as the Commune can be exemplified by Tarde's differentiation of crowd activities into three types of social upheaval, all of which reminded the author, we are told, of *disguised epilepsy*. These upheavals included: (a) *social convulsion* and/or civil war; (b) enthusiasm, such as cult, nation, and religion; (c) external war against nations…. Such a focus highlights the deliberate choice made, considering the availability of portrayals of crowds at the same time…. We had already remarked that simultaneous to the crowd psychology there was an abundant literature on syndicalism and positive collective behaviour, which viewed masses constructively, but in an ideological view not shared by Tarde and Le Bon.[15]

Late-nineteenth-century scientism followed a different pattern in Italy. Although the French debate on hypnotism was not unknown, and produced some important effects, the main influence was from Darwinism through its fusion with the criminological theses of Cesare Lombroso, whose book *L'Uomo delinquente* was published in 1876. Lombroso, a professor of clinical psychiatry and later of criminal anthropology in Turin, had started as a medical officer measuring Italian army recruits with the aim of discovering in them possible criminal atavistic features. After undertaking physical – especially cranial – measurements on a considerable number of criminals he concluded that a set of distinguishing physical features were stigmas of criminality, and were transmissible by heredity. He affirmed the possibility that 'Injurious characters … tend to reappear through reversion, such as blackness in sheep; and with mankind some of the worst dispositions, which occasionally without any assignable cause make their appearance in families, may perhaps be reversions to a savage state, from which we are not removed by very many generations. This view seems indeed recognised in the common expression that such are the black sheep of the family'.[16] He later extended his studies to mob crimes during political upheavals (especially the French Revolution), and, not surprisingly, cites Taine as a major influence.

In the early 1880s, the positivist criminological school inspired by Lombroso started publication of its own journal, the *Archivio di Psichiatria, Antropologia Criminale e Scienze Penali*, followed later on by *La Scuola Positiva nella Giurisprudenza Civile e Penale*. The main topic of discussion was the question of the penal responsibility of crowd criminals. Scipio Sighele, a younger and prominent member of the school, established in his influential book *La Folla deliquente* the distinction between 'born criminals', organized around sects of bandits whose criminal motivations have anthropological/biological roots, and 'occasional criminals', led to criminal actions by a variety of ambient factors. According to Sighele, born criminals should be punished with all the rigour of the law, while occasional criminals should receive only half-sentences. The criterion for discriminating between the two had to be whether the criminal had or had not been previously convicted. (As has frequently been pointed out, this criterion is rather dubious: the same person could have committed several offences for purely circumstantial reasons.[17]) On the whole, Sighele, who was well versed in the French debate, gave a somewhat eclectic explanation of the sources of crowd behaviour. To the classical causes – moral contagion, social imitation and hypnotic suggestion – he added primitive emotional tendencies and the quantitative factor, derived from the number of people participating in crowd activities. Enrico Ferri, Sighele's mentor, identified five types of criminals: 'born' criminals, insane, habitual, occasional and passional.

The more the discussion went on, however, the more the tendency was increasingly to question the relation between anatomic features and criminality as proposed by Lombroso. Lombroso himself, in successive editions of *L'Uomo deliquente*, tended to increase the importance of ambient factors over purely biological ones. The First International Congress on Criminal Anthropology, which took place in Rome in 1885, saw a first confrontation between Italian and French criminologists, the latter putting into question for the first time the anatomico-biological model of the former. The confrontation was even more acute at the Second International Congress in Paris in 1889, when the Italians' entire anatomical evidence came under fire. After the 1890s, biological explanations of crowd behaviour were clearly in retreat. The Italian positivist school maintained some positions of power in Italy, and even obtained some victories in the reform of penal law at the beginning of the Fascist period, but internationally its influence declined. This decline was partly due to the emergence of new trends in crowd-behaviour research resulting from the disintegration of the pathological model.

The decisive development in this disintegration took place in the country where the whole tradition of crowd psychology had started: France. In the last decade of the nineteenth century, the whole issue between the rival psychiatric currents of Charcot and Bernheim was definitely settled: the victory went to the Nancy school. The consequences of this are of considerable importance for our research. In the first place, the collapse of the physiological model dissolved the pathological terrain in which crowd psychology had traditionally been grounded. Whatever the novelties – even the dangers – that the transition to a mass society involved, it became increasingly clear that they could not be addressed with the pathological approach that had dominated early crowd theory. Mass society required a positive characterization, not one dominated by the language of social disintegration. But there was something else which was perhaps more important. Whatever its shortcomings, crowd psychology *had* touched on some crucially important aspects in the construction of social and political identities – aspects which had not been properly addressed before. The relationship between words and images, the predominance of the 'emotive' over the 'rational', the sense of omnipotence, the suggestibility and the identification with the leaders, and so on, are all too real features of collective behaviour.

To focus on them was the most original contribution made by crowd theory to the understanding of social agency and social action. Why, however, did crowd psychologists ultimately fail? It is not difficult to find the reason: because of their ideological anti-popular bias; because they framed their discourses within stark and sterile dichotomies – the individual/ the crowd; the rational/the irrational; the normal/the pathological. It is enough, however, to introduce some *souplesse* into these rigid oppositions, to let each of their two poles partially contaminate the other, for an entirely different picture to emerge. For in that case the mass behaviour described by crowd theorists will be a catalogue not of social aberrations but of processes which, in different degrees, structure *any* kind of socio-political life. It was necessary to integrate their findings into a comprehensive theory of politics, one which did not relegate them to the aberrant, the marginal and the irrational. A radical change of perspective was necessary to make this breakthrough possible. This Rubicon was crossed a few years later in Vienna: Freud would tell us that psychopathology holds the key to the understanding of normal psychology. And to prove his point, he would start his study of mass psychology not with the *canaille* described by Taine and Le Bon, but with two highly organized groups: the Army and the Church. Before moving on to Freud, however, I must mention some other developments which, to some extent, made the Freudian breakthrough possible.

Tarde and McDougall

The advance towards a more complex approach to social psychology followed a pattern whose main defining characteristics were: (1) an increasing differentiation in the typology of groups; (2) the transference of many features of the Le Bonian crowds to more permanent groups, and the redefinition of those features when applied to these new social entities; (3) the transference to the group of many features which had been considered as belonging exclusively to the individual – a transference which started to blur the stark opposition group/individual which had dominated early group psychology. If the first two characteristics are associated mainly with the theoretical intervention of Gabriel Tarde, the third is to be found in the work of William McDougall.

Tarde's intellectual trajectory is symptomatic of this change of perspective.[18] At the beginning, his central category of 'imitation' is still entirely dominated by the notion of 'suggestion'. His *Les lois de l'imitation*, published in 1890, establishes a strict analogy between imitation and somnambulism. The role of the leader (the equivalent of the hypnotist) is central in determining the possibility of imitation. A sharp distinction is drawn between *invention*, which involves the introduction of novelties (a role corresponding to the leader), and *imitation*, which is the mode of social reproduction corresponding to the mass of people. Social cohesion results from these imitative laws, which operate at a plurality of levels, but always tend in the direction of subordinating the rational and creative moments to the lower and non-creative ones. The cognitive aspects of beliefs [*croyances*], for instance, occupy a secondary role *vis-à-vis* the affective ones [*désirs*], and the very possibility of imitation depends on the reinforcement of lower mental functions at the expense of the higher ones. The description of mass behaviour given by Tarde, at this stage of his career, repeats all the shibboleths of early crowd theorists: crowds are incapable of rational thought (following Henry Fournial, he calls them 'spinal creatures'); they are assimilated to savages and women; and any kind of collective gathering is systematically debased.

Even at this early stage, however, Tarde established a set of differentiations which anticipate his later thought. In what follows, we will discuss two essays by Tarde. An early one, 'Les foules et les sectes criminelles', was originally published in 1893; the second, 'Le public et la foule', appeared in the volume *L'Opinion et la foule* (1901).[19] A comparison between them helps us to perceive the increasingly more nuanced nature of the distinctions that Tarde introduces.

Tarde starts the first essay by establishing a distinction between various forms of human aggregation according to the degree of internal organization they reach. Walkers in the same street, people occupying the same coach in a train, or those who silently share the same table in a restaurant are virtual social groups which become actual only if a sudden event fuses them in a single emotion (the derailment of the train, an explosion in the street, etc.). 'In those cases that first degree of association will be born which we call the crowd. Through a series of intermediary degrees one raises from that rudimentary, transient and amorphous aggregation to that organized, hierarchical, lasting and regular crowd which one can call the *corporation*, in the widest sense of the term.'[20] Neither of these two extreme poles – crowd and corporation – manages totally to prevail at the expense of the other. This already arouses our suspicion that Tarde is describing not so much different *types* of social organization as different *social logics* which, to various extents, are always present in the structuration of the social body. One common feature is, however, shared by both crowds and corporations: the group's foundation is provided by the presence of a leader. Thus: 'all kinds of true associations have this common and permanent character of being produced, of being more or less led by a visible or concealed chief; concealed, very often, in the case of crowds, always apparent and visible in the case of corporations'.[21] This gives us some criteria for distinguishing the degree to which the dominant idea unifying a group can be imprinted on to the latter: 'One can affirm that any form of human association can be distinguished: 1 – by the manner in which a thought or will among one thousand becomes a leading one, by the conditions of the confluence of thoughts and wills from which it achieves victory; 2 – by the more or less great facility which is offered to the leading thought and will.'[22] The degree of hegemonization of the group by the idea is clearly higher in the corporation than in the crowd.

Thus crowd and corporation are the two extremes of a continuum which admits many variations and temporary groupings. But mass events, anyway, are the result of the combined action of both crowds and corporations. Without the presence of the latter, the former would lack any intelligent direction, and would not go beyond mob explosions. Without its propagation in crowd-like events, the social effects of the corporation would necessarily be limited (let us just think of the nineteenth-century anarchist attempts, which Tarde discusses in some detail). What is important for our purposes, however, is to underline the mechanisms through which the idea originating in a corporation (in Tarde's term: a sect, criminal or not) is propagated. This propagation depends on the previous constitution of an ideological terrain ready to receive it. What is essential is 'a preparation of souls by conversations or readings, by the regular visiting of clubs, of cafés, which have thrown on them, in a long contagion of slow imitation, the seal of previous ideas appropriate to receive the newcomer'.[23] Even in the embryonic stage of the idea's propagation, in the association between two people, suggestion is needed to consolidate it: one of the two members of the couple [suggestionnaire] has the active role, while the other [suggestionné] has the passive one. When the propagation of the idea extends to larger groups, we can have either of two phenomena: suggestion operates as a reciprocal phenomenon among all the members of the group, the leader included; or there is a unilateral action of suggestion by the latter.

There is also an important distinction to be introduced here: the mechanism of suggestion can in some cases require the physical presence of the two parts, but it can also operate at a distance (this last possibility, Tarde points out, implies that one should not exaggerate the assimilation of social suggestion to hypnotism). This group cohesion brought about by suggestion at a distance leads Tarde to establish another set of distinctions, concerning group leadership. Primitive groups required from leaders 'an iron will, an eagle's sight and a strong faith, a powerful imagination and an intractable pride'. These features, however, are dissociated once the process of civilization tends to privilege, as far as leadership is concerned, intellectual or imaginative superiority over undifferentiated strengths. Thus, mass action becomes less violent and traumatic, and more controllable: 'Civilization has, fortunately, the effect of constantly increasing the actions at a distance over other people, through the ceaseless extension of the territorial field and of the numbers of those addressed, as a result of the diffusion of the book and the newspaper, and this is not the smallest service that it performs … as a compensation for so many evils.'[24]

We can draw from this brief summary of 'Les foules et les sectes criminelles' the following conclusions: (1) the mechanism of imitation tends to create equivalential relations across the whole social spectrum; (2) that which explains imitation is a human predisposition which is to be understood in terms of *suggestibility*; (3) this suggestibility, however, is not found only within a limited set of social phenomena – crowd behaviour – but is operative in all human institutions (conceived, in a wide sense, as corporations); (4) civilization brings about an increasing social differentiation which results in the expanded role played by action at a distance. This changes neither the centrality of suggestion nor the basic structure of the leaders/led dyad, but it makes the ways in which both operate more complex. We are clearly moving away from the simplicity of Le Bon's dualism.

Tarde's conception of imitation changes over the 1890s.[25] Of the two forms of suggestion I have described – the mutual suggestion between all members of the group, the leader included, and the unilateral suggestion of the group members by the leader – it is the former which is given increasing centrality. This centrality, as we have seen, results from what Tarde considers the dominant line in the development of civilization: the advance towards a type of social organization in which action at a distance replaces direct physical contact. As Van Ginneken points out, the prefix 'inter-' is very often used by Tarde: 'interspiritual, intermental, interpsychological'. The result is that imitation is conceived less and less in terms of suggestion: 'Where social influence in assembled groups may well be conceived as a form of suggestion, he felt, social influence in dispersed groups is better thought of as a form of interaction. By continuing to shift emphasis, Tarde cut loose from the old paradigms of crowd psychology and made it possible to bypass and transcend Le Bon's limited approach.'[26]

This new approach is clearly evident in Tarde's 1898 essay on 'Le public et la foule'. The contrast between crowds and publics is stated at the beginning: 'The psychology of crowds has been established; one has now to establish the psychology of publics, conceived in this new sense, as a purely spiritual collectivity, as a dissemination of physically separated individuals whose cohesion is entirely mental.'[27] Publics, in that sense, were unknown in the Ancient World and in the Middle Ages, and the precondition for their emergence was the invention of the printing press in the sixteenth century. This public of readers was, however, reduced, and it started a process of generalization and fragmentation only in the eighteenth century – a process which would be deepened and consolidated with the advent of political journalism during the French Revolution. At that time, however, the revolutionary public was mainly Parisian; it was necessary to wait until the twentieth century, until the development of rapid means of transportation and communication, to see the emergence of truly national and even international publics. According to Tarde, the crowd – which, with the family, is the most ancient of social groups – belongs to the past; it is in the public that the future of our societies is to be found.: 'Thus it has been formed, by the joint action of three inventions interacting with each other, the printing press, railways, telegraph, the formidable power of the press, this prodigious telephone which has so incredibly enlarged the old audience of tribunes and preachers. So I cannot concede to a vigorous writer, Dr Le Bon, that our age is the "age of crowds". It is the age of the public or publics, which is very different'.[28]

The structural differences between publics and crowds are clearly determined by Tarde. One can belong to many publics, but to only one crowd. The consequence of this plurality is that publics represent 'a progress in tolerance, if not in scepticism'. And although the movements of retrogression from public to crowd can be highly dangerous, they are quite exceptional, and 'without examining whether the crowds born from a public are not slightly less brutal than those previous to any publics, it is evident that the opposition of two publics, always ready to coalesce over their undecided frontiers, is a much lesser danger to social peace than the encounter of two confrontational crowds'.[29] Publics are less subjected to the influence of natural factors, as well as racial factors.[30] The influence that the publicist exercises over his public, although it is less intense than the one the leader exercises at a given moment over his crowd, is, in the long run, more profound and persistent. It gives expression to, and crystallizes in images, a diffuse state of feeling which had not previously found any form of discursive representation:

[F]or Édouard Drummond to awaken anti-Semitism, it was necessary that his mobilizing attempt corresponded to a certain state of spirit disseminated in the population, but since no voice was raised which loudly gave a common expression to that state of spirit, it remained purely individual, not very intense, even less contagious, unconscious of itself.... I know of French regions where people have never seen a Jew; this does not prevent anti-Semitism from flourishing because they have read anti-Semitic newspapers.[31]

The emergence of the publics not only *adds* a new social entity to those already existing, but changes the social logics which governed the relations between the latter. All former groups – religious, economic, aesthetic, political, and so on – want to have their own press, and constitute their own public. By doing this, however, they profoundly change both their own identity and their relations with other groups. From pure expression of professional interests, they tend to become the expression of divisions conceived in terms of ideal aspirations, sentiments, theoretical ideas. 'Interests are only expressed by it [the press] ... as always concealed or sublimated in theories and passions; it spiritualizes and idealizes them.'[32] In the same way, political parties cease to be the stable reference points of the past and, as they become publics, are crisscrossed by a variety of ideological influences which lead to their division and reaggregation within a matter of years. Let me state clearly the main implication, crucial to our analysis of populism, that this transformation of social groups involves: while crowds were presented by previous mass theorists as leading towards the dissolution of those differentiations proper to a rational organization of society, and towards the absorption of the individual by an undifferentiated mass, this logic of homogenization operates, according to Tarde, *not only in the case of crowds but also in that of publics*. Thus:

> In spite of all the differences that we have pointed out, the crowd and the public, these two extremes of social evolution, have in common the fact that the bond of the different individuals who integrate them does not consist

in *harmonizing* them through their very diversities, through specialities which are mutually useful, but in reflecting themselves one in the other, in coalescing themselves through their innate or acquired similitude in a simple and powerful *unicity*, – but with how much more force in the public than in the crowd! – in a communion of ideas and passions which, moreover, does not interfere with the free play of their individual differences.[33]

I omit Tarde's lengthy discussion of the various types of crowd and their comparable features in the case of publics, because – important as it is – it would take us too far away from our main purpose. There is only one final distinction that Tarde introduces which is highly relevant here: the one between crowds of love and crowds of hatred. Here, again, the differentiation between crowds and publics has to be stressed: 'What the irate crowds demand is one or more heads. The activity of the public is, however, less simplistic, since it moves as easily towards an ideal of reforms or utopias, as towards ideas of ostracism, persecution and exspoliation.' But even in the case of publics, hatred plays a central role: 'To discover or invent for the public a new and great object of hatred is still one of the surest means of becoming one of the kings of journalism.'[34] Tarde's conclusion is not, however, entirely pessimistic. The advantages of publics are to be found not only in replacing custom by mode, tradition by innovation; 'they also replace the neat and persistent division between the many varieties of human association, with their endless conflicts, by an incomplete and variable segmentation whose limits are blurred, in a process of perpetual renovation and mutual penetration'.[35]

While early crowd theorists opposed the mental life of crowds to that of the individual, William McDougall would introduce the distinction between the crowd and the highly organized group – the former lowering individual achievements, the latter enhancing them. As Freud observed, McDougall's picture of the crowd is as unflattering as the one we find in the work of Le Bon-style crowd theorists. He emphasizes the dimension of homogeneity to be found in any crowd which is more than a mere fortuitous gathering: 'There must, then, be some degree of similarity of mental constitution, of interest and sentiment, among the persons who form a crowd, a certain degree of mental homogeneity of the group. And the higher the degree of this mental homogeneity of any gathering of men, the more readily they form a psychological crowd and the more striking and intense are the manifestations of collective life.'[36]

The formation of a crowd requires the exaltation and intensification of emotions. McDougall cites as typical the panic that a group of individuals experiences when it is confronted with an impending danger. McDougall explains this rapid spread of the same emotion in a crowd as resulting from what he calls 'the principle of direct induction of emotion': 'The principle of direct induction of emotion by way of the primitive sympathetic response enables us to understand the fact that a concourse of people (or animals) may be quickly turned into a panic-stricken crowd by some threatening object which is perceptible by only a few of the individuals present.'[37] In the same way, a few fearless individuals who occupy a prominent position in a crowd can arrest panic.

The same principle of direct induction explains the spread of other emotions, and this gives all those who share in them a sense of a mighty and irresistible power. This is related to two peculiarities of the crowd mind:

> In the first place, the individual, in becoming one of a crowd, loses in some degree his self-consciousness, his awareness of himself as a distinct personality, and with it goes also something of his consciousness of his specifically personal relations; he becomes to a certain extent depersonalised. In the second place, and intimately connected with this last change, is a diminution of the sense of personal responsibility: the individual feels himself enveloped and overshadowed and carried away by forces which he is powerless to control.[38]

Crowds have the effect of lowering the average intelligence of their members, as a result of the lowest minds establishing the level to which all have to submit, and of the increased suggestibility of crowd members. The result is a description which is already familiar to us:

> We may sum up the psychological character of the unorganised or simple crowd by saying that it is excessively emotional, impulsive, violent, fickle, inconsistent, irresolute and extreme in action, displaying only the coarser emotions and the less refined sentiments; extremely suggestible, careless in deliberation, hasty in judgement, incapable of any but the simpler and imperfect forms of reasoning; easily swayed and led, lacking in self-consciousness, devoid of self-respect and of sense of responsibility, and apt to be carried away by the consciousness of its own force, so that it tends to produce all the manifestations we have learned to expect of any irresponsible and absolute power.[39]

And so on.

When we move on to the highly organized group, however, the situation is altogether different: 'There is ... one condition that may raise the behaviour of a temporary and unorganised crowd to a higher plane, namely the presence of a clearly defined common purpose in the minds of all its members.'[40] Before describing the structurally defining features of such a common purpose, let me briefly mention what are, for McDougall, the five preconditions for raising the consciousness of the group above the level of the unorganized crowd.[41] The first is that the group needs to have some kind of temporal continuity. The second is that the members of the group should have 'formed some adequate idea of the group, of its nature, composition, functions and capacities, and of the relations of the individuals to the group'. The third – although this is not essential – is that, through interaction with other groups, the members have elaborated some comparative vision of the group to which they belong. The fourth is 'the existence of a body of traditions and customs and habits in the minds of the members of the group determining their relations to one another and to the group as a whole'. The fifth and last is the existence of an internal differentiation or organization of the group, which can either rest on the traditions or customs specified by condition four, or be imposed on the group by an external power.

As an example of a well-organized group, McDougall cites the Japanese Army in the Russo–Japanese war. This kind of group combines a functional differentiation, by which the individual sees himself as a part of a whole, with the attribution of the capacity of deliberation and choice to the most capable members of the group (in the case of the army, to the commander in chief). This combination of the best attributes of collective action with individual deliberation and decision raises the intellectual and moral standards of the organized group far above those of its individual members. Here is the key passage:

> This is the essential character of the effective organisation of any human group; it secures that while the common end of collective action is willed by all, the choice of means is left to those best qualified and in the best position for deliberation and choice; and it secures that co-ordination of the voluntary actions of the parts which brings about the common end by the means so chosen. In this way the collective actions of the well-organised group, instead of being, like those of the simple crowd, merely impulsive or instinctive actions, implying a degree of intelligence and morality far inferior to that of the average individual of the crowd, become truly volitional actions expressive of a degree of intelligence and morality much higher than that of the average member of the group: i.e. the whole is raised above the level of its average member; and even, by reason of exaltation of emotion and organised co-operation in deliberation, above that of its highest members.[42]

Finally, I must say something about McDougall's notion of collective will – that is to say, the common purpose present in the minds of the members of the group. He starts by making a quasi-Rousseauian distinction between a general or collective will and the will of all the individuals. A common purpose is not enough to constitute a collective will. He gives as an example a crowd of white people in the South of the USA lynching a Negro who has supposedly committed a crime. Even if the group is dominated by the common will to carry out the execution with ruthless determination, that is not enough to constitute a collective will. What is missing? The identification with some highly cathected image of the identity of the group as such. How can this arise? Here we must consider the relation between individual and collective volition in McDougall's social psychology. What he calls the 'self-regarding sentiment', the sentiment of self-identity, can, he argues, be extended to other objects:

> to all objects with which the self identifies itself, which are regarded as belonging to the self or as part of a wider self. This extension depends largely on the fact that others identify us with such an object, so that we feel ourselves to be an object of all the regards and attitudes and actions of others directed towards that object, and are emotionally affected by them in the same way that we are affected by similar regards, attitudes, and actions directed towards us individually. It was shown also that such a sentiment may become wider and emotionally richer than the purely self-regarding sentiment, through fusing with a sentiment of love for the object that has grown up independently.[43]

McDougall illustrates the point through a comparison between a patriot and a mercenary army. It is quite central to his conception that there is no strict separation between self-regard and identification with the group, because self-regard is always the regard of an already socialized self which presupposes the presence of objects as part of the very construction of that self:

> The main difference between the self-regarding sentiment and the developed group sentiment is that the latter commonly involves an element of devotion to the group for its own sake and the sake of one's fellow members. That is to say the group sentiment is a synthesis of the self-regarding and the altruistic tendencies in which they are harmonised to mutual support and re-enforcement: the powerful egoistic impulses being sublimated to higher ends than the promotion of the self's welfare.[44]

The important point is that, for McDougall, the very unity of the group is grounded in a common object of identification which establishes equivalentially the unity of the group members. We had already found something similar in Tarde's assertion that a homogenizing 'communion of ideas and passions' – the equivalence that this communion brings about – operates not only in the case of crowds, but also in that of publics. This notion of equivalence – developed, of course, far beyond McDougall's and Tarde's theorization – is crucial to the concept of populism that I shall propose in Part II of this book. Before that, however, we have to consider the decisive intervention of Freud.

The Freudian breakthrough

Freud's *Group Psychology* (1921) was, no doubt, the most radical break-through which had so far been accomplished in mass psychology – despite, as we must recognize from the start, several deadlocks which prevented its insights from developing their full potential. Freud begins his work by asserting that the contrast between individual and social psychology loses, on careful consideration, most of its sharpness because the individual, from the beginning of his or her life, is invariably linked to somebody else 'as a model, as an object, as a helper, as an opponent, and so from the very first individual psychology ... is at the same time social psychology as well'.[45] Freud relativizes the constitutive character of this social link, however, when he argues, in the following paragraph, that these social links with parents, siblings, the object of love and the physician 'may be contrasted with certain other processes, described by us as "narcissistic", in which the satisfaction of the instincts is partially or totally withdrawn from the influence of other people'.[46] It is on the difference between social and narcissistic drives that Freud establishes the distinction between social and individual psychology. This, as we shall see, has important consequences, for he concludes that the two psychologies have evolved in a parallel way, and apply to different aspects of the social bond: while regular members of the group would fall, as far as their mutual link is concerned, under the label of social psychology, narcissism (as the terrain of individual psychology) would fully apply only to the leader of the group.[47] One could, however, wonder, even at this early stage of the argument, whether, if the satisfaction of the drives is *withdrawn*, in narcissism, from the influence of other people, this 'withdrawing' does not retain, in its very rejection, the traces of a reference to the other, and in that sense remains part of a social process.

We will come back to this point. First, however, we have to reconstruct the main steps of Freud's argument. Freud asserts that the social psychology of his predecessors had been concerned more with describing the changes the individual experiences in becoming part of a crowd than with the nature of the social tie. 'Suggestion' had been the limit of all efforts to determine the nature of this tie. Freud proposes to put aside 'suggestion' as a term which itself requires explanation, and to appeal to *libido* as the key category explaining the nature of the social bond. The social bond would be a libidinal bond; as such, it relates to everything that concerns 'love'. Its nucleus consists, of course, of sexual love, but psychoanalysis has shown that we should not separate sexual love from 'on the one hand self-love, and on the other, love for parents and children, friendship and love for humanity in general, and also devotion to concrete objects and abstract ideas'. Although the drives tend, in relations between the sexes, towards sexual union, 'in other circumstances they are diverted from this aim or are prevented from reaching it, though always preserving enough of their original nature to keep their identity recognizable'.[48] A description ensues of the libidinal ties operating in the Church and in the Army, which, on the one hand, link the members of these institutions to one another and, on the other, link all of them to their leaders, Christ or the commander in chief; as well as a description of the disintegrative processes which follow from a sudden disappearance of those leading figures.

Freud goes on to discuss the feeling of aversion or hostility which inhabits all close ties with other people, and is kept out of perception only through repression. In cases where this hostility is directed towards people with whom we are in close association, we talk about ambivalent feelings; but when it is directed at strangers, we can clearly recognize in it an expression of self-love – of narcissism. Self-love is, however, limited or suspended in the case of group formation, in which, in Freud's words: 'Individuals in the group behave as though they were uniform, tolerate the peculiarities of its other members, equate themselves with them, and have no feeling of aversion towards them. Such a limitation of narcissism can, according to our theoretical views, only be produced by one factor, a libidinal tie with other people. Love for oneself knows only one barrier – love for others, love for objects'.[49] This requires that we study the kind of emotional bond which is established between members of a group, and this in turn involves looking more closely at the phenomena of being in love. These emotional ties which pull the group together are obviously love drives which have been diverted from their original aim and which follow, according to Freud, a very precise pattern: that of *identification*.

Identification is, Freud says, 'the earliest expression of an emotional tie with another person',[50] linked to the early history of the Oedipus complex. There are three main forms of identification. The first is identification with the father. The second is identification with the object-choice of love. The third arises, according to Freud, 'with any new perception of a common quality shared with some other person who is not an object of the sexual instinct. The more important this common quality is, the more successful may this partial identification become, and it may thus represent the beginning of a new tie.'[51] This third type of identification is the one to be found in the mutual tie between members of the group, and Freud adds – decisively, albeit problematically – that the common quality on which this identification is based 'lies in the nature of the tie with the leader'.[52] How should the tie with the leader be conceived? Freud approaches this question in terms of the various forms of 'being in love'. The primary way of being in love is experiencing sexual satisfaction in an object. The cathexis invested in the object is, however, exhausted every time satisfaction is obtained. Thus, consciousness of the periodic renewal of the need leads to love as an 'affectionate' feeling, attached to the object even during the passionless intervals. The love of the child for his or her parents once the repression of the original sexual drives has set in is of this 'affectionate' nature. The future life of the individual will be dominated by this sensual love/affection duality, which can either overdetermine the same object or have its two poles invested in different objects. Investment in the object of love means that the narcissistic libido overflows on to the object. This can take various forms or show various degrees, their common denominator being the *idealization* of the object, which thus becomes immune to criticism. So the situation arises 'in many forms of love choice, that the object serves as a substitute for some unattained ego ideal of our own. We love it on account of the perfections which we have striven to reach for our own ego, and which we should now like to procure in this roundabout way as a means of satisfying our narcissism.'[53]

Once this point in the argument has been reached, Freud weighs, in three particularly dense paragraphs, the system of alternatives that his previous *démarche* has opened. When we are in love, 'the ego becomes more and more unassuming and modest, and the object more and more sublime and precious, until at last it gets possession of the entire self-love of the ego, whose self-sacrifice thus follows as a natural consequence. The object has, so to speak, consumed the ego.... The whole situation can be completely summarised in a formula: *The object has been put in the place of the ego ideal.*[54] So what about the relation between being in love and identification? Here Freud's argument becomes somewhat hesitant, but these hesitations are what make it particularly illuminating. He starts by saying that the difference between identification and the extreme forms of being in love – which he describes as 'fascination' and 'bondage' – are to be found in the fact that, in identification, the ego has introjected the object into itself, while in being in love 'it has surrendered itself to the object, it has substituted the object for its own most important constituent'.[55]

Here, however, his hesitations start, for this description 'creates an illusion of distinctions which have no real existence. Economically there is no question of impoverishment or enrichment; it is even possible to describe an extreme case of being in love as a state in which the ego has introjected the object into itself.'[56] So he tries to displace this distinction into a different one: while in identification the object has been lost and introjected into the ego which makes an alteration into itself 'after the model of the lost object', in the case of being in love there would be a hypercathexis of the object by the ego at the ego's expense. This alternative, however, does not quite satisfy Freud who, at this point, asks himself the crucial question: 'Is it quite certain that object-cathexis has been given up? Can there not be identification while the object is retained?'[57] Here he glimpses the possibility of another alternative: 'namely, *whether the object is put in the place of the ego or of the ego ideal*'.[58]

With this, we reach the climax of Freud's argument. He moves from there to a brief comparison between hypnosis and being in love, and to a characterization of group formation in terms of equivalential attachments forged between people as a result of their common love for a leader (a love which has, of course, been inhibited of its sexual impulses). The definition of the social bond follows from this analysis: *'A primary group of this kind is a number of individuals who have put one and the same object in the place of their ego ideal and have consequently identified themselves with one another in their ego.'*[59] We have to retain two conclusions implicit in this analysis for our further discussion. First, if we follow Freud's argument strictly at this point, identification takes place between those who are led, but not between them and the leader. So the possibility for the latter to be *primus inter pares* would be closed. Second, that the ground of any identification would exclusively be the common love for the leader. Freud's tortuous and somewhat hesitant elaboration of the distinction between identification and being in love is apparently resolved in a strict differentiation of functions in the constitution of the social bond: identification between brothers, love for the father. We can easily move from there to the myth of the horde as constitutive of society and to the distinction between individual and social psychology in terms of the differentiation between narcissistic and social mental acts.

What are we to think of this remarkable theoretical sequence? One possible conclusion is the one reached by Mikkel Borch-Jacobsen.[60] In his view, Freud, far from approaching the political in a critical way, seeing in it the alienation of the essence of the social bond, conceives of the social as moulded by the political, as depending for its constitution on the presence of a beloved chief. Society would be conceived as a homogeneous mass whose coherence would be exclusively assured by the presence of the leader. It is true that, for Freud, the political has a founding role as far as the instauration of the social bond is concerned. It is also true that Freud's view of the common love for the leader as being the feature shared by those who identify with each other somehow invites Borch-Jacobsen's reading. I think, however, that his conclusion is excessive, for the unilateral emphasis on the relationship with the leader simply ignores all the places in Freud's text where different social arrangements are suggested as actual possibilities. They do not necessarily question the role of the political in the institution of the social tie, but they do evoke different kinds of politics, not all of which have the authoritarian implications that Borch-Jacobsen detects. If we develop the full implications of these alternative possibilities, a far more complex picture of the social emerges, and the meaning of *Group Psychology*'s theoretical intervention appears in a new light. Freud's attempt at limiting the social validity of his own model moves essentially in two directions.

In the first place, we have those passages in which he opens up the possibility – as an alternative mode of social aggregation – that, through organization, society acquires the characteristics of the individual. The definition of the group – quoted above – as consisting of individuals putting an object in the place of the ego ideal, and mutually identifying through their egos, is preceded by this important limitation: 'We are quite in a position to give the formula for the libidinal constitution of groups or at least of such groups as we have hitherto considered – namely, those that have a leader and have not been able by means of too much "organisation" to acquire secondarily the characteristics of an individual.'[61] Freud also takes issue with McDougall's view that the intellectual disadvantages of the group can be overcome 'by withdrawing the performance of intellectual tasks from the group and reserving them for individual members of it'. The alternative that Freud has in mind is far more radical: 'The problem consists in how to procure for the group precisely those features which were characteristic of the individual and which are extinguished in him by the formation of the group.'[62] That Freud meant this literally, not in a merely analogical sense, is further proved by his straight rejection, in a footnote added to the 1923 edition, of a criticism by Hans Kelsen, who had adduced that providing the group mind with such an organization would be a hypostasis (attributing to society a mental function which belongs only to individuals).

So how are we to conceive of this opposition between two modes of social aggregation – one based in 'organization', by which society acquires the secondary characteristics of the individual; the other grounded in the libidinal tie with the leader? Do they apply to different kinds of group? Or, rather, are they social logics which, to various extents, enter into the constitution of all social groups? I think that this second hypothesis is the correct one. In my view, the fully organized group and the *purely* narcissistic leader are simply the *reductio ad absurdum* – that is, impossible – extremes of a continuum in which the two social logics are articulated in various ways. To prove, however, that 'organiza-tion' and the 'narcissistic leader' have such a status in the economy of Freud's text, I should be able to show some textual instances of such a combination of both principles. This is my next task.

In fact it is not a difficult task, because Freud gives many examples of such a combination. In a chapter suggestively called 'A Differentiating Degree in the Ego', he discusses the prodigy of the disappearance of individual acquirements in the crowd, prodigy to be interpreted – we are told again – 'as meaning that the individual gives up his ego ideal and substitutes for it the group ideal as embodied in the leader'. He has to add, however, immediately:

And we must add by way of correction that the prodigy is not equally great in every case. In many individuals the separation between the ego and the ego ideal is not very far advanced; the two still coincide readily; the ego has often preserved its earlier narcissistic self-complacency. The selection of the leader is very much facilitated by this circumstance. He need often only possess the typical qualities of the individuals concerned in a particularly clearly marked and pure form, and need only give an impression of greater force and more freedom of libido; and in that case the need for a strong chief will often meet him half-way and invest him with a predominance to which he would otherwise perhaps have had no claim.[63]

What exactly is Freud telling us with this new account? Simply that whenever the need for a strong leader meets the individual only halfway, the leader will be accepted only if he presents, in a particularly marked fashion, features that he shares with those he is supposed to lead. In other words: the led are, to a considerable extent, *in pari materia* with the leader – that is to say, the latter becomes *primus inter pares*. And three momentous consequences follow from this structural mutation. First, that 'something in common' which makes the identification between members of the group possible cannot consist exclusively in love for the leader, but in some positive feature that both leader and led share. Second, identification does not take place only between egos, because the separation between ego and ego ideal is far from complete. This means that a certain degree of identification with the leader becomes possible. In the 'Postscript' to *Group Psychology*, Freud hints at that possibility when he compares the Army and the Catholic Church. While in the Army the soldier would become ridiculous if he identified himself with the commander in chief, the Church requires from the believer more than identification with other Christians: 'He has also to identify with Christ and love all other Christians as Christ loves them. At both points, therefore, the Church requires that the position of the libido which is given by group formation should be supplemented. Identification has to be added where object-choice has taken place, and object-love where there is identification.'[64] Third, if the leader leads because he presents, in a particularly marked way, features which are common to all members of the group, he can no longer be, in all its purity, the despotic, narcissistic ruler. On the one hand, as he participates in that very substance of the community which makes identification possible, his identity is split: he is the father, but also one of the brothers.

On the other hand, since his right to rule is based on the recognition by other group members of a feature of the leader which he shares, in a particularly pronounced way, with all of them, the leader is, to a considerable extent, accountable to the community. The need for leadership could still be there – for structural reasons that Freud does not really explore, but to which we shall return in a moment – but it is a far more democratic leadership than the one involved in the notion of the narcissistic despot. We are, in fact, not far away from that peculiar combination of consensus and coercion that Gramsci called hegemony.

Let us finish this discussion by stressing that Freud was so acutely aware of the impossibility of reducing the process of group formation to the central role of the authoritarian chief of the horde that at the beginning of Chapter 6 of *Group Pyschology* he provides us with an inventory of other possible situations and social combinations – it is, in fact, a sort of programmatic description of a virgin terrain to be intellectually occupied. It is worthwhile quoting it *in extenso*:

> Now much else remains to be examined and described in the morphology of groups. We should have to give our attention to the different kinds of groups, more or less stable, that arise spontaneously, and to study the conditions of their origin and of their dissolution. We should above all be concerned with the distinction between groups which have a leader and leaderless groups. We should consider whether groups with leaders may not be the more primitive and complete, whether in the others an idea, an abstraction, may not take the place of the leader (a state of things to which religious groups, with their invisible head, form a transitional stage), and whether a common tendency, a wish in which a number of people can have a share, may not in the same way serve as a substitute. This abstraction, again, may be more or less completely embodied in the figure of what we may call a secondary leader and interesting varieties would arise from the relation between the idea and the leader. The leader or the leading idea might also, so to speak, be negative; hatred against a particular person or institution might operate in just the same unifying way, and might call up the same kind of emotional ties as positive attachment. Then the question

would also arise whether a leader is really indispensable to the essence of a group – and other questions besides.[65]

Conclusion: towards a starting point

Is there a recurrent theme that gives coherence to reflections on mass society from Taine to Freud? I think there is, and it is to be found in the progressive theoretical renegotiation of the duality between social homogeneity (or indistinctness) and social differentiation. At the beginning of the process, in what we have called the zero degree of any positive evaluation of mass action, this *duality* is actually a *dualism*: for Taine, society can open the door to homogenizing forces only at the expense of its internal cohesion. Equalization of conditions can only mean the breakdown of all hierarchy and differentiation – that is to say, the collapse of the social order. As we have seen, the bloodbath which had, for him, been the French Revolution was the direct result of the uniformity brought about by Absolutism, which had done away with all the intermediate bodies linking the individual to the state. For him, social homogeneity and the breakdown of any kind of social organization were synonymous.

From that uncompromising starting point, the story I have narrated is one of successive efforts to make homogenizing (or equivalential) social logics compatible with the actual working of a viable social body. The homogenization/differentiation duality was maintained, but it adopted less and less the character of a dualism. First, there was a blurring of the sharp distinction between the normal and the pathological and, parallel to this, a transference to the group of many functions which had previously been conceived as belonging exclusively to the individual. Le Bon saw the crowd as an inevitable part of the community, and devised some kind of manipulative catechism to keep it within its limits. For Tarde, the equivalential moment of homogenization is to be found in what he called 'imitation' – in the repetitive practices which usually follow the moments of creation or invention. So the equivalential moment is the very cement of the social fabric. This, as we have seen, was even more the case when he later established the distinction between crowds and publics: although publics are more compatible than crowds with an orderly functioning of society, they are equally based in the homogenizing logic of similitude. As for McDougall if, on the one hand, he established a sharp distinction between crowd and organized group, on the other, through a notion of 'collective will' based on a common identification with an object, he introduced the equivalential principle as a condition of the constitution of the highly organized group. Differentiation and homogeneity, which had been antipodes for Taine, were no longer in opposition to each other. With this we are on the borders of Freud's theorization.

With Freud, the last vestiges of dualism disappear. What he contributed was an intellectual framework within which everything that had so far been presented as a heterogeneous summation of incommensurable principles could now be thought out of a unified theoretical matrix. If my reading of his text is correct, everything turns around the key notion of identification, and the starting point for explaining a plurality of socio-political alternatives is to be found in the *degree* of distance between ego and ego ideal. If that distance increases (why? – this is a question we will have to ask ourselves), we will find the central situation described by Freud: identification between the peers as members of the group and transference of the role of ego ideal to the leader. In that case, the grounding principle of the communal order would be transcendent to the latter and, *vis-à-vis* that principle, the equivalential identification between members of the group would increase. If, on the contrary, the distance between ego and ego ideal is narrower, the process I described above will take place: the leader will be the object-choice of the members of the group, but he will also be part of the group, participating in the general process of mutual identification. In that case there would be a partial immanentization of the ground of the communitarian order. Finally, in the imaginary (*reductio ad absurdum*) case in which the breach between ego and ego ideal was *entirely* bridged, we would have a situation also contemplated by Freud's theory as a limit case: the total transference – through organization – of the functions of the individual to the community. The various myths of the *totally* reconciled society – which invariably presuppose the absence of leadership, that is, the withering away of the political – share this last type of vision.

With this system of alternatives at hand, we can now come back to the question of populism. We started our reflection with an enumeration of the discursive strategies through which populism was either dismissed or downgraded as a political phenomenon, but in any case never really thought in its specificity as one legitimate way among others of constructing the political bond. And we can already entertain a strong suspicion that the reasons for the dismissal of populism are not entirely unrelated to those invoked in what I have called 'the denigration of the masses'. In both cases we see the same accusations of marginality, transitoriness, pure rhetoric, vagueness, manipulation, and so forth. There is also another suspicion creeping into our mind: that in both cases the dismissal is linked to an identical prejudice – that is, the repudiation of the undifferentiated milieu which is the 'crowd' or the 'people' in the name of social structuration and institutionalization. It is true that populist mobilizations do not have the utterly formless expression of the mass actions described by Taine, but when we move from him to the more organized phenomena described by Le Bon, Tarde or McDougall, the differences between populism and group behaviour reduce markedly. With Freud, however, we have reached a more complex and promising approach in which these variations can be seen as alternatives that can be explained within a unified theoretical matrix. This will be my starting point for elaborating a concept of 'populism' in Part II of this book.

Two remarks, however, before I engage on this task. The first is that Freud, as a result of the psychoanalytic framework within which he constructs his theory, has a predominantly genetic approach to the object of his study. Therefore his categories obviously require a structural reformulation if they are going to be useful as tools of socio-political analysis. We cannot fully engage, in the context of our discussion on populism, in this task, although some minimal steps in this direction will be taken at the beginning of Chapter 4. Secondly, although I take Freud as my point of departure, this book should not be conceived as a 'Freudian' venture. There are many issues that Freud did not engage with, and many avenues, quite important for our purposes, which he did not follow. So my research has to appeal to a plurality of intellectual traditions. My hope is that this intertextuality does not make it unduly eclectic.

Part II

CONSTRUCTING THE 'PEOPLE'

The 'People' and the Discursive Production of Emptiness

Some ontological glimpses

Let us go back, for a moment, to the end of Chapter 1. I suggested there that one possible way of approaching populism would be to take at face value some of the pejorative labels which have been attached to it, and to show that those pejorative connotations can be maintained only if one accepts, as a starting point of the analysis, a set of rather questionable assumptions. The two pejorative propositions to which I referred were: (1) that populism is vague and indeterminate in the audience to which it addresses itself, in its discourse, and in its political postulates; (2) that populism is mere rhetoric. To this I opposed two different possibilities: (1) that vagueness and indeterminacy are not shortcomings of a discourse *about* social reality, but, in some circumstances, inscribed in social reality as such; (2) that rhetoric is not epiphenomenal *vis-à-vis* a self-contained conceptual structure, for no conceptual structure finds its internal cohesion without appealing to rhetorical devices. If this is so, the conclusion would be that populism is the royal road to understanding something about the ontological constitution of the political as such. This is what I shall try to prove in this chapter. Before doing so, however, I must make explicit some more general ontological assumptions which will govern my analysis. I have explored these aspects, in a preliminary way, in other works,[1] so here I will simply summarize the main conclusions of these works, and only in so far as they are relevant to the argument of this book.

Three sets of categories are central to my theoretical approach:

1. *Discourse.* Discourse is the primary terrain of the constitution of objectivity as such. By discourse, as I have attempted to make clear several times, I do not mean something that is essentially restricted to the areas of speech and writing, but any complex of elements in which *relations* play the constitutive role. This means that elements do not pre-exist the relational complex but are constituted through it. Thus 'relation' and 'objectivity' are synonymous. Saussure asserted that there are no positive terms in language, only differences – something is what it is only through its differential relations to something else. And what is true of language conceived in its strict sense is also true of any signifying (i.e. objective) element: an action is what it is only through its differences from other possible actions and from other signifying elements – words or actions – which can be successive or simultaneous. Only two types of relation can possibly exist between these signifying elements: combination and substitution. Once the schools of Copenhagen and Prague radicalized linguistic formalism, it was possible to go beyond the Saussurean enthralment to the phonic and conceptual substances, and to develop the full ontological implications of this fundamental breakthrough: all purely regional linguistic reference was, to a large extent, abandoned.

Given this centrality of the category of 'relation' to my analysis, it is clear how my theoretical horizon differs from other contemporary approaches. Alain Badiou, for instance, sees set theory as the terrain of a fundamental ontology. Given the centrality to set theory of the notion of extensionality, however, the category of relation can, at best, play only a marginal role. But in various holistic approaches, too, there is something that is ultimately incompatible with my perspective. Functionalism, for instance, has a relational conception of the social whole, but here relations are subordinated to function and, in this way, teleologically reintegrated to a structural whole which is necessarily previous to and more than the givenness of the differential articulations. And even in a classical structuralist perspective such as Lévi-Strauss's – from which teleology is certainly absent – the whole reaches its unity in something other than the play of differences, this other being the basic categories of the human mind, which reduce all variation to a combination of elements governed by an underlying set of oppositions. In my perspective, there is no beyond the play of differences, no ground which would a priori privilege some elements of the whole over the others. Whatever centrality an element acquires, it has to be explained by the play of differences as such. How? This leads to my second set of categories.

2. *Empty signifiers and hegemony.* I present these categories in the most cursory way, for we will have to come back to them several times in this chapter. A more developed version of the theoretical argument can be found in 'Why Do Empty Signifiers Matter to Politics?'.[2] Our dual task is as follows:

(i) Given that we are dealing with purely differential identities, we have, in some way, to determine the whole within which those identities, as different, are constituted (the problem would not, obviously, arise if we were dealing with positive, only externally related, identities).

(ii) Since we are not postulating any necessary structural centre, endowed with an a priori 'determination in the last instance' capacity, 'centring' effects that manage to constitute a precarious totalizing horizon have to proceed from the interaction of the differences themselves. How is this possible?

In 'Why Do Empty Signifiers Matter to Politics?' I present an argument structured around the following steps. First, if we have a purely differential ensemble, its totality has to be present in each individual act of signification. Conceptually grasping that totality is the condition of signification as such. Secondly, however, to grasp that totality conceptually, we have to grasp its limits – that is to say, we have to differentiate it from something *other* than itself. This other, however, can only be another difference, and since we are dealing with a totality that embraces *all* differences, this *other* difference – which provides the outside that allows us to constitute the totality – would be internal, not external, to the latter – that is to say, it would be unfit for the totalizing job. So, thirdly, the only possibility of having a true outside would be that the outside is not simply one more, neutral element but an *excluded* one, something that the totality expels from itself in order to constitute itself (to give a political example: it is through the demonization of a section of the population that a society reaches a sense of its own cohesion). This, however, creates a new problem: *vis-à-vis* the excluded element, all other differences are equivalent to each other – equivalent in their common rejection of the excluded identity. (As we should remember, this is one of the possibilities of group formation anticipated by Freud: that the feature making the mutual identification between members of the group possible is a common hatred for something or somebody.) But equivalence is precisely what subverts difference, so that all identity is constructed within this tension between the differential and the equivalential logics. Fourthly, this means that in the locus of the totality we find only this tension. What we have, ultimately, is a failed totality, the place of an irretrievable fullness. This totality is an object which is both impossible and necessary. Impossible, because the tension between equivalence and difference is ultimately insurmountable; necessary, because without some kind of closure, however precarious it might be, there would be no signification and no identity. Fifthly: we have shown, however, only that there are no *conceptual* means of fully determining that object. But representation is wider than conceptual grasping. The need remains for this impossible object somehow to have access to the field of representation. Representation has, however, as its only means, particular differences. The argument I have developed is that, at this point, there is the possibility that one difference, without ceasing to be a *particular* difference, assumes the representation of an incommensurable totality. In that way, its body is split between the particularity which it still is and the more universal signification of which it is the bearer. This operation of taking up, by a particularity, of an incommensurable universal signification is what I have called *hegemony*. And, given that this embodied totality or universality is, as we have seen, an impossible object, the hegemonic identity becomes something of the order of an *empty* signifier, its own particularity embodying an unachievable fullness. With this it should be clear that the category of totality cannot be eradicated but that, as a failed totality, it is a horizon and not a ground. If society were unified by a determinate ontic content – determination in the last instance by the economy, spirit of the people, systemic coherence, or whatever – the totality could be *directly* represented at the strictly conceptual level. Since this is not the case, a hegemonic totalization requires a radical investment – that is, one that is not determinable a priori – and engagement in signifying games that are very different from purely conceptual apprehension. As we shall see, the affective dimension plays a central role here.

3. *Rhetoric.* There is a rhetorical displacement whenever a literal term is substituted by a figural one. Let me just point out one aspect of rhetoric which is highly relevant to the discussion above. Cicero, reflecting on the origin of rhetorical devices,[3] imagined a primitive stage of society in which there were more things to be named than the words available in language, so that it was necessary to use words in more than one sense, deviating them from their literal, primordial meaning. For him, of course, this shortage of words represented a purely empirical lack. Let us imagine, however, that this lack is not empirical, that it is linked to a *constitutive* blockage in language which requires naming something which is *essentially* unnameable as a condition of language functioning. In that case the original language would not be literal but figural, for without giving names to the unnameable there would be no language at all. In classical rhetoric, a figural term which cannot be substituted by a literal one was called a *catachresis* (for instance, when we talk about 'the *leg* of a chair'). This argument can be generalized if we face the fact that any distortion of meaning has, at its root, the need to express something that the literal term would simply not transmit. In that sense, catachresis is more than a particular figure: it is the common denominator of rhetoricity as such. This is the point where I can link this argument with

my earlier remarks on hegemony and empty signifiers: if the empty signifier arises from the need to name an object which is both impossible
and necessary, from that zero point of signification which is nevertheless the precondition for any signifying process, the hegemonic
operation will be catachrestical through and through. As we shall see,
the political construction of 'the people' is, for that reason, essentially
catachrestical.

Although a lot more will need to be said later about rhetoric in order
to reveal the discursive devices intervening in the production of 'the
people', we can leave the matter here for the moment. Just one more
point needs, however, to be brought into focus. I have asserted that, in
a hegemonic relation, one particular difference assumes the representation of a totality that exceeds it. This gives clear centrality to a particular
figure within the arsenal of classical rhetoric: synecdoche (the part representing the whole). It also suggests that synecdoche is not simply one
more rhetorical device, simply to be taxonomically added to other figures
such as metaphor and metonymy, but has a different ontological
function. I cannot embark here on a discussion of this matter which,
since it pertains to the general foundations of rhetorical classification,
far exceeds the theme of this book. Let me just say, in passing, that the
classifications of rhetoric have been ancillary to the categories of classical ontology, and that the questioning of the latter cannot fail to have
important consequences for the principles of the former.

We now have most of the necessary preconditions for our discussion
of populism.

Demands and popular identities

A first decision has to be taken. What is our minimal unit of analysis
going to be? Everything turns around the answer to this question. We
can decide to take as our minimal unit the group as such, in which case
we are going to see populism as the ideology or the type of mobilization
of an *already* constituted group – that is, as the expression (the epiphe-
nomenon) of a social reality different from itself; or we can see

populism as one way of constituting the very unity of the group. If we opt for the first alternative, we are immediately confronted with all the pitfalls that I have described in Chapter 1. If we choose the second – as I think we should – we have to accept its actual implications: 'the people' is not something of the nature of an ideological expression, but a real relation between social agents. It is, in other terms, one way of constituting the unity of the group. Obviously, it is not the only way of doing so. There are other logics operating within the social, and making possible types of identity different from the populist one. So, if we want to gauge the specificity of a populist articulatory practice, we have to isolate units smaller than the group, and to determine the kind of unity that populism brings about.

The smallest unit from which we will start corresponds to the category of 'social demand'. As I have pointed out elsewhere,[4] the notion of 'demand' is ambiguous in English: it can mean a request, but it can also mean a claim (as in 'demanding an explanation'). This ambiguity of meaning, however, is useful for our purposes, because it is in the transition from request to claim that we are going to find one of the first defining features of populism.

Let me give an example of how isolated demands emerge, and how they start their process of articulation. This example, although it is imaginary, corresponds pretty well to a situation widely experienced in Third World countries. Think of a large mass of agrarian migrants who settle in the shantytowns on the outskirts of a developing industrial city. Problems of housing arise, and the group of people affected by them request some kind of solution from the local authorities. Here we have a *demand* which initially is perhaps only a *request*. If the demand is satisfied, that is the end of the matter; but if it is not, people can start to perceive that their neighbours have other, equally unsatisfied demands – problems with water, health, schooling, and so on. If the situation remains unchanged for some time, there is an accumulation of unfulfilled demands and an increasing inability of the institutional system to absorb them in a *differential* way (each in isolation from the others), and an *equivalential* relation is established between them. The result could easily be, if it is not circumvented by external factors, a widening chasm separating the institutional system from the people.

So we have here the formation of an internal frontier, a dichotomization of the local political spectrum through the emergence of an equivalential chain of unsatisfied demands. The *requests* are turning into *claims*. We will call a demand which, satisfied or not, remains isolated a *democratic demand*.[5] A plurality of demands which, through their equivalential articulation, constitute a broader social subjectivity we will call *popular demands* – they start, at a very incipient level, to constitute the 'people' as a potential historical actor. Here we have, in embryo, a populist configuration. We already have two clear preconditions of populism: (1) the formation of an internal antagonistic frontier separating the 'people' from power; and (2) an equivalential articulation of demands making the emergence of the 'people' possible. There is a third precondition which does not really arise until the political mobilization has reached a higher level: the unification of these various demands – whose equivalence, up to that point, had not gone beyond a feeling of vague solidarity – into a stable system of signification.

If we remain for one more moment at the local level, we can clearly see how these equivalences – without which there cannot be populism – could be consolidated only when some further steps are taken, both through the expansion of the equivalential chains and through their symbolic unification. Let us take as an example the pre-industrial food riots described by George Rudé.[6] At the more elementary level it is the 'force of the example' – corresponding to the 'contagion' of mass theorists – which can establish an ephimerous equivalence. In the Corn Riots of 1775 in the Paris region, for instance, 'far from being a simultaneous eruption touched off at some central point in control, they [the riots] were a series of minor explosions, breaking out not only in response to local initiative but to the force of example.... At Magny, for example, it was reported that the people had been "excited by the revolt at Pontoise" (17 miles away); at Villemomble, south of Gonesse, it was argued in support of the lower prices offered by buyers "that the price of bread had been fixed at 2 sous in Paris and wheat at 12 francs at Gonesse"; and other such cases could be cited.'[7] The lack of success of these early riots, compared with those which took place during the Revolution, is explained by the fact that, on the one hand, their equivalential chains had not extended to the demands of other social sectors; and on the other, that no national anti-status-quo discourses were available in which the peasantry could inscribe their demands as one more equivalential link. Rudé is quite explicit on this point:

> this [their failure] was due to the isolation of these early rioters, who found themselves confronted ... by the combined opposition of army, Church, government, urban bourgeoisie, and peasant proprietors.... Again – and this is of the greatest importance – the new ideas of 'liberty', popular sovereignty, and the Rights of Man, which were later to align the lower and middle classes against a common enemy, had not yet begun to circulate among the urban and rural poor.... The sole target was the farmer or prosperous peasant, the grain merchant, miller or baker.... There was no question of overthrowing the government or established order, of putting forward new solutions, or even of seeking redress of grievances by political action. This is the eighteenth-century food riot in its undiluted form. Similar movements will appear under the Revolution, but they will never have quite the same degree of spontaneity and political innocence.[8]

Here we see a double pattern: on the one hand, the more extended the equivalential chain, the more mixed will be the nature of the links entering into its composition: 'The crowd may riot because it is hungry or fears to be so, because it has some deep social grievance, because it seeks an immediate reform or the millennium, or because it wants to destroy an enemy or acclaim a "hero"; but it is seldom for any single one of these reasons alone.'[9] On the other hand, if the confrontation is going to be more than purely episodic, the forces engaged in it have to attribute to *some* of the equivalential components a role of anchorage which distinguishes them from the rest. From this perspective, Rudé makes the distinction between the ostensible motives of a riot and 'the underlying motives and traditional myths and beliefs – what crowd psychologists and social scientists have termed "fundamental" or "generalized" beliefs – that played a not inconsiderable part in such disturbances'.[10] He discusses the 'levelling' instinct, the antipathy to capital innovation, the identification of 'justice' with the King as protector or 'father' of his people, as well as a set of recurrent religious or millenarian themes. All these themes show a clearly discernible pattern: they have a different role from the actual material contents of the demands at stake – otherwise they could not ground or give consistency to these demands. About the 'levelling instinct', for instance, Rudé asserts:

> There is the traditional 'levelling instinct' … which prompts the poor to seek a degree of elementary social justice at the expense of the rich, *les grands*, and those in authority regardless of whether they are government officials, feudal lords, capitalists, or middle-class revolutionary leaders. It is the common ground on which, beyond the slogans of contending parties, the militant *sans-culotte* meets the 'Church and King' rioter or the peasant in search of his millennium …. [T]he 'levelling' instinct of the crowd might as readily be harnessed to an anti-radical as to a radical cause.[11]

The other examples he mentions are equally telling: during the Gordon Riots, the crowds attacked *rich* Catholics rather than Catholics in general; during the 'Church and King' disturbances, people in Naples attacked Jacobins not just because they were allies of the atheistic French, but mainly because they went around in carriages; and during the Vendée, if peasants revolted against revolutionary Paris, it was because they hated the wealthy city more than the local landlord. The conclusion is unmistakable: if this 'levelling instinct' can be attached to the most diverse social contents, it cannot, in itself, have a content of its own. This means that those images, words, and so on through which it is recognized, which give successive concrete contents a sense of temporal continuity, function exactly as what I have called empty signifiers.

This provides us with a good starting point for an approach to populism. All the three structural dimensions which are necessary to elaborate its developed concept are contained, *in nuce*, in the local mobilizations to which I have just referred: the unification of a plurality of demands in an equivalential chain; the constitution of an internal frontier dividing society into two camps; the consolidation of the equivalential chain through the construction of a popular identity which is something qualitatively more than the simple summation of the equivalential links. The rest of this chapter will be devoted to the successive discussion of each of these three aspects. The concept of populism at which we shall arrive at the end of that exploration will, however, be a provisional one, for it will be based on the operation of two – heuristically necessary – simplifying assumptions. These two assumptions will be successively eliminated in Chapter 5. Only then shall we be in a position to present a fully developed concept of populism.

The adventures of equivalences

When we move from our localized riots to populism, we necessarily have to widen the dimensions of our analysis. Populism, in its classical forms, presupposes a larger community, so the equivalential logics will cut across new and more heterogeneous social groups. This widening, however, will reveal more clearly some features of those logics that the more restricted mobilizations tended to conceal.

Let us go back to the previously established distinction between democratic and popular demands. We already know something about the latter: they presuppose, for their constitution, the equivalence of a plurality of demands. But about democratic demands we have said very little: the only thing we know is that they remain in isolation. Isolation *vis-à-vis* what? Only *vis-à-vis* the equivalential process. This is not, however, a monadic isolation, for we know that if it does not enter into an equivalential relation with other demands, it is because it is a *fulfilled* demand (in Chapter 5 I shall discuss a different type of isolation, linked to the status of floating signifiers). Now, a demand which is met does not remain isolated; it is inscribed in an institutional/differential totality. So we have two ways of constructing the social: either through the assertion of a particularity – in our case, a particularity of demands – whose only links to other particularities are of a differential nature (as we have seen: no positive terms, only differences); or through a partial surrender of particularity, stressing what all particularities have, equiv-alentially, in common. The second mode of construction of the social involves, as we know, the drawing of an antagonistic frontier; the first does not. I have called the first mode of constructing the social *logic of difference*, and the second, *logic of equivalence*. Apparently, we could draw the conclusion that one precondition for the emergence of populism is the expansion of the equivalential logic at the expense of the differential one. This is true in many respects, but to leave the matter there would be to win the argument too cheaply, for it would presuppose that equiva-lence and difference are simply in a zero-sum relation of exclusion of each other. Things are far more complex.

At this point we can go back to our discussion of discursive totaliza-tion. We saw that there is no totalization without exclusion, and that such an exclusion presupposes the split of all identity between its differential nature, which links/separates it from other identities, and its equivalential bond with all the others *vis-à-vis* the excluded element. The partial total-ization that the hegemonic link manages to create does not eliminate that split but, on the contrary, has to operate out of the structural possibilities deriving from it. So both difference and equivalence have to reflect them-selves into each other. How can this be? Let me give two opposing examples, in order to draw from them later a theoretical conclusion.

A society which postulates the welfare state as its ultimate horizon is one in which only the differential logic would be accepted as a legitimate way of constructing the social. In this society, conceived as a continuously expanding system, any social need should be met differentially; and there would be no basis for creating an internal frontier. Since it would be unable to differentiate itself from anything else, that society could not totalize itself, could not create a 'people'. What actually happens is that the obstacles identified during the establishment of that society – private entrepreneurial greed, entrenched interests, and so on – force their very proponents to identify enemies and to reintroduce a discourse of social division grounded in equivalential logics. In that way, collective subjects constituted around the defence of the welfare state can emerge. The same can be said about neo-liberalism: it also presents itself as a panacea for a fissureless society – with the difference that in this case, the trick is performed by the market, not by the state. The result is the same: at some point Margaret Thatcher found 'obstacles', started denouncing the parasites of social security and others, and ended up with one of the most aggressive discourses of social division in contemporary British history.

From the viewpoint of the equivalential logics, however, the situation is similar. Equivalences can weaken, but they cannot domesticate differences. In the first place, it is clear that equivalence *does not attempt* to eliminate differences. In our initial example, it was because a series of particular social demands were frustrated that the equivalence was established in the first place – if the particularity of the demands disappears, there is no ground for the equivalence either. So difference continues to operate within equivalence, both as its ground and in a relation of tension with it. Let me give an example. In the course of the French Revolution, and especially during the Jacobin period, the 'people', as we know, is an equivalential construction, and the whole political dynamic of the period is unintelligible if we do not see it in terms of the tension between the universality of the equivalential chain and the particularity of the demands of each of its links. Let us consider the case of the workers' demands in such a chain.[12] The whole revolutionary period is punctuated by the tension – one among others – of workers' demands and the equivalential discourse of radical popular democracy. On the one hand, the demands of workers, who belonged to the revolutionary camp, were contradictorily reflected in the official revolutionary discourse: the latter could not simply ignore them, and this led to a zigzag movement of partial recognition and partial repression. On the other hand, some hesitations are also detectable in the workers' actions. While the *sansculottes* – through Hébert and his associates – controlled the Paris Commune, there was political recognition, to a large extent, of workers' social demands; but after their fall in April 1794, and the subsequent closing down of the *sans-culottes*' 'popular societies', a disbanding of the incipient workers' organizations took place. Later in the year, the workers' protest movements re-emerge as a result of the publication of the General Maximum law establishing the new wage rates in Paris; they were an important element in the fall of Robespierre and later of the Commune, whose councillors were taken to the place of execution surrounded by a hostile mass of workers who shouted at them as they passed: '*Foutu maximum!*' But later, the new rulers let the laws of the market operate; this led to rapid inflation and the deterioration of wage values. This time, in the midst of an unemployment crisis, social protest took the form of more traditional food riots. What this complex history shows is that the tension equivalence/difference was not really broken at any time during the revolutionary period. Those who were in control of the state did not surrender to the workers' demands, but could not ignore them either; and the workers, for their part, could not afford at any point to push their autonomy to the point of abandoning the revolutionary camp. There was no question at any moment of initiating a new chapter of an independent class struggle, as Daniel Guérin has argued in a now discredited book.[13]

Where, however, does all this leave us? I have shown that equivalence and difference are ultimately incompatible with each other; none the less, they require each other as necessary conditions for the construction of the social. The social is nothing but the locus of this irreducible tension. What, in that case, about populism? If no ultimate separation between the two logics is possible, in what sense would the privileging of the equivalential moment be specific to it? And, especially, what would 'privileging' mean in this context? Let us consider the matter carefully. What I said above about totalization, hegemony and the empty signifier gives us the clue required to solve this riddle. On the one hand, *all* social (that is, discursive) identity is constituted at the meeting point of difference and equivalence – just as linguistic identities are the seat of both syntagmatic relations of combination and paradigmatic relations of substitution. On the other hand, however, there is an essential unevenness in the social, for, as we have seen, totalization requires that one differential element should assume the representation of an impossible whole. (The *Solidarność* symbols, for instance, did not remain the particular demands of a group of workers in Gdansk, but came to signify a much wider popular camp against an oppressive regime.) Thus a certain identity is picked up from the whole field of differences, and made to embody this totalizing function. This – to answer the previous question – is exactly what *privileging* means. Resurrecting an old phenomenological category, we could say that this function consists in posing the *horizon* of the social, the limit of what is representable within it (we have already discussed the relation between limit and totality).

The difference between a populist and an institutionalist totalization is to be found at the level of these privileged, hegemonic signifiers which structure, as nodal points, the ensemble of a discursive formation. Difference and equivalence are present in both cases, but an institutionalist discourse is one that attempts to make the limits of the discursive formation coincide with the limits of the community. So the universal principle of 'differentiality' would become the dominant equivalence within that homogeneous communitarian space. (Think, for instance, of Disraeli's 'one nation'.) The opposite takes place in the case of populism: a frontier of exclusion divides society into two camps. The 'people', in that case, is something less than the totality of the members of the community: it is a partial component which nevertheless aspires to be conceived as the only legitimate totality. Traditional terminology – which has been translated into common language – makes this difference clear: the people can be conceived as *populus*, the body of all citizens; or as *plebs*, the underprivileged. Even this distinction, however, does not exactly capture what I am driving at. For the distinction could easily be seen as a *juridically* recognized one, in which case it would simply be a differentiation within a homogeneous space giving universal legitimacy to all its component parts – that is to say, the relation between its two terms would not be an antagonistic one. In order to have the 'people' of populism, we need something more: we need a *plebs* who claims to be the only legitimate *populus* – that is, a partiality which wants to function as the totality of the community. ('All power to the Soviets' – or its equivalent in other discourses – would be a strictly populist claim.) In the case of an institutionalist discourse, we have seen that differentiality claims to be the only legitimate equivalent: all differences are considered equally valid within a wider totality. In the case of populism, this symmetry is broken: there is a part which identifies itself with the whole.

So, as we already know – a radical exclusion will take place *within* the communitarian space. In the first case the principle of differentiality can remain as the only dominant equivalence; in the second that is not enough: the rejection of a power that is very active within the community requires the identification of all links in the popular chain with an identity principle which crystallizes all differential claims around a common denominator – and the latter requires, of course, *a positive symbolic expression*. This is the transition from what we have called *democratic* demands to *popular* demands. The first can be accommodated within an expanding hegemonic formation; the second presents a challenge to the hegemonic formation as such. In Mexico, during the period of hegemony of the Partido Revolucionario Institucional (PRI), political jargon used to distinguish between the punctual demands which the system could absorb in a *transformistic* way (to use the Gramscian term) and what was called *el paquete* (the parcel) – a large set of simultaneous demands presented as a unified whole. It was only with the latter that the regime was not prepared to negotiate – they were usually met with ruthless repression.

At this point, we can return for a moment to our discussion of Freud. Freud's notion of a group which, through organization, has assumed all functions of the individual and eliminated the need for a leader corresponds, almost point by point, to a society entirely governed by what I have called the logic of difference. We know that such a society is an impossibility and, as I said above, I think there are good grounds to think that Freud also saw it as a limit concept, not as an actually viable alternative. But its antipode, a durable group whose *only* libidinal tie is love for the leader, is equally impossible. The dimension of differential particularity – which, as we have seen, continues to operate under the equivalential relation – would have vanished, and equivalence would have collapsed into simple identity. And in that case there would be no group at all. I think Freud moves too quickly from pointing to love of the leader as a central condition for *consolidating* the social bond to asserting that it is the *origin* of that bond. The only examples Freud can provide of groups based *just* on love for the leader involve rather fleeting situations, such as the contagion of a fit of hysterics in a group of girls because one of them has received a disappointing letter from a lover; or, in a second example, another group of girls in love with a singer or a pianist – identification in these cases being just a way of surmounting envy or jealousy. But whenever we move to any of the other groups he discusses, this explanation is patently insufficient. Soldiers do not join the Army *because* of their love for the commander in chief, however important that love later becomes in consolidating the unity of the group. However, if we complement this analysis with Freud's own references to a differentiated grade in the ego, which I have discussed above, we come up with a very different picture – one that actually corresponds, in all substantive respects, with our analysis of the necessary articulation between equivalence and difference.

We have advanced one step – and only one – in approaching the notion of populism. We know, so far, that populism requires the dichotomic division of society into two camps – one presenting itself as a part which claims to be the whole; that this dichotomy involves the antagonistic division of the social field; and that the popular camp presupposes, as a condition of its constitution, the construction of a global identity out of the equivalence of a plurality of social demands. The exact meaning of these findings remains, however, necessarily undetermined until we establish more precisely what is involved in the discursive construction both of an antagonistic frontier and of that particular articulation of equivalence and difference that we call 'popular identity'. This is what I will turn to next.

Antagonism, difference and representation

What does our notion of the antagonistic frontier require in order that it should fulfil the role that we have assigned to it – namely, to think society as two irreducible camps structured around two incompatible equivalential chains? Clearly, we cannot move from one camp to the other in terms of any differential continuity.[14] If, through the internal logic of a certain camp, we were able to move to the other, we would be dealing with a differential relation, and the chasm separating the two camps would not be truly radical. Radicality of the chasm involves its conceptual irrepresentability. It is like the Lacanian dictum that 'there is no sexual relationship': the statement does not mean, obviously, that people do not have sexual relations; what it *does* mean is that the two sides of such a relationship cannot be subsumed under a single formula of sexuation.[15] The same happens with antagonism: the strict moment of the chasm – the antagonistic moment as such – eludes conceptual apprehension. A simple example will demonstrate this. Let us suppose a historical explanation proceeding according to the following sequence: (1) in the world market, a growth in the demand for wheat pushes wheat prices up; (2) so wheat producers in country X have an incentive to increase production; (3) as a result, they start occupying new land, and to this end they have to dispossess traditional peasant communities; (4) so the peasants have no alternative but to resist this dispossession, and so on. There is a clear hiatus in this exposition: the first three points follow naturally one from the other as part of an objective sequence; the fourth, however, is of a completely different nature: it is an appeal to our common sense, or to our knowledge of 'human nature', to add to the sequence a link that the objective explanation is unable to provide. We have a discourse that actually *incorporates* this link, but that incorporation does not take place through conceptual apprehension.

It is not difficult to detect the meaning of this conceptual hiatus. If we were able to reconstitute the whole series of events through purely conceptual means, the antagonistic chasm could not be constitutive. The conflictual moment would be the epiphenomenal expression of an underlying and fully rational process – as in the Hegelian cunning of reason. Between the way people 'live' their antagonistic relations and the 'true meaning' of the latter there would be an unbridgeable gap. This is why 'contradiction', in its dialectical sense, is entirely unable to capture what is at stake in a social antagonism. B can be – dialectically – the negation of A, but I can move to B only through the development of something which was already contained, from its very inception, in A. And when A and B are *aufgehoben* in C, we can see even more clearly that the contradiction is part of a dialectical sequence which is, conceptually, entirely masterable. If, however, antagonism is strictly constitutive, the antagonistic force shows an exteriority which certainly can be overcome, but cannot be dialectically retrieved.

One could perhaps argue that this is the case only because we have identified objectivity with what is conceptually masterable in a consistent whole, while other notions of a seamless objective terrain – for example, semiological distinctions – are not exposed to the same kind of criticism. Saussure's differences, for instance, do not presuppose logical connections between them. This is true, but it is irrelevant to the question we are raising. We are putting into question not the universality of the *logical* terrain, but of objectivity as such. Saussurean differences still presuppose a continuous space within which they are, as such, constituted. A notion of constitutive antagonism, of a radical frontier, requires, on the contrary, a *broken* space. We have to see the various dimensions of this break, and their consequences for the emergence of popular identities.

Here I shall discuss only those dimensions that are inherent to the break as such, reserving for the next section the question of the discursive construction of the 'people'. Let us go back to our original scene: the frustration of a series of social demands makes possible the movement from isolated democratic demands to equivalential popular ones. One first dimension of the break is that, at its root, there is the experience of a *lack*, a gap which has emerged in the harmonious continuity of the social. There is a fullness of the community which is missing. This is decisive: the construction of the 'people' will be the attempt to give a name to that absent fullness. Without this initial breakdown of something in the social order – however minimal that something could initially be – there is no possibility of antagonism, frontier, or, ultimately, 'people'. This initial experience is not only, however, an experience of lack. Lack, as we have seen, is linked to a demand which is not met.[16] But this involves bringing into the picture the power which has not met the demand. A demand is always addressed to somebody. So from the very beginning we are confronted with a dichotomic division between unfulfilled social demands, on the one hand, and an unresponsive power, on the other. Here we begin to see why the *plebs* sees itself as the *populus*, the part as the whole: since the fullness of the community is merely the imaginary reverse of a situation lived as *deficient being*, those who are responsible for this cannot be a legitimate part of the community; the chasm between them is irretrievable.

This leads us to our second dimension. As we have seen, the movement from democratic to popular demands presupposes a plurality of subject positions: demands, isolated at the beginning, emerge at different points of the social fabric and the transition to a popular subjectivity consists in establishing an equivalential bond between them. These popular struggles, however, confront us with a new problem, which we were not facing when we were dealing with precise democratic demands. The meaning of such demands is determined largely by their differential positions within the symbolic framework of society, and it is only their frustration that presents them in a new light. But if there is a very extensive series of social demands which are not met, it is that very symbolic framework which starts to disintegrate. In that case, however, the popular demands are less and less sustained by a pre-existing differential framework: they have, to a large extent, to construct a new one. And for the same reason, the identity of the enemy also depends increasingly on a process of political construction. I can be relatively certain about who the enemy is when, in limited struggles, I am fighting against the local council, those responsible for the health system, or the university authorities. But a popular struggle involves the equivalence between all those partial struggles, and in that case the global enemy to be identified becomes much less obvious. The consequence is that the internal political frontier will become much less determinate, and the equivalences intervening in that determination can operate in many different directions.

The true dimensions of this indeterminacy can best be apprehended if we take into account the following consideration. As we have seen, no particular content has inscribed, in its ontic specificity, its actual meaning within a discursive formation – everything depends on the system of differential and equivalential articulations within which it is located. A signifier like 'workers', for instance, can, in certain discursive configurations, exhaust itself in a particularistic, sectional meaning; while in other discourses – the Peronist would be an example – it can become the name *par excellence* of the 'people'. What has to be stressed is that this mobility also involves another possibility which is crucially important to an understanding of the way populist variations operate. We know, from our previous analysis, that populism involves the division of the social scene into two camps. This division presupposes (as we shall see in more detail below) the presence of some privileged signifiers which condense in themselves the signification of a whole antagonistic camp (the 'regime', the 'oligarchy', the 'dominant groups', and so on, for the enemy; the 'people', the 'nation', the 'silent majority', and so on, for the oppressed underdog – these signifiers acquire this articulating role according, obviously, to a contextual history). In this process of condensation, however, we have to differentiate between two aspects: the *ontological* role of discursively constructing social division and the *ontic* content which, in certain circumstances, plays that role. The important point is that, at some stage, the ontic content can exhaust its ability to play the role, while the need for this nevertheless remains; and that – given the indeterminacy of the relation between ontic content and ontological function – this function can be performed by signifiers of an entirely opposite political sign. That is why, between left-wing and right-wing populism, there is a nebulous no-man's-land which can be crossed – and has been crossed – in many directions.

Let me give one example. There had traditionally been, in France, a left-wing vote of protest, channelled mainly through the Communist Party, which fulfilled what Georges Lavau has called a 'tribunicial function',[17] being the voice of those who were excluded from the system. So it clearly was an attempt to create a *'peuple de gauche'*, grounded in the construction of a political frontier. With the collapse of Communism and the formation of a Centre establishment in which the Socialist Party and its associates were not very different from the Gaullists, the division between Left and Right became increasingly blurred. The need, however, for a radical vote of protest remained and, as the left-wing signifiers had abandoned the camp of social division, this camp was occupied by signifiers of the Right. The ontological need to express social division was stronger than its ontic attachment to a left-wing discourse which, anyway, did not attempt to build it up any longer. This was translated into a considerable movement of former Communist voters to the National Front. As Mény and Surel have put it: 'In the case of the French National Front [FN], many works have tried to show that the transfers of votes in favour of the extreme right-wing party followed deeply atypical logics. Thus the notions of "left-lepenism" [*gaucho-lepénisme*] and "workers-lepenism" [*ouvriero-lepénisme*] proceed both from finding that a sizeable proportion of the FN votes come from voters who previously "belonged" to the electorate of the classical Left, especially the Communist Party.'[18] I think that today's resurgence of a right-wing populism in Western Europe can largely be explained along similar lines.[19] Given that I am talking about populism, I have presented this asymmetry between ontological function and its ontic fulfilment in relation to discourses of radical change, but it can also be found in other discursive configurations. As I have argued elsewhere,[20] when people are confronted with radical *anomie*, the need for *some kind* of order becomes more important than the actual ontic order that brings it about. The Hobbesian universe is the extreme version of this gap: because society is faced with a situation of *total* disorder (the state of nature), whatever the Leviathan does is legitimate – irrespective of its content – as long as order is the result.

There is a final important dimension in the construction of political frontiers which requires our attention. It concerns the tension we have detected between difference and equivalence within a complex of demands which have become 'popular' through their articulation. For any democratic demand, its inscription within an equivalential chain is a mixed blessing. On the one hand, that inscription undoubtedly gives the demand a corporeality which it would not otherwise have. It ceases to be a fleeting, transient occurrence, and becomes part of what Gramsci called a 'war of position': a discursive/institutional ensemble which ensures its long-term survival. On the other hand, the 'people' (the equivalential chain) has strategic laws of movement of its own, and nothing guarantees that these laws would not lead to sacrify, or at least substantially compromise, the requests involved in some of the individual democratic demands. This possibility is even more real because each of these demands is linked to the others *only* through the equivalential chain, which results from a contingent discursive construction, not from an aprioristically dictated convergence. Democratic demands are, in their mutual relations, like Schopenhauer's porcupines, to which Freud refers:[21] if they are too far apart, they are cold; if they approach each other too closely in order to get warmer, they hurt each other with their quills. Not only that, however: the terrain within which this uneasy alternation between cold and warm takes place – that is, the 'people' – is not just a neutral terrain which acts as a clearing-house for the individual demands, for it is transformed in most cases into a hypostasis which starts to have demands of its own. We will come back to some possible political variations in this unended – and unending – game of differential and equivalential articulations. I would like now, however, to refer to only one of them, which is a very real – albeit an extreme – possibility, because it involves the dissolution of the 'people': namely, the absorption of each of the individual demands, as pure differentiality, within the dominant system – with its concomitant result, the dissolution of its equivalential links with other demands. So the destiny of populism is strictly related to the destiny of the political frontier: if this frontier collapses, the 'people' as a historical actor disintegrates.

I shall take as an illustration the analysis of the disintegration of British Chartism by Gareth Stedman Jones in a pathbreaking and now classic essay.[22] His starting point is the critique of the dominant version of Chartism as a *social* movement, responding to the dislocations brought about by the Industrial Revolution. What this image of Chartism does not take into account, according to Stedman Jones, is its specific discourse (language, in his terms), which locates it within the main current of British radicalism. This tradition, which has its roots in the eighteenth-century Tory opposition to Whig oligarchy, was given a radical turn at the time of the French Revolution and the Napoleonic wars. Its dominant leitmotiv is to situate the evils of society not in something that is inherent in the economic system, but quite the opposite: in the abuse of power by parasitic and speculative groups which have control of political power – 'old corruption', in Cobbett's words: 'If the land could be socialised, the national debt liquidated, and the banker's monopoly control over the supply of money abolished, it was because all these forms of property shared the common characteristic of not being the product of labour. It was for this reason that the feature most strongly picked out in the ruling class was its idleness and parasitism.'[23] This being the dominant discourse dividing society into two camps, workers' demands could only be one more link in that equivalential chain – although the sequence of events would give it an increasing centrality. What is, anyway, characteristic of that discourse is that it was not a *sectional* discourse of the working class but a *popular* discourse addressed, in principle, to all the producers against the 'idlers': 'The distinction was not primarily between ruling and exploited classes in an economic sense, but rather between the beneficiaries and the victims of corruption and monopoly political power. The juxtaposition was in the first instance moral and political, and dividing lines could be drawn as much within classes as between them.'[24] Dominant themes in denouncing the enemy were the consolidation of the landowners' power through a historical sequence whose stepping stones were the Norman occupation, the loss of suffrage right in medieval times, the dissolution of the monasteries and the eighteenth-century enclosures; the increase of the national debt during the French wars and the return to the gold standard after them; and so on. Although after 1832 there was, as Stedman Jones points out, an increasing identification of the 'people' with the working classes, and also an extension of the notion of 'old corruption' to the capitalists themselves, neither the political and moral character of the denunciation nor the hopes of winning back the middle classes was ever abandoned.

In this saga, there were two moments of crucial signification for the theoretical issue under discussion. The first was the wave of centralizing administrative reforms which took place in the 1830s. In a short time there was a succession of measures which broke all structures of local power as inherited from the eighteenth century. This authoritarian centralization met a violent reaction, and the anti-statist discourse of Chartism would apparently have been ideal to galvanize and amalgamate social protest. This, however, did not happen, because the fracture in the popular camp after 1832 had become unbridgeable. The middle classes preferred to look for alternatives within the existing institutional framework rather than risk an alliance with forces which they saw as increasingly threatening.[25]

What happened next, however, was even more revealing. The confrontational state policy of the 1830s was discontinued in the 1840s. On the one hand, we have a more humane type of legislation dealing with issues such as housing, health and education; on the other, there was an increasing recognition that political power should not tamper with the actual working of market forces. This undermined the two bases of Chartist political discourse. Social actors now had to discriminate between one piece of legislation and another. This means, in our terms, that there was less of a confrontation with a global enemy, since isolated demands had a chance of succeeding in their dealings with a power which was no longer unequivocally unsympathetic. We know what that means: the loosening up of the equivalential bonds and the disaggregation of the popular demands into a plurality of democratic ones. But something more also happened: the opposition between the producers and the parasites, which had been the foundation of the Chartist equivalential discourse, lost its meaning once the state relaxed its grip on the economy – in a not entirely dissimilar way from the one the Chartists had advocated – and could no longer be presented as the source of all economic evils. Here, as Stedman Jones has pointed out, we have the beginning of that separation between state and economy which would be the trademark of mid-Victorian liberalism:

If Chartist rhetoric was ideally suited to concert the opposition to the Whig measures of the 1830s, by the same token it was ill-equipped to modify its position in response to the changed character of state activity in the 1840s. The Chartist critique of the state and the class oppression it had engendered was a totalising critique. It was not suited to the discrimination between one legislative measure and another, since this would be to concede that not all measures pursued by the state were for obviously malign class purposes and that beneficial reforms might be carried by a selfish legislature in an unreformed system.[26]

We perceive, through this last quotation, where the pattern of disintegration of the 'people' is to be found – not just in the fact that the political (state power) ceased to play its totalizing role in the discursive construction of the enemy, but in the fact that no other power could play the same role. The popular crisis was more than a simple failure by the state to function as the linchpin keeping together a system of domination. It was, rather, a crisis in the ability of the 'people' to totalize at all – either the identity of the enemy or its own 'global' identity. The increasing separation between the economy and state intervention was not in itself an insurmountable obstacle to the construction of both a political frontier and a 'people': it was just a matter of giving less weight to 'idlers' and 'speculators' and more to capitalists as such – a transition that the Chartist discourse had, in any case, already started. This, however, would have presupposed that the structural location of the people within the opposition us/them would have survived the progressive substitution of its actual content. And this is exactly what did not happen. As we have indicated, the chasm between middle and working classes became deeper, several state measures were able to meet *individual* social demands, and – this is crucial – this break of equivalential links had long-term repercussions for the identity of the working classes themselves. This is the true meaning of the transition to mid-Victorian liberalism: politics became less a matter of confrontation between two antagonistic blocs and more a question of negotiating differential demands within an expansive social state. When working-class organizations re-emerged as modern trade unions, they found that their *specific* demands could be more advantageously advanced through negotiation with the state than through a head-on confrontation with it. This did not, of course, exclude moments of violent explosion, but even they could not conceal their *sectional* character. And, although the construction of a bourgeois hegemony in the second half of the nineteenth century was anything but a peaceful process, the long-term line is unmistakable: the primacy of differential logic over equivalential ruptures.

The internal structuration of the 'people'

I have explained two of the *sine qua non* dimensions of populism: the equivalential bond and the need for an internal frontier. (The two are, in fact, strictly correlated.) I now have to explain the precipitator of the equivalential link: popular identity as such. I said above that equivalential relations would not go beyond a vague feeling of solidarity if they did not crystallize in a certain discursive identity which no longer represents democratic demands *as* equivalent, but the equivalential link as such. It is only that moment of crystallization that constitutes the 'people' of populism. What was simply a mediation between demands now acquires a consistency of its own. Although the link was originally ancillary to the demands, it now reacts over them and, through an inversion of the relationship, starts behaving as their ground. Without this operation of inversion, there would be no populism. (This is similar to what Marx describes in *Capital* as the transition from the general form of value to the money form.)

Let us explore the different moments of this construction of the 'people' as a crystallization of a chain of equivalences in which the crystallizing instance has, in its autonomy, as much weight as the infrastructural chain of demands which made its emergence possible. A good starting point could be my earlier reference to a breach in the continuity of the communitarian space resulting from the *plebs* presenting itself as the totality of the *populus*. This essential asymmetry at the root of popular action is also stressed by Jacques Rancière, in comparable terms:

The demos attributes to itself as its proper lot the equality that belongs to all citizens. In so doing, this party that is not one identifies its improper property with the exclusive principle of community, and identifies its name – the name of the indistinct mass of men of no position – with the name of the community itself …. [T]he people appropriates the common quality as their own. What they bring to the community strictly speaking is contention.[27]

What, however, is the meaning of this aspiration of a partiality to be seen as the social totality? Where does its ontological possibility lie? For the totality to have the status of an aspiration, it must, to start with, differentiate itself from the factually given ensemble of social relations. We already know why this is so: because the moment of antagonistic break is irreducible. It cannot be led back to any deeper positivity which would transform it into the epiphenomenal expression of something different from itself. This means that no institutional totality can inscribe within itself, as positive moments, the ensemble of social demands. That is why the unfulfilled, uninscribable demands would, as we have seen, have a *deficient* being. At the same time, however, the *fullness* of communitarian being is very much present, for them, as that which is absent; as that which, under the existing positive social order, has to remain unfulfilled. So the *populus* as the given – as the ensemble of social relations *as* they actually are – reveals itself as a false totality, as a partiality which is a source of oppression. On the other hand, the *plebs*, whose partial demands are inscribed in the horizon of a fully fledged totality – a just society which exists only ideally – can aspire to constitute a truly universal *populus* which the actually existing situation negates. It is because the two visions of the *populus* are strictly incommensurable that a certain particularity, the *plebs*, can identify itself with the *populus* conceived as an ideal totality.

What is involved in this identification? I have already described how the transition from individual to popular demands operates – through the construction of equivalential links. Now I have to explain how this plurality of links becomes a singularity through its condensation around a popular identity. What, in the first place, are the raw materials entering into that process of condensation? Obviously, only the individual demands in their particularism. But if an equivalential link is going to be established between them, some kind of common denominator has to be found which embodies the totality of the series. Since this common denominator has to come from the series itself, it can only be an individual demand which, for a set of circumstantial reasons, acquires a certain centrality. (Let us remember our *Solidarność* example, above.) This is the hegemonic operation, which I have already described. There is no hegemony without constructing a popular identity out of a plurality of democratic demands. So let us locate the popular identity within the relational complex which explains the conditions of both its emergence and its dissolution.

Two aspects of the constitution of popular identities are important for us. First, the demand which the popular identity crystallizes is internally split: on the one hand, it remains a particular demand; on the other, its own particularity comes to signify something quite different from itself: the total chain of equivalential demands. While it remains a particular demand, it also becomes the signifier of a wider universality. (For a short time after 1989, for instance, the 'market' signified, in Eastern Europe, much more than a purely economic arrangement: it embraced, through equivalential links, contents such as the end of bureaucratic rule, civil freedoms, catching up with the West, and so forth.) But this more universal signification is necessarily transmitted to the other links of the chain, which are thus also split between the particularism of their own demands and the popular signification imparted by their inscription within the chain. This is the site of a tension: the weaker a demand, the more it depends for its formulation on its popular inscription; conversely, the more discursively and institutionally autonomous it becomes, the more tenuous will be its dependence on an equivalential articulation. The breaking of this dependence can lead, as we have seen in the case of Chartism, to an almost complete disintegration of the popular-equivalential camp.

Secondly, our argument has to dovetail, at this point, with what I said above about the production of 'empty signifiers'. As we know, any popular identity needs to be condensed around some signifiers (words, images) which refer to the equivalential chain as a totality. The more extended the chain, the less these signifiers will be attached to their original particularistic demands. That is to say, the function of representing the relative 'universality' of the chain will prevail over that of expressing the particular claim which is the material bearer of that function. In other words: popular identity becomes increasingly full from an *extensional* point of view, for it represents an ever-larger chain of demands; but it becomes *intensionally* poorer, for it has to dispossess itself of particularistic contents in order to embrace social demands which are quite heterogeneous. That is: a popular identity functions as a tendentially empty signifier.

What is crucially important, however, is not to confuse *emptiness* with *abstraction* – that is to say, not to conceive of the common denominator expressed by the popular symbol as an ultimate positive feature shared by all the links in the chain. If it were, we would not have transcended the logic of difference. We would be dealing with an *abstract* difference, which would nevertheless belong to the differential order and would be, as such, conceptually graspable. But in an equivalential relation, demands share nothing positive, just the fact that they all remain unfulfilled. So there is a specific negativity which is inherent to the equivalential link.

How does this moment of negativity enter into the constitution of a popular identity? Let us go back for a moment to a point I discussed above: in a situation of radical disorder, the demand is for *some kind of* order, and the *concrete* social arrangement that will meet that request is a secondary consideration (the same can also be said of similar terms such as 'justice', 'equality', 'freedom', etc.). It would be a waste of time trying to give a positive definition of 'order' or 'justice' – that is, to ascribe to them a conceptual content, however minimal it might be. The semantic role of these terms is not to express *any* positive content but, as we have seen, to function as the names of a fullness which is constitutively absent. It is because there is no human situation in which injustice of some kind or another does not exist that 'justice', as a term, makes sense. Since it names an undifferentiated fullness, it has no conceptual content whatsoever: it is not an *abstract* term but, in the strictest sense, *empty*. A discussion of whether a just society will be brought about by a fascist or by a socialist order does not proceed as a logical deduction starting from a concept of 'justice' accepted by the two sides, but through a radical investment whose discursive steps are not logico-conceptual connections but attributive-performative ones. If I refer to a set of social grievances, to widespread injustice, and attribute its source to the 'oligarchy', for instance, I am performing two interlinked operations: on the one hand, I am constituting the 'people' by finding the common identity of a set of social claims in their opposition to the oligarchy; on the other, the enemy ceases to be purely circumstantial and acquires more global dimensions. This is why an equivalential chain *has* to be expressed through the cathexis of a *singular* element: because we are dealing not with a conceptual operation of *finding* an abstract common feature underlying all social grievances, but with a performative operation constituting the chain as such. It is like the process of condensation in dreams: an image does not express its own particularity, but a plurality of quite dissimilar currents of unconscious thought which find their expression in that single image. It is well known that Althusser[28] used this notion of condensation to analyse the Russian Revolution: all the antagonisms within Russian society were condensed in a ruptural unity around demands for 'bread, peace and land'. The moment of emptiness is decisive here: without empty terms such as 'justice', 'freedom', and so on being invested into the three demands, the latter would have remained closed in their particularism; but because of the radical character of the investment, something of the emptiness of 'justice' and 'freedom' was transmitted to the demands, which thus became the *names* of a universality that transcended their actual particular contents. Particularism is not, however, eliminated: as in all hegemonic formations, popular identities are always the points of tension/negotiation between universality and particularity. It should now be clear why we are dealing with 'emptiness', not with 'abstraction': peace, bread and land were not the *conceptual* common denominator of all Russian social demands in 1917. As in all processes of overdetermination, grievances which had nothing to do with those three demands nevertheless expressed themselves through them.

At this point I can deal with two aspects of populism to which the literature on the subject frequently refers but for which, as we have seen, no satisfactory explanation has been provided. The first concerns the so-called 'imprecision' and 'vagueness' of populist symbols. This has usually been – as is clearly shown by the authors whose analyses I have quoted – the step preceding their dismissal. If, however, the matter is approached from the perspective that I have outlined, concerning the social production of empty signifiers, the conclusions are altogether different. The empty character of the signifiers that give unity or coherence to a popular camp is not the result of any ideological or political under-development; it simply expresses the fact that any populist unification takes place on a radically heterogeneous social terrain. This heterogeneity does not tend, out of its own differential character, to coalesce around a unity which would result from its mere *internal* development; so any kind of unity is going to proceed from an inscription, the surface of inscription (the popular symbols) being irreducible to the contents which are thereon inscribed. The popular symbols are, no doubt, the expression of the democratic demands that they bring together; but the expressing medium cannot be reduced to what it expresses: it is not a *transparent* medium. To go back to my earlier example: to say that the oligarchy is responsible for the frustration of social demands is not to state something which can possibly be read out of the social demands themselves; it is provided from *outside* those social demands, by a discourse on which they can be inscribed. This discourse, of course, will increase the efficacy and coherence of the struggles deriving from them. But the more heterogeneous those social demands, the less the discourse providing them with a surface of inscription will be able to appeal to the common differential framework of a concrete local situation. As I have said, in a local struggle I can be relatively clear about both the nature of my demands and the force against which we are fighting. But when I am trying to constitute a wider popular identity and a more global enemy through an articulation of sectorial demands, the identity of both the popular forces and of the enemy becomes more difficult to determine. It is here that the moment of emptiness necessarily arises, following the establishment of equivalential bonds. *Ergo*, 'vagueness' and 'imprecision', but these do not result from any kind of marginal or primitive situation; they are inscribed in the very nature of the political. Should proof be needed, let us just think of the outburst of populist mobilizations which take place periodically at the heart of *over*developed societies.

A second problem that is not completely solved in the literature on populism concerns the centrality of the leader. How do we explain it? The two most common types of explanation are 'suggestion' – a category taken from crowd theorists – and 'manipulation' – or, quite frequently, a combination of the two (a combination which presents no major problems since each shades easily into the other). In my view, this kind of explanation is useless. For even if we were going to accept the 'manipulation' argument, the most it would explain is the subjective intention of the leader, but we would remain in the dark as to why the manipulation succeeds – that is to say, we would know nothing about the kind of relation which is subsumed under the label of 'manipulation'. So, following our method, we will adopt a structural approach and will ask ourselves whether there is not something in the equivalential bond which already pre-announces key aspects of the leader's function. We already know that the more extended the equivalential tie is, the emptier the signifier unifying that chain will be (that is, the more specific particularism of the popular symbol or identity will be subordinated to the 'universal' function of signifying the chain as a totality). But we also know something else: that the popular symbol or identity, being a surface of inscription, does not *passively express* what is inscribed in it, but actually *constitutes* what it expresses through the very process of its expression. In other words: the popular subject position does not simply *express* a unity of demands constituted outside and before itself, but is the decisive moment in establishing that unity. That is why I said that this unifying element is not a neutral or transparent medium. If it were, whatever unity the discursive/hegemonic formation could have would have preceded the moment of naming the totality (that is to say, the name would be a matter of complete indifference). But if – given the radical heterogeneity of the links entering into the equivalential chain – the only source of their coherent articulation is the chain as such, and if the chain exists only in so far as one of its links plays the role of condensing all the others, in that case the unity of the discursive formation is transferred from the conceptual order (logic of difference) to the nominal one. This, obviously, is more the case in situations where there is a breakdown or retreat of the differential/institutional logic. In those cases, the name becomes the ground of the thing. An assemblage of heterogeneous elements kept equivalentially together only by a name is, however, necessarily a *singularity*. The less a society is kept together by immanent differential mechanisms, the more it depends, for its coherence, on this transcendent, singular moment. But the extreme form of singularity is an individuality. In this way, almost imperceptibly, the equivalential logic leads to singularity, and singularity to identification of the unity of the group with the name of the leader. To some extent, we are in a situation comparable to that of Hobbes's sovereign: in principle there is no reason why a corporate body could not fulfil the functions of the Leviathan; but its very plurality shows that it is at odds with the indivisible nature of sovereignty. So the only 'natural' sovereign could be, for Hobbes, an individual. The difference between that situation and the one we are discussing is that Hobbes is talking about actual ruling, while we are talking about constituting a signifying totality, and the latter does not lead automatically to the former. Nelson Mandela's role as the symbol of the nation was compatible with a great deal of pluralism within his movement. However, the symbolic unification of the group around an individuality – and here I agree with Freud – is inherent to the formation of a 'people'.

The opposition between 'naming' and 'conceptual determination' has crept, almost surreptitiously, into our argument. It is this opposition that I now have to clarify further, for several issues of capital importance for our subject depend on it.

Naming and affect

I have talked about the *name* becoming the ground of the thing. What, exactly, is the meaning of this assertion? We will explore the matter from two successive angles: the first concerns the *signifying operations* which are required for a name to play such a role; the second the *force*, behind those operations, which makes them possible. This last issue could be reformulated in terms which are already familiar to us: what does 'investment' mean when we talk about 'radical investment'? These questions will be approached through two contemporary developments in Lacanian theory: the work of Slavoj Žižek and that of Joan Copjec.

Žižek's starting point is the discussion, in contemporary analytical philosophy, of how names relate to things.[29] Here we have a classical approach (descriptivism), originally to be found in the work of Bertrand Russell but later adopted by most analytical philosophers, according to which every name has a content given by a cluster of descriptive features. The word 'mirror', for instance, has an intensional content (the ability to reflect images, etc.), so I use that word whenever I find an actually existing object which displays such a content. John Stuart Mill had distinguished between common names, which have a describable content, and proper names, which do not. This distinction, however, was put into question by Russell, who maintained that 'ordinary' proper names – as distinct from 'logical' ones (the deictic categories) – are abbreviated descriptions. 'George W. Bush', for instance, would be an abbreviated description of 'the US President who invaded Iraq'. (Later descriptivist philosophers and logicians started to wonder whether a descriptive content could not be attached even to logical proper names.) Difficulties arose within this approach in relation to the plurality of descriptions which can be attached to the same object. Bush, for instance, could equally be described as 'the man who became a teetotaller after being a drunkard'. John Searle has argued that any description is just one within a cluster of alternative options; while for Michael Dummett there should be a 'fundamental' description to which all others are subordinate. This discussion, however, is not our concern. What is important for us is to differentiate the descriptivist from the anti-descriptivist approach, whose main exponent is Saul Kripke.[30] According to Kripke, words refer to things not through their shared descriptive features, but through a 'primal baptism' which does away with description entirely. Names would, in this sense, be rigid designators. Let us suppose that Bush had never gone into politics: the name 'Bush' would still apply to him, even in the absence of all descriptive features that we associate with him today; conversely, if a new individual turned up who actually had the totality of those features, we would nevertheless say that he is not Bush. The same applies to common names: gold – to use one of Kripke's examples – would remain gold even if it were proved that all the properties traditionally attributed to it are an illusion. In that case we would say that gold is different from what we thought it was, not that this substance is not gold. If we translate these arguments into a Saussurean terminology, what the descriptivists are doing is to establish a fixed correlation between signifier and signified; while the anti-descriptivist approach involves emancipating the signifier from any enthralment to the signified. It becomes clear, at this point, that the opposition with which I closed the last section – the one between 'conceptual determination' and 'naming' – re-emerges here in terms of the descriptivism/anti-descriptivism opposition. And it is equally clear that the premisses of our argument locate it firmly within the anti-descriptivist camp.

Not, however, without a crucial change of terrain. This is where Žižek enters into the picture. While he agrees on the whole with the anti-descriptivist approach, he poses – following his Lacanian stance – a new question to Kripke and his followers: granted that the object remains the same beyond all its descriptive changes, *what* is it that exactly remains the same; what is the 'X' which receives the successive descriptive attributions? Žižek's answer, following Lacan, is: the X is a retroactive effect of naming:

> The basic problem of antidescriptivism is to determine what constitutes the identity of the designated object beyond the ever-changing cluster of descriptive features – what makes the object identical-to-itself even if all its properties have changed; in other words, how to conceive the objective

correlative of the 'rigid designator', to the name in so far as it denotes the same object in all possible worlds, in all counterfactual situations. What is overlooked, at least in the standard version of antidescriptivism, is that this guaranteeing the identity of an object in all counterfactual situations – *through a change of all its descriptive features* – is the retroactive effect of naming itself: it is the name itself, the signifier, which supports the identity of the object.[31]

Now, we have to recognize that whatever the merits of Žižek's solution, it is not one that could be accepted within a Kripkean perspective, for it involves introducing ontological premises which are incompatible with this perspective. Not only would Kripke not accept Žižek's solution, he would not even recognize the problem as a valid one. His is not – as Lacan's is – a theory of the productivity of naming, but a theory of a *pure* designation in which the referent – Žižek's X – is simply taken for granted. But if the notion of naming as a retroactive production of the object would not make any sense for Kripke, it makes a lot of sense for us, given that our approach to the question of popular identities is grounded, precisely, in the performative dimension of naming. So let us take leave of Kripke, and go on to Žižek's own argument.

According to Žižek, the quilting point (the *point de capiton*) whose name brings about the unity of a discursive formation – Lacan's *objet petit a* – has no positive identity of its own: 'we search in vain for it in positive reality because it has no positive consistency – because it is just an objectification of a void, of a discontinuity open in reality by the emergency of the signifier'.[32] It is not through a wealth of signifieds but, on the contrary, through the presence of a pure signifier that this quilting function is fulfilled.

If we maintain that the *point de capiton* is a 'nodal point', a kind of knot of meanings, this does not imply that it is simply the 'richest' word, the word in which is condensed all the richness of meaning of the field it 'quilts': the *point de capiton* is rather the word which, *as a word*, on the level of the signifier itself, unifies a given field, constitutes its identity: it is, so to speak, the word to which 'things' themselves refer to recognise themselves in their unity.[33]

Two of the examples given by Žižek are very revealing, since they show the inversion which is a distinctive feature of the quilting function. In the first, referring to Marlboro advertisements, all allusions to America – 'a land of hard, honest people, of limitless horizons' – are quilted through the inversion of its relation to Marlboro: it is not that Marlboro expresses American identity, but that the latter is constructed through the recognition of America as Marlboro country. The same mechanisms can be seen in Coca-Cola advertisements: 'Coke, this is America' cannot be inverted into 'America, this is Coke', because it is only in the role of Coke as a pure signifier that American identity crystallizes.

If we look at the intellectual sequence I have described, from classical descriptivism to Lacan, we can see a movement of thought with a clear direction: the increasing emancipation of the order of the signifier. This transition can also be presented as the progressive autonomy of naming. For descriptivism, the operations that naming can perform are strictly limited by the straitjacket within which they take place: the descriptive features inhabiting any name reduce the order of the signifier to the transparent medium through which a purely conceptual overlapping between name and thing (the concept being their common nature) expresses itself. With anti-descriptivism we have the beginning of an autonomization of the signifier (of the name). This parting of the ways between naming and description, however, does not lead to any increase in the complexity of the operations that 'naming' can perform, for although designation is no longer ancillary to description, the identity of what is designated is ensured before and quite independently of the process of its being named. It is only with the Lacanian approach that we have a real breakthrough: the identity and unity of the object result from the very operation of naming. This, however, is possible only if naming is not subordinated either to description or to a preceding designation. In order to perform this role, the signifier has to become, not only contingent, but empty as well.

These remarks, I think, show very clearly why the name becomes the ground of the thing. We can now return to the question of popular identities, and link it to some of the theoretical conclusions which follow my earlier analysis. There are four points to be made in this connection. The first concerns the relationship between the Lacanian *point de capiton* (the nodal point) and the other elements of a discursive configuration. It is clear that, without nodal points, there would be no configuration at all. Without Marlboro, Americanness – in Žižek's example – would be a set of diffuse themes which would not be articulated into a meaningful totality. This is exactly what we have seen in the case of popular identities: without the quilting point of an equivalential identification, democratic equivalences would remain merely virtual. In the second place, there is the question of the relationship between universality and particularism in determining the identity of the quilting point. To this we must add the related question of whether, if the quilting function is associated with universality, it is a universality that expresses fullness or emptiness. Žižek is inclined to opt for the second alternative: 'Historical reality is, of course, always symbolized; the way we experience it is always mediated through different modes of symbolization; all Lacan adds to this phenomenological common wisdom is the fact that the unity of a given "experience of meaning", itself the horizon of an ideological field of meaning, is supposed to be some "pure", meaningless "signifier without the signified".'[34]

My answer to this question is different. The notion of 'a signifier without a signified' is, to start with, self-defeating: it could only mean 'noise' and, as such, would be outside the system of signification. When we talk about 'empty signifiers', however, we mean something entirely different: we mean that there is a place, within the system of signification, which is constitutively irrepresentable; in that sense it remains empty, but this is an emptiness which I can signify, because we are dealing with a void *within* signification. (Compare Paul de Man's analysis of the Pascalian *zero*:[35] 'zero' is the absence of number, but by giving a name to that absence, I am transforming the 'zero' into a 'one'.) Moreover, my earlier analysis of popular identities as empty signifiers allows me to show that the exclusive fullness/emptiness alternative is a spurious one: as we have seen, the popular identity expresses/constitutes – through the equivalence of a plurality of unfulfilled demands – the fullness of the community as that which is denied and, as such, remains unachieved – an empty fullness, if you like. If we were not dealing with the signifier of emptiness as a particular location, but with one that is not attached to *any* signified while nevertheless remaining within signification, that could only mean that it is the name of a *fully achieved* totality which, as such, would have no structural fails.

So what form does the representation of 'emptiness' take? I have argued that the totalization of the popular camp – the discursive crystallization of the moment of fullness/emptiness – can take place only if a partial content takes up the representation of a universality with which it is incommensurable. This is crucial. Even in the examples Žižek gives, we can see this articulation between particular content and universal function: Marlboro and Coca-Cola can work as quilting points within the images of advertising, and thus be the signifiers of a certain totalization, but there are still the *particular* entities, Marlboro and Coca-Cola, the ones that perform this role. It is because it is not possible either to reduce them to their mere particularistic identity or to eliminate the latter totally in the name of their quilting role (if that total elimination were possible we would, indeed, have a signifier without a signified) that something like a hegemonic operation becomes possible.[36]

This leads me to the third point that I would like to make. The articulation between universality and particularity which is constitutively inherent to the construction of a 'people' is not something which takes place just at the level of words and images: it is also sedimented in practices and institutions. As I said above, our notion of 'discourse' – which is close to Wittgenstein's 'language games' – involves the articulation of words and actions, so that the quilting function is never a merely verbal operation but is embedded in material practices which can acquire institutional fixity. This is the same as saying that any hegemonic displacement should be conceived as a change in the configuration of the state, provided that the latter is conceived, not in a restrictive juridical sense, as the public sphere, but in an enlarged, Gramscian sense, as the ethico-political moment of the community. Any state will manifest that combination of particularism and universality which is inherent to the hegemonic operation. This clearly shows how both the Hegelian and the Marxian conceptions of the state try to untie this necessary articulation between the universal and the particular. For Hegel, the sphere of the state is the highest form of universality achievable in the terrain of social ethics: bureaucracy is the universal class, while civil society – the system of needs – is the realm of pure particularity. For Marx, the situation is reversed: the state is the instrument of the dominant class, and a 'universal class' can emerge only in a civil society that is reconciled with itself – one in which the state (the political power) has necessarily to wither away. In both cases, particularity and universality exclude one another. It is only with Gramsci that the articulation of both instances becomes thinkable: for him there is a particularity – a *plebs* – which claims hegemonically to constitute a *populus*, while the *populus* (the abstract universality) can exist only as embodied in a *plebs*. When we reach that point, we are close to the 'people' of populism.

There is a fourth and final point to be made concerning particularity/universality/naming in connection with the constitution of popular identities. Let us go back for a moment to my argument about *singularity*. Singularity, in my approach, is strictly linked to the question of heterogeneity. I shall deal in Chapter 5 with the main dimensions and effects of the logic of heterogeneity, but I can anticipate some of them here in so far as they are required to illuminate the centrality of naming in populism. Social homogeneity is what constitutes the symbolic framework of a society – what we have called the logic of difference. I can move from one institution to another, from one social category to another, not because there is a *logical* connection between them – although several rationalizations could try later on to reconstruct institutional interconnections in terms of logical links – but because all differentiations require and refer to each other within a systematic ensemble. Language as a system of differences is the archetypical expression of this symbolic interconnection. A first form of heterogeneity emerges when, as we have seen, a particular social demand cannot be met within that system: the demand is in *excess* of what is differentially representable within it. The heterogeneous is what lacks any differential location within the symbolic order (it is equivalent to the Lacanian real).

There is, however, another type of heterogeneity which is equally important: the one that derives from the mutual relations between unfulfilled demands. These demands are no longer united/separated from each other through the symbolic system, because it is precisely the dislocation of that system that has generated them in the first place. But they do not tend spontaneously to coalesce with each other either, for as far as their specificity is concerned, they can be entirely heterogeneous in nature. What gives them an initial and weak equivalential tie is the mere fact that they all reflect the failure of the institutional system. I have already dealt *in extenso* with this matter, and I shall not go back to it. *What I can add now, however, is that the unity of the equivalential ensemble, of the irreducibly new collective will in which particular equivalences crystallize, depends entirely on the social productivity of a name.* That productivity derives exclusively from the operation of the name *as a pure signifier* – that is to say, not *expressing* any conceptual unity that precedes it (as would be the case if we had adopted a descriptivist perspective).

Here we can strictly follow the Lacanian view as presented by Žižek: the unity of the object is a retroactive effect of naming it. Two consequences follow: first, the name, once it has become the signifier of what is heterogeneous and excessive in a particular society, will have an irresistible attraction over *any* demand which is lived as unfulfilled and, as such, as excessive and heterogeneous *vis-à-vis* the existing symbolic framework; second, since the name – in order to play that constitutive role – has to be an empty signifier, it is ultimately unable to determine what kind of demands enter into the equivalential chain. In other words: if the names of the 'people' constitute their own object – that is, give unity to a heterogeneous ensemble – the reverse movement also operates: they can never fully control which demands they embody and represent. Popular identities are always *loci* of the tension between these two opposite movements, and of the precarious equilibria that they manage to establish between them. From this results a necessary ideological ambiguity, whose political consequences will become apparent as our argument progresses.

At this point, I can go back to the argument concerning rhetoric which I have already broached a couple of times. It is closely related to the question of the 'singular' and the 'heterogeneous' that we have just discussed, for a rhetorical displacement or reaggregation has precisely the function of emancipating a name from its univocal conceptual attachments. Let me bring to the discussion an example which I have discussed elsewhere. Let us think of a certain neighbourhood where there is racial violence, and the only local forces capable of organizing an anti-racist counter-offensive are the trade unions. Now, in a strictly literal sense, the function of the unions is not to fight racism but to negotiate wages and other related issues. If, however, the anti-racist campaign is taken up by the unions, it is because there is a relation of *contiguity* between the two issues in the same neighbourhood. A relation of displacement between terms, issues, agents, and so on, is what is called, in rhetoric, a metonymy. Let us suppose, next, that this connection between anti-racist and trade union struggles continues for a certain time: in that case, people will start to feel that there is a natural link between the two types of struggle. So the relation of *contiguity* will start to shade into one of *analogy*, the *metonymy* into a *metaphor*. This rhetorical displacement involves three main changes. First, despite the differential particularism of the initial two kinds of struggles and demands, a certain equivalential homogeneity between them is being created. Second, the nature of the trade unions changes in this process: they cease to be the pure expression of sectorial interests at a given moment, and become more – if a variety of equivalential articulations develops – a nodal point in the constitution of a 'people' (using the Gramscian distinction: they move from being a 'corporative' class to being a 'hegemonic' one). Third, the term 'trade union' becomes the name of a *singularity*, in the sense defined above: it no longer designates the name of an *abstract* universality, whose 'essence' would be repeated, beyond accidental variations, in all historical contexts, and becomes the name of a *concrete* social agent, whose only essence is the specific articulation of heterogeneous elements which, through that name, crystallize in a unified collective will. Another way of saying the same thing is that there is no social element whose meaning is not overdetermined. As a result, this meaning cannot be *conceptually* apprehended, if by 'conceptual' we understand a signified which would entirely eliminate the opaqueness of the signifying process. This shows again that rhetorical mechanisms, as I have asserted from the beginning of this book, constitute the anatomy of the social world.

A final and crucial dimension must, however, be added to our analysis. Our whole approach to populism turns, as we have seen, around the following theses: (1) the emergence of the 'people' requires the passage – via equivalences – from isolated, heterogeneous demands to a 'global' demand which involves the formation of political frontiers and the discursive construction of power as an antagonistic force; (2) since, however, this passage does not follow from a mere analysis of the heterogeneous demands themselves – there is no logical, dialectical or semiotic transition from one level to the other – something qualitatively new has to intervene. This is why 'naming' can have the retroactive effect I have described. This qualitatively differentiated and irreducible moment is what I have called 'radical investment'. What this notion of 'investment' would involve is, however, something we have not yet explored . The different signifying operations to which I have referred so far can explain the *forms* the investment takes, but not the *force* in which the investment consists. It is clear, however, that if an entity becomes the object of an investment – as in being in love, or in hatred – the investment belongs necessarily to the order of *affect*. It is this affective dimension that I now have to bring into the picture.

Not, however, without a caveat. It would be a mistake to think that, by adding affect to what I have said so far about signification, I am putting together two different types of phenomena which would – at least analytically – be separable. The relation between signification and affect is in fact far more intimate. As we have already seen, the paradigmatic pole of language (Saussure's associative pole) is an integral part of language functioning – that is to say, there would be no signification without paradigmatic substitutions. But paradigmatic relations consist, as we have seen, of substitutions operating at the level of both the signifier and the signified, and these associations are governed by the unconscious. There is no possibility of a language in which the *value* relations would be established only between *formally* specifiable units. So affect is required if signification is going to be possible. But we arrive at the same conclusion if we consider the matter from the viewpoint of affect. Affect is not something which exists on its own, independently of language; it constitutes itself only through the differential cathexes of a signifying chain. This is exactly what 'investment' means. The conclusion is clear: the complexes which we call 'discursive or hegemonic formations', which articulate differential and equivalential logics, would be unintelligible without the affective component. (This is a further proof – were one still needed – of the inanity of dismissing emotional populist attachments in the name of an uncontaminable rationality.)

So we can conclude that any social whole results from an indissociable articulation between signifying and affective dimensions. But in discussing the constitution of popular identities, we are dealing with a very particular type of whole: not one which is just composed of parts, but one in which a part functions as the whole (in our example: a *plebs* claiming to be identical with the *populus*). It is exactly the same if we see the matter from the hegemonic angle: as we know, a hegemonic relation is one in which a certain particularity signifies an unachievable universality. What, however, is the ontological possibility of such a relationship? To approach the issue, I shall examine two highly illuminating analyses in the recent work of Joan Copjec. They belong to the psychoanalytic field, but their consequences for our political analysis are visible and far-reaching.[37]

The first essay by Copjec, 'The Tomb of Perseverance: on *Antigone*', discusses, in those passages which are relevant to our theme, the death drive in Freud. For Freud, as she asserts, death is the aim of every drive. What does this mean? Essentially, that every drive 'aims at the past, at a time before the subject found itself where it is now, imbedded in time and moving toward death' (p. 33). This earlier state of inanimation or inertia, which is a retrospective illusion (Copjec refers here to the myth of the *Timaeus*, where the Earth, being a globe comprising everything, does not need organs of any kind – it has no outside), is read by psychoanalysis in terms of the primordial mother/child dyad, 'which supposedly contained all things and every happiness and to which the subject strives throughout life to return'. (We can easily recognize in this picture something that is already present in our political analysis: the idea of a fullness which unfulfilled demands constantly reproduce as the presence of an absence.) If this fullness is a mythical one, the actual search for it could lead only to destruction, except for two facts that Copjec stresses: '(1) that there is no single, complete drive, only partial drives and thus *no realisable will to destruction*; and (2) the second paradox of the drive, which states that the drive inhibits, as part of its activity, the achievement of its aim. So some inherent obstacle – the object of the drive – simultaneously *brakes* the drive and *breaks it up*, curbs it, thus preventing it from reaching its aim, and divides it up into partial drives' (p. 34). So the drives content themselves with these partial objects which Lacan calls *objets petit a*.

It is important to see how Copjec's argument is constructed within the Freudian and Lacanian texts. To start with, we have Freud's notion of the *Nebenmensch* (the primordial mother) and the initial split between *das Ding* (the Thing), the irretrievable fullness, and what is representable. Something of the primordial mother cannot be translated into representation; thus a hole is opened up within the order of the signifier. If the matter remained there, however, we would be within the terrain of a Kantian opposition between the noumenon and its phenomenal representation, between being and thinking. It is at this point that Lacan radicalizes Freudian thought: the lost Thing is not an *impossibility of thought*, but a *void of Being*: 'it is not that the mother escapes representation or thought, but that the *jouissance* that attached me to her has been lost, and this loss depletes the whole of my being' (Copjec, p. 36). If, however, *jouissance* is not lost, this is because traces of it remain in the partial objects. The nature of these traces, however, must be carefully explored, because they no longer follow the noumenon/phenomenal representation schema. The partial object becomes itself a totality; it becomes the structuring principle of the whole scene:

> The development of the concept of *Vorstellungrepräsentanz* [ideational representative in Freud's English translation] appears, then, to sever the *Ding*-component of the *Nebenmensch* complex into two parts, into *das Ding* and *Vorstellungrepräsentanz*, although *das Ding* is no longer conceivable as a noumenal object and is retained only by the description of *Vorstellungrepräsentanz* as *partial*. It is clear from the theory that when this partial object arrives on the scene, it blocks the path to the old conception of *das Ding*, which is now only a retrospective illusion.... The traitorous delegate and the partial object act not as evidence of a body or a Thing existing elsewhere, but as evidence of the fact that the body and satisfaction have lost the support of the organic body and the noumenal thing. (p. 37)

Copjec is very careful to stress that this mutation breaks with the notion that the partial object of *jouissance* would act as a representative of the inaccessible Thing. Quoting Lacan's definition of sublimation as 'the elevation of an ordinary object to the dignity of the Thing', she reads it in the sense that 'elevation does not seem to entail [the] function of representation, but rather entails – in a reversal of the common understanding of sublimation – the substitution of an ordinary object for the Thing' (p. 38).

In a second essay in the same volume, 'Narcissism, Approached Obliquely', Copjec adds the important observation that the partial object is not *a part of a whole* but *a part which is the whole*. She quotes Béla Balász and Deleuze, for whom close-ups do not simply entail focusing on a detail within a whole – rather, it is as if, through that detail, the whole scene were re-dimensioned: 'Deleuze is claiming that the close-up is *not* a closer look at a part of a scene, that is, it does not disclose an object that can be listed as an element of that scene, a *detail* plucked from the whole and then blown up in order to focus our attention. The close-up discloses, rather, the *whole* of the scene itself, or as Deleuze says, its entire "expressed".... The partial object of the drive, I will argue, exemplifies the same logic; it does not form part of the organism, but implies an absolute change' (p. 53). In this way, the partial object ceases to be a partiality evoking a totality, and becomes – using our earlier terminology – the *name* of that totality. Lacan breaks with the notion of a mother/child dyad by adding a third component, detached from the mother: the breast – properly speaking, the object of the drive:

> This term, 'object of lack', cannot be understood outside the Timaean/ *lamellian* myth from which it derives. The partial object or object of lack is the one that emerges out of the lack, the void, opened by the loss of the original Plenum or *das Ding*. In place of the mythical satisfaction derived from being at one with the maternal Thing, the subject now experiences satisfaction in this partial object.... The elevation of the external object of the drive – let us stay with the example of milk – to the status of breast (that is, to the status of an object capable of satisfying something more than the mouth or stomach) does not depend on its cultural or social value in relation to other objects. Its surplus 'breast value', let us say, depends solely on the drive's election of it as an object of satisfaction. (p. 60)

The reader would perhaps ask herself: what has all this to do with popular identities? The answer is very simple: everything. Copjec is perfectly aware that psychoanalytic categories are not regional, but belong to the field of what could be called a general ontology. She asserts, for instance, that the theory of the drives in Freud occupies the terrain of classical ontological questions. It is true that her account – as frequently in psychoanalysis – has a predominantly genetic character, but it can easily be recast in structural terms. The mythical wholeness of the mother/child dyad corresponds to the unachieved fullness evoked – as its opposite – by the dislocations brought about by the unfulfilled demands. The aspiration to that fullness or wholeness does not, however, simply disappear; it is transferred to partial objects which are the objects of the drives. In political terms, that is exactly what I have called a hegemonic relation: a certain particularity which assumes the role of an impossible universality. Because the partial character of these objects does not result from a particular story but is inherent in the very structure of signification, Lacan's *objet petit a* is the key element in a social ontology. The whole is always going to be embodied by a part. In terms of our analysis: there is no universality which is not a hegemonic one. There is, however, something more: as in the examples of the close-ups and the 'breast value' of the milk discussed by Copjec, there is nothing in the materiality of the particular parts which predetermines one or the other to function as a whole. Nevertheless, once a certain part has assumed such a function, it is its very materiality as a part which becomes a source of enjoyment. Gramsci formulated the political argument in similar terms: which social force will become the hegemonic representation of society as a whole is the result of a contingent struggle; but once a particular social force becomes hegemonic, it remains so for a whole historical period. The object of the investment can be contingent, but it is most certainly not indifferent – it cannot be changed at will. With this we reach a full explanation of what radical investment means: making an object the embodiment of a mythical fullness. Affect (that it, enjoyment) is the very essence of investment, while its contingent character accounts for the 'radical' component of the formula.

Let me press this point once more. We are dealing not with casual or external homologies but with the same discovery taking place from two different angles – psychoanalysis and politics – of something that concerns the very structure of objectivity. The main ontological consequence of the Freudian discovery of the unconscious is that the category of representation does not simply reproduce, at a secondary level, a fullness preceding it which could be grasped in a direct way but, on the contrary, representation is the absolutely primary level in the constitution of objectivity. That is why there is no meaning which is not overdetermined from its very inception. With the fullness of the primordial mother being a purely mythical object, there is no achievable *jouissance* except through radical investment in an *objet petit a*. Thus *objet petit a* becomes the primary ontological category. But the *same* discovery (not merely an *analogous* one) is made if we start from the angle of political theory. No social fullness is achievable except through hegemony; and hegemony is nothing more than the investment, in a partial object, of a fullness which will always evade us because it is purely mythical (in our terms: it is merely the positive reverse of a situation experienced as 'deficient being'). The logic of the *objet petit a* and the hegemonic logic are not just similar: they are simply identical. This is why, within the Marxist tradition, the Gramscian moment represents such a crucial epistemological break: while Marxism had traditionally had the dream of access to a systemically closed totality (determination in the last instance by the economy, etc.), the hegemonic approach breaks decisively with that essentialist social logic. The only possible totalizing horizon is given by a partiality (the hegemonic force) which assumes the representation of a mythical totality. In Lacanian terms: an object is elevated to the dignity of the Thing. In that sense, the object of the hegemonic investment is not a second-best *vis-à-vis* the *real* thing which would be an *entirely* reconciled society (which, as a systemic totality, would require no investment and no hegemony): it is simply the name that fullness receives within a certain historical horizon, which as partial object of a hegemonic investment it is not an *ersatz* but the rallying point of passionate attachments. Copjec's argument about the drive being able to achieve satisfaction is highly relevant here because, in a different register, it asserts the very political point that I am trying to make.

All this has a clear implication for the main theme of this book, because – as should be evident at this stage of the argument – there is no populism without affective investment in a partial object. If a society managed to achieve an institutional order of such a nature that all demands were satisfied within its own immanent mechanisms, there would be no populism but, for obvious reasons, there would be no politics either. The need to constitute a 'people' (a *plebs* claiming to be a *populus*) arises only when that fullness is not achieved, and partial objects within society (aims, figures, symbols) are so cathected that they become the name of its absence. Why the affective dimension is decisive in this process is, I think, abundantly clear from the earlier discussion.

Populism

I have now introduced all the theoretical variables needed to attempt a first and provisional conceptualization of populism. Three aspects should be taken into account.

1. First, it should be clear at this stage that by 'populism' we do not understand a *type* of movement – identifiable with either a special social base or a particular ideological orientation – but a *political logic*. All the attempts at finding what is idiosyncratic in populism in elements such as a peasant or small-ownership constituency, or resistance to economic modernization, or manipulation by marginalized elites are, as we have seen, essentially flawed: they will always be overwhelmed by an avalanche of exceptions. What do we understand, however, by a 'political logic'? As I have asserted elsewhere,[38] I see social logics as involving a rarefied system of statements – that is to say, a system of rules drawing a horizon within which some objects are representable while others are excluded. So we can talk about the logics of kinship, of the market – even of chess-playing (to use Wittgenstein's example). A political logic, however, has something specific to it which is important to stress. While social logics consist in rule-following, political logics are related to the institution of the social. Such an institution, however, as we already know, is not an arbitrary *fiat* but proceeds out of social demands and is, in that sense, inherent to any process of social change. This change, as we also know, takes place through the variable articulation of equivalence and difference, and the equivalential moment presupposes the constitution of a global political subject bringing together a plurality of social demands. This in turn involves, as we have seen, the construction of internal frontiers and the identification of an institutionalized 'other'. Whenever we have this combination of structural moments, whatever

the ideological or social contents of the political movement in question, we have populism of one sort or another.

2. There are two other aspects from our previous discussion which have to come into our conceptual characterization of populism: those which concern naming and affect. Naming, in the first place. If the construction of the 'people' is a *radical* one – one which constitutes social agents as such, and does not express a previously given unity of the group – the heterogeneity of the demands that the popular identity brings to a precarious unity has to be irreducible. This does not necessarily mean that these demands are not analogous, or at least comparable at some level; it *does*, however, mean that they cannot be inscribed in a structural system of differences which would provide them with an infrastructural ground. This point is crucial: heterogeneity does not mean differentiality. There cannot be a priori system unity, precisely because the unfulfilled demands are the expression of systemic dislocation. This involves two consequences that I have analysed: (1) the moment of unity of popular subjects is given at the nominal, not at the conceptual, level – that is, popular subjects are always singularities; (2) precisely because that name is not conceptually (sectorially) grounded, the limits between the demands it is going to embrace and those it is going to exclude will be blurred, and subjected to permanent contestation. From this we can deduce that the language of a populist discourse – whether of Left or Right – is always going to be imprecise and fluctuating: not because of any cognitive failure, but because it tries to operate performatively within a social reality which is to a large extent heterogeneous and fluctuating. I see this moment of vagueness and imprecision – which, it should be clear, does not have any pejorative connotation for me – as an essential component of any populist operation.

Let us now move on to affect. Our previous discussion implicitly entails that there is no affect without a constitutive unevenness. If, to use Lacanian terminology, we had a Real before the Symbolic, we would have a continuous fullness without internal differentiations. But the presence of the Real *within* the Symbolic involves unevenness: *objets petit a* presuppose a differential cathexis, and it is this cathexis that we call affect. Freud quotes George Bernard Shaw as saying that to be in love is considerably to exaggerate the difference between one woman and another. Pure harmony would be incompatible with affect. As Ortega y Gasset said, history would be destroyed if we were fair to all its internal moments. Affect, in that sense, means radical discontinuity between an object and the one next to it, and this discontinuity can be conceived only in terms of a differential cathexis. We have to pay attention to all the moments of this structural sequence if we are going to approach the question of popular identities correctly. First we have the moment of the mythical fullness for which we search in vain: the restoration of the mother/child unity or, in political terms, the fully reconciled society. Then we have the partialization of the drives: the plurality of *objets petit a* which, at some point, embody that ultimately unachievable fullness. Here we must be careful in our analysis, because to embody something can mean several different things. This is the point where Copjec's analysis reveals all its relevance. She rightly rejects a purely external notion of representation according to which something which cannot show itself as such would be substituted by a succession of indifferent *ersatzs*. So what could be a more intimate relationship between what is being embodied and the very act of embodying it? All our previous analyses allow us to give a proper answer to this question. Embodying something can only mean giving a *name* to what is being embodied; but, since what is embodied is an impossible fullness, something which has no independent consistency of its own, the 'embodying' entity becomes the full object of the cathectic investment. The embodying object is thus the ultimate horizon of what is achievable – not because there is an unachievable 'beyond', but because that 'beyond', having no entity of its own, can be present only as the phantasmatic excess of an object through which satisfaction is achievable – this excess would, in Copjec's words, be the 'breast value' of the milk. In psychoanalytic terms: while desire knows no satisfaction, and lives only by reproducing itself through a succession of objects, the drive can find satisfaction, but this is achievable only by 'sublimating' an object, raising it to the dignity of the Thing. Let us translate this into political language: a certain demand, which was perhaps at the beginning only one among many, acquires at some point an unexpected centrality, and becomes the name of something exceeding it, of something which it cannot control by itself but which, however, becomes a 'destiny' from which it cannot escape. When a democratic demand has gone through this process, it becomes a 'popular' one. But this is not achievable in terms of its own initial, material particularity. It has to become a nodal point of sublimation; it has to acquire a 'breast value'. It is only then that the 'name' becomes detached from the 'concept', the signifier from the signified. Without this detachment, there would be no populism.

3. Finally, there is a third aspect to take into consideration. Although I shall deal with its full implications in Chapter 5, I must address here some remarks which cannot be skipped even in a preliminary approach to populism. I asserted earlier that the logics of difference and equivalence, although they are ultimately antagonistic to one another, none the less need one another . They inhabit the space of a tension between mutually related dimensions. I have already indicated the reason: an equivalential chain can weaken the particularism of their links, but cannot do away with it altogether. It is because a *particular* demand is unfulfilled that with other unfulfilled demands a solidarity is established, so that without the active presence of the particularism of the link, there would be no equivalential chain.

I have described this aspect as difference and equivalence reflecting themselves in each other. This reflection is constitutive, but so is the tension between its two poles. Tension and reflection can be contingently combined in unstable equilibria, but neither is entirely able to eliminate the other. Let us think of an apparent example of equivalence at its purest: a millenarian peasant revolt. We would tend to think that here we have no contamination between difference and equivalence, no reflection in each other: since on the one hand, the enemy is a total one, the relation with him aims at his entire destruction; on the other, since the meaning of the confrontation is given by the defence, against a threat, of something the community *already* was, it looks as if all communitarian particularism would precede the equivalential confrontation, and would not depend on this confrontation for its constitution. Since the clash of the two worlds is an uncompromising one, it would look as if whatever substantial reality each of them had would precede the clash, not result from it. In other words, the communitarian space would be *exclusively* organized by a differential logic, and the equivalential moment would become *entirely* external – that is to say, difference and equivalence would cease to reflect in each other; what was a tension between two dimensions would be resolved into a total separation between them. This, however, would be the wrong conclusion. For even in the extreme case of the millenarian revolt, the reflecting moment is operating. Once the revolt starts, nothing in the community remains as it was before. Even if the aim of the rebellion is the restoration of a previous identity, it has to reinvent that identity; it cannot simply rely on something entirely given beforehand. The defence of the community against an external threat has dislocated that community, which, in order to persist, cannot simply repeat something that preceded the dislocatory moment. That is why someone who wants to defend an existing order of things has already lost it through its very defence. In our terms: the perpetuation of a threatened order can no longer rely on a purely differential logic; its success depends on the inscription of those differences within an equivalential chain.

This conclusion has some crucial consequences for the question of popular identities and populism. The example of millenarianism is, admittedly, an extreme one, but by showing that even in this case the double reflective moment we are discussing is present, we can throw light on a whole game of variations which is inscribed in the very nature of populism. If the equivalential logic does not dissolve differences but inscribes them within itself, and if the relative weight of the two logics largely depends on the autonomy of what is inscribed *vis-à-vis* the hegemony exercised by the surface of inscription, the room for variation opened by the double reflection is, indeed, very substantial. In other words: any social level or institution can operate as a surface of equivalential inscription. The essential point is that, since the dislocation at the root of the populist experience requires an equivalential inscription, any emerging 'people', whatever its character, is going to present two faces: one of rupture with an existing order; the other introducing 'ordering' where there is basic dislocation. Let me give two examples which, I hope, will make these somewhat abstract propositions fully understandable.

Let us take, as one extreme, Mao Tse-Tung's 'Long March'. Here, we have 'populism' in the sense described above: the attempt to constitute the 'people' as a historical actor out of a plurality of antagonistic situations. Mao even talks about 'contradictions within the *people*', so that the 'people', an entity which would have been anathema to classic Marxist theory, is brought into the picture. This is the double reflection discussed above: the 'people', far from having the homogeneous nature that one would attribute to pure class actors (defined by precise locations within the relations of production), is conceived as the articulation of a plurality of ruptural points. These ruptural points, however, arising within a shattered symbolic framework – as a result of the civil war, the Japanese invasion, the confrontation between war lords, and so on – depend for their very constitution on a popular surface of inscription that transcends them. Here are the two dimensions I mentioned above: on the one hand, the attempt to break with the status quo, with the preceding institutional order; on the other, the effort to constitute an order where there was anomie and dislocation. So the equivalential chain necessarily plays a double role: it makes the emergence of the particularism of the demands possible but, at the same time, it subordinates them to itself as a necessary surface of inscription.

Let us now move on to an example that apparently belongs to the opposite extreme: the political mobilizations of the followers of Adhemar de Barros, a corrupt politican from the south of Brazil whose campaigns in the 1950s had as their motto '*Rouba mais faz*' ('He steals, but he keeps things going'). De Barros's inscription of grass-roots demands was essentially clientelistic: an exchange of votes for political favours. We find *prima facie* very little in common between Mao's global emancipatory project and Adhemar de Barros's *cosa nostra*. I would argue, however, that we have populism in both cases. How? The common element is given by the presence of an anti-institutional dimension, of a certain challenge to political normalization, to 'business as usual'. In both cases there is an appeal to the underdog. Walter Benjamin evokes the popular attraction to the high criminal, to the bandit,[39] whose appeal stems from the fact that the bandit is outside the legal system, and challenging it. Since any kind of institutional system is inevitably at least partially limiting and frustrating, there is something appealing about any figure who challenges it, whatever the reasons for and forms of the challenge. There is in any society a reservoir of raw anti-status-quo feelings which crystallize in some symbols *quite independently of the forms of their political articulation*, and it is their presence we intuitively perceive when we call a discourse or a mobilization 'populistic'. Clientelism – to go back to the example – is not necessarily populistic; it can adopt purely institutional forms, but it is enough that it is constructed as a public appeal to the underdog outside the normal political channels for it to acquire a populist connotation. In that case, however, what I have called the 'popular surface of inscription' can be any institution or ideology: it is a certain inflection of its themes that makes it populistic, not the particular character of the ideology or institution. I shall deal with some of these typological variations in Part III.

We have now reached a preliminary notion of populism. As I anticipated, however, my analysis has been based, for heuristic reasons, on two simplifying assumptions which I now have to eliminate. The first is that my whole approach to empty signifiers has assumed the presence of a stable dichotomic frontier within society (without such a frontier there would be no equivalences and, *ergo*, no empty signifiers either). Is this, however, an assumption that we can take for granted? What if forces on the two sides of the frontier displace it in new directions? The second is that I have not explored the full consequences of the permanence of the particularism of the demands within the equivalential chain. I have, in particular, taken it for granted that *any* anti-system demand could be incorporated as a new link in an already existing chain of equivalences.

What, however, if the particularism of the demands which are already part of the chain clashes with the new demands which attempt to incorporate themselves into it? Does this not create the conditions for an outside of a new type, one which can no longer be conceived as a camp within a stable space of representation dominated by a dichotomic frontier? These are the two questions which I must now explore. If the first is going to lead us to the notion of the 'floating signifier', the second will involve a more thorough study of the question of social heterogeneity which has arisen at several points in my presentation.

APPENDIX: WHY CALL SOME DEMANDS 'DEMOCRATIC'?

Readers of early drafts of this chapter have been puzzled by the category of 'democratic demands'. Why call them 'democratic' rather than 'specific' or simply 'isolated'? What is particularly democratic about them? These are legitimate questions which call for an answer. Let me say, in the first place, that by 'democratic' I do not mean, in this context, anything related to a democratic *regime*. As my text abundantly shows, these demands are not teleologically destined to be articulated in any particular political way. A Fascist regime can absorb and articulate democratic demands as much as a liberal one. Let me also say that the notion of 'democratic demands' has even less to do with any normative judgement concerning their legitimacy. It remains strictly descriptive. The only features I retain from the usual notion of democracy are: (1) that these demands are formulated *to* the system *by* an underdog of sorts – that there is an equalitarian dimension implicit in them; (2) that their very emergence presupposes some kind of exclusion or deprivation (what I have called 'deficient being').

Is this not a rather idiosyncratic notion of democracy? I do not think so. I shall try to defend it by saying something about the pedigree of my use of the concept. The starting point of this genealogical reconstruction should be the Marxian category of 'bourgeois-democratic revolution'. In this conception, democracy was linked to the struggle of the rising bourgeoisies against feudalism and Absolutism. So democratic demands were inherently bourgeois, and essentially linked to the establishment of 'liberal-democratic' regimes. Different from the (bourgeois)-democratic demands were the socialist ones, which involved transcending capitalist society and corresponded to a more advanced stage of historical development. So in those countries where the main item on the political agenda was the overthrow of feudalism, the task of the socialist forces was to support the bourgeois-democratic revolution which would establish, for a whole period, a fully fledged capitalist society. Only later, as a result of the internal contradictions of capitalism, would socialist demands come to the forefront of political struggle. So the main distinction was between socialist and democratic demands; the inscription of the latter within bourgeois hegemony and the establishment of a liberal state were taken for granted.

The neatness of these distinctions was tarnished with the emergence of those phenomena which were later to be subsumed under the label of 'combined and uneven development'. What happens if, in a certain country, the task of overthrowing feudalism retains all its centrality, but the bourgeoisie as a social force is too weak to bring about its own democratic revolution? In that case the democratic revolution remains on the historical agenda, but its bourgeois character becomes increasingly problematic. Its leadership needs to be transferred to different historical actors, and all kinds of non-orthodox articulations between agents and tasks become possible. The Bolshevik formula of a 'democratic dictatorship of workers and peasants' twisted the notion of 'democracy' in new and unexpected directions, and Trotsky's 'permanent revolution' required an even looser connection between revolution, democratic tasks and agents. The anti-Fascist struggles of the 1930s and the wave of Third World revolutions after 1945 made this process of disintegration of the 'bourgeois-democratic revolution' notion even more pronounced: on the one hand, the connection between democratic demands and liberalism was revealed as purely contingent (many formally anti-liberal regimes were the only possible framework for the advance of democratic demands); on the other, in those cases in which democratic demands required the defence of liberal institutions against the authoritarian onslaught, the 'bourgeois' character of those institutions could no longer be easily asserted. There was a changing articulating mediation on which the meaning of forces, institutions and events depended. I remember reading in Argentina, in the 1960s, a newspaper with the front-page headline: 'The National Constitution is becoming subversive'.

It is within this vast historical mutation that we can appreciate the whole significance of Gramsci's intervention. His entire theory of hegemony makes sense only if the popular inscription of democratic demands does not proceed according to an a priori given or teleologically determined *diktat*, but is a contingent operation which can move in a plurality of directions. This means that there is no demand with a 'manifest destiny' as far as its popular inscription is concerned – and in fact it is not just a question of the contingency of the inscription, because no demand is fully a demand without *some* kind of inscription. When we reach this point in the Gramscian theorization we are not far from the notion of 'democratic demand' presented in this text. This is not entirely true, however, because for Gramsci, the final core of the articulating instance – or the collective will – is always what he calls a fundamental class of society, and the identity of this core is not itself thought as resulting from articulating practices: that is to say, it still belongs to a different ontological order from that of the democratic demands. This is what Chantal Mouffe and I, in *Hegemony and Socialist Strategy*, called the last remainder of essentialism in Gramsci. If we eliminate it, the 'people' as the articulating instance – the locus of what we have called popular demands – can result only from the hegemonic overdetermination of a particular democratic demand which functions, as we have explained, as an empty signifier (as an *objet petit a* in the Lacanian sense).

This explains, I hope, why I have called these demands 'democratic' – not because of any nostalgic attachment to the Marxian tradition, but because there is an ingredient of the notion of 'democracy' in that tradition which it is vital to retain: the notion of the non-fulfilment of the demand, which confronts it with an existing status quo and makes possible the triggering of equivalential logics leading to the emergence of a 'people'. Let us suppose that instead of 'democratic' demands, we talked about 'specific' ones. This last denomination would immediately evoke the idea of a full positivity, closed in itself. But we know that there is no such positivity: either the demand is differentially constructed – which means that its positivity is not monadic, but positioned within a relational ensemble – or it is equivalentially related to other demands. We also know that this alternative overlaps with the one between fulfilled and unfulfilled demands. But a fulfilled demand ceases to be a demand. It is only the lack of fulfilment – which can oscillate between downright rejection and just 'being in the balance' – that gives a demand materiality and discursive presence. The 'democratic' qualification (which is not, in fact, a qualification because it repeats as an adjective what was already included in the notion of demand) points to that equivalential/discursive environment which is the condition of emergence of the demand, while 'specific' or 'isolated' do not.

The problem remains, of course, of the relation between popular and democratic demands, as stated in the text, and the more conventional notion of democracy. I shall partially address this question in Chapter 6.

5

Floating Signifiers and Social Heterogeneity

Floating: nemesis or destiny of the signifier?

Let us start by restating those conditions of emergence of a popular identity that we have discovered so far. First, there is the presence of an empty signifier which both expresses and constitutes an equivalential chain. Second, there is an autonomization of the equivalential moment *vis-à-vis* its integrating links, given that, although there is equivalence only because there is a plurality of demands, this equivalential moment is not merely ancillary to these demands, but has a crucial role in making their plurality possible. As we have seen, the equivalential inscription tends to give solidity and stability to the demands, but also restricts their autonomy, for it has to operate within strategic parameters established for the chain as a whole. To give one example: during the 1940s and 1950s the Italian Communist Party pushed democratic demands in a large variety of fronts. By so doing it gave them a surface of inscription which made them better defined in their aims and more efficient in their tactical moves but, by the same token, they became less autonomous and more subordinated to Communist strategic aims. The tension between these two moments is inherent in the establishment of any political frontier and, indeed, in any construction of the 'people' as a historical agent. Finally, there is the question of limits of this double game of sub-ordination and autonomization of the particular demands. The chain can live only within the unstable tension between these two extremes, and disintegrates if one of them entirely imposes itself over the other. The unilateralization of the moment of subordination transforms the popular signifiers into an inoperative entelechy incapable of acting as a *ground* for the democratic demands. This is what happened to many populist discourses in African countries with the emergence of bureaucratic elites after the process of decolonialization. Autonomization beyond a certain point, on the other hand, leads to a pure logic of differences and to the collapse of the popular equivalential camp. (This, as we have seen, was the case with the crisis of the Chartist discourse.)

There is, however, a simplifying assumption in this picture that we must now eliminate. For the way I have presented the matter would presuppose that the only alternative to a demand being articulated within an equivalential chain is that it is differentially absorbed, in a non-antagonistic way, within the existing symbolic system. This, however, presupposes that the internal frontier remains the same, without displacements – obviously a rather unrealistic assumption, which was acceptable only for heuristic reasons, in order to present the notion of 'empty signifier' at its purest. This initial, simplified model can be illustrated with the following diagram, which I have used in another work:[1]

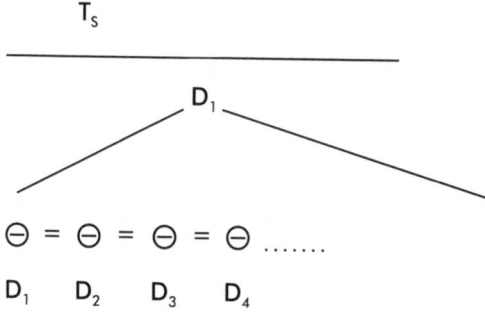

The example I had in mind was that of an oppressive regime – in that case Tsarism – separated by a political frontier from the demands of most sectors of society (D_1, D_2, D_3 ... etc.). Each of these demands, in its particularity, is different from all the others (this particularity is shown in the diagram by the lower semicircle in the representation of each of them). All of them, however, are equivalent to each other in their common opposition to the oppressive regime (this is what the upper semicircle represents). This, as we have seen, leads to one of the demands stepping in and becoming the signifier of the whole chain – a tendentially empty signifier. But the whole model depends on the presence of the dichotomic frontier: without this, the equivalential relation would collapse and the identity of each demand would be exhausted in its differential particularity.

What happens, however, if the dichotomic frontier, without disappearing, is blurred as a result of the oppressive regime itself becoming hegemonic – that is, trying to interrupt the equivalential chain of the popular camp by an alternative equivalential chain, in which some of the popular demands are articulated to entirely different links (for example, as we shall see in a moment, the defence of the 'small man' against power ceases to be associated to a left discourse, as in the American New Deal, and becomes linked to the 'moral majority')? In that case, the *same* democratic demands receive the structural pressure of *rival* hegemonic projects. This generates an autonomy of the popular signifiers different from the one we have considered so far. It is no longer that the particularism of the demand becomes self-sufficient and independent of any equivalential articulation, but that its meaning is indeterminate between alternative equivalential frontiers. I shall call signifiers whose meaning is 'suspended' in that way 'floating signifiers'. We could represent their operation, following the previous diagram, in this way:

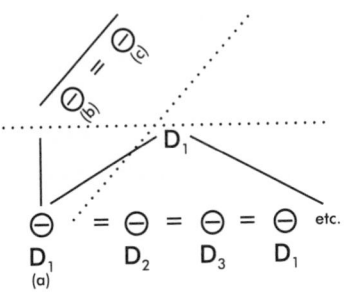

As we can see, D_1 is submitted to the structural pressure of two antagonistic equivalential chains represented by the dotted lines: the horizontal corresponds to the popular camp opposing Tsarism, as in the first diagram. The diagonal, however, establishes an equivalential link between D_1, belonging to the popular camp, and two other demands that the latter would oppose as belonging to the camp of Tsarism. So we have two antagonistic ways of constituting the 'people' as a historical actor. The way in which the meaning of D_1 is going to be fixed will depend on the result of a hegemonic struggle. So the 'floating' dimension becomes most visible in periods of organic crisis, when the symbolic system needs to be radically recast. And, for that reason, that dimension has, as a necessary pattern, the unfixing of the relationship between the two semicircles in the representation of the demands: the upper semicircle is always the one that becomes autonomous in any floating, for it is in its equivalential virtualities that the representation of the (absent) fullness of society lies. In a recent semi-autobiographical article, the British Conservative politician Michael Portillo writes:

> At the age of 11 I was interested in politics. In the election year of 1964 I helped to run a Labour Party committee room in my parents' house. I had a poster of Harold Wilson on my bedroom wall .... But by the middle 1970s Labour was threadbare. Mrs Thatcher took over the Tories in 1975 with a gleam of revolution in her eye. For me it was alluring. Perhaps I've never changed: I have some left-of-centre views mingled with a zest for radicalism.[2]

The move could not be clearer: Portillo was both a left-of-centre militant and a radical. Once a left-of-centre alternative ceased to be experienced as radical, he had to choose between the *content* of a politics and its radical *form*, even if that radicalism was of an opposite sign. The discussion of *'gaucho-lepénisme'* in Chapter 4 points in the same direction. This distance between the ontic contents of a politics and their ability to represent radical fullness is always present but, as I said, it becomes particularly visible in critical periods, when radical conversions and sudden shifts in the public mood are quite common.

As we can see, the categories of 'empty' and 'floating' signifiers are structurally different. The first concerns the construction of a popular identity once the presence of a stable frontier is taken for granted; the second tries conceptually to apprehend the logic of the displacements of that frontier. In practice, however, the distance between the two is not that great. Both are hegemonic operations and, most importantly, the referents largely overlap. A situation where only the category of empty signifier was relevant, with total exclusion of the floating moment, would be one in which we would have an entirely immobile frontier – something that is hardly imaginable. Conversely, a purely psychotic universe, where we would have a pure floating without any partial fixation, is not thinkable either. So floating and empty signifiers should be conceived as partial dimensions – and so as analytically distinguishable – in any process of hegemonic construction of the 'people'.

Let us take as an example of the way floating signifiers operate during the emergence in America of a right-wing populism in the decades after the Second World War. One of the strategists of Richard Nixon's presidential campaign in 1968, Kevin Phillips, wrote a global interpretation of American political history based on the centrality of the phenomenon of populism:

> With the imaginative use of a voluminous array of statistics, Phillips argued that ethnic, racial and regional antagonisms have been the keys to party supremacy in every electoral cycle from the era of Jefferson to the 1960s. When a party convincingly placed itself on the side of the hard-working, culturally mainstream masses and against the moneyed, Northeastern establishment, it usually gained national dominance for a generation or more.[3]

This cause of the 'small man' would have been abandoned, according to Phillips, by the dominant coalition of liberal-oriented Democrats and poor blacks and Latinos who depended for their survival on Government subsidies. Contemporary Democrats, argued Phillips, had made a fatal political error. They foolishly leaped 'beyond programs taxing the few for the benefit of the many (the New Deal)' to pass 'programs taxing the many on behalf of the few (the Great Society)'. In response, whites across the Sunbelt (a term he invented) and Catholics in the North and Midwest were moving towards the GOP (Grand Old Party – the Republicans). The establishment – which Phillips defined as 'Wall Street, the Episcopal Church, the great metropolitan newspapers, the US Supreme Court, and Manhattan's East Side' – had opposed FDR (Roosevelt). But now it was composed of genteel liberals who disdained the conservative wave that 'has invariably taken hold in the ordinary (now middle class) hinterlands of the nation'.[4] The pattern of this process, as described by Kazin, could not be more revealing for our theme: the same populist strands were present – in different articulations – in both the discourse of the New Dealers and that of the new conservative Right – or, rather, they were progressively taken by the latter from the former. That is to say, we are dealing with floating signifiers in the strict sense of our definition. Thus:

> There *was* a close resemblance between the *rhetoric* of Populist campaigners [at the end of the nineteenth century] and that of conservative anti-Communists [in the 1950s]. Both appealed to the will and interests of a self-reliant, productive majority whose spiritual beliefs, patriotic ideals, and communities were judged to be under attack at the hand of a modernizing elite, a 'civilized minority', in the historian Christopher Lasch's ironic term. To neglect the presence of common threads of expression that stretched beyond the People's Party itself is as mistaken as to force that tradition into a container brimming with repugnant beliefs. John T. Flynn and Patrick Scanlan were pursuing quite different ends than were Ignatius Donnelly and Tom Watson in the 1890s. But, as a language, populism could leap ideological boundaries and attract Americans hostile to modern liberalism as well as those who continue to think fondly of labor unions and FDR's Four Freedoms.[5]

The process through which the populist signifiers were hegemonized by a right-wing discourse was long and complex, but we can recognize some critical turning points. As Kazin points out, until 1940 the notion of a conservative populism was an oxymoron. There was no connection between populism and the discourse of the traditional Right, which was centred on the defence of unregulated capitalism and the discouragement of any kind of grass-roots mobilization. The first moment in which a conservative discourse with populist connotation arises is in the anti-Communist crusades of the 1950s, whose epicentre was McCarthyism but which had been preceded by a series of molecular processes on a variety of fronts. There was certainly an anti-Communist component, but it was immediately associated with the conservative fear of a powerful government machine controlled by the liberal elites of the Northwest. Once these two components started feeding on each other, it was easy to move from the second to some traditional populist themes:

> Conservatives thus found in the storehouse of populist language a potent weapon for their anti-statist crusade. A conspiratorial elite organized both inside government and in the wider culture was forcing Americans into a regimented system that would destroy their livelihoods and tear down their values. The power of big business, implied the Right, looked puny compared to that of the new leviathan.... This was quite a departure. For the first time in United States history, large numbers of activists and politicians were employing a populist vocabulary to oppose social reform instead of support it.[6]

These new associations obviously required a different modulation of the old populist themes. The opposition between 'parasites' and 'producers' had to lose its centrality, while the link between 'people' and 'workers' was replaced by an appeal to the average man: 'working man' and 'Joe worker' tended to be replaced by 'regular guy', 'average Joe' and 'average American'.[7] The important point is that this conservative turn took place via a change in the emphasis, but not necessarily the content, of the former left-orientated populist language. This means, in our terminology, that a new regime of equivalences was being constructed. From this viewpoint, the career of John T. Flynn is typical. He had started as a left-wing writer in the 1930s, attacking financial speculation and demanding government protection for small firms against the big corporations. His hatred of big money, however, led him also to reject the dominant elite – including its governmental component – *in toto* and, in this way, to maintain a populist discourse, but of an opposing sign. Following this path, he became one of the main theoreticians of a new breed of conservatism. 'After the war, this visceral suspicion of the governing elite allowed Flynn to update his enemies list without departing too much from his original script. The victories of Communists and social-democrats after World War II simply allowed him to draw a frightening image of a state run amuck'.[8]

A similar path was followed by other intellectuals who started their careers as Marxists – James Burnham, Whittaker Chambers, Max Eastman, Will Herberg, Wilmore Kendall, Eugene Lyons and James Rorty – or as more traditional conservatives – Brent Bozell, William F. Buckley Jr, and Russell Kirk. If to this we add the new popularity of communitarian themes, the new wave of religious organizations – especially within the Catholic Church – and the expansion of veterans' associations, we have the whole spectrum of phenomena which was going to lead to the severing of the links between liberalism and populism. The first public crystallization of this new mood was, of course, McCarthyism, which consciously used every type of weapon in the populist ideological arsenal. After the fall of McCarthy, the type of mobilization he had fostered quickly disintegrated, but the break between liberalism and populism remained as a lasting effect. The discourse of the New Deal was in clear retreat. The void it left would be occupied by new forces from the Right.

The second important moment in the disintegration of the New Deal discourse was the electoral campaigns of George C. Wallace.[9] If we are to understand their relative success, we must understand the crisis of representation that America was experiencing in the 1960s. Underdogs of various sorts were emerging – the civil rights movement, the New Left, and so on – but, for our purposes, it is important to realize that what later, in Nixon's campaigns, would be called 'middle America' also felt under-represented – asphyxiated between an almighty bureaucracy in Washington and the demands of several minorities. Kazin describes the mood of the group in these terms:

> They were defensively proud of people like themselves – whites with steady jobs or small, local businesses. While not overtly racist, they were also not particularly sensitive to or concerned about the specific problems of black people. Their attitudes toward the world of politics ranged from a cynical disgust at elected officials who 'wasted' tax money on welfare programs and the war in Indochina to a flickering hope that, left to themselves, ordinary people could fix whatever the establishment had screwed up.... A movement or party that could channel the growing resentment of such people – as had the grassroots reformers and insurgent politicians of an earlier day – might break the grip of the New Deal order.[10]

The crisis of representation which is at the root of any populist, anti-institutional outburst was clearly in embryo in the demands of these people. Some kind of radical discourse had to emerge which was able to inscribe those demands. Where was this discourse going to come from? Or – to put it differently – how could these demands cohere in an equivalential whole? The radical Left was not in a position to enter into this hegemonic competition: 'Based in university enclaves, New Leftists included few who comprehended the tangled emotions of envy and indignation that shaped the response of less privileged whites to ghetto rebellions and anti-war demonstrations.'[11] As for the trade unions, they were seen as depending too much on the support of the liberal Democratic establishment to be the source of any radical anti-status-quo upsurge. So this was clearly an opportunity for the Right, if it could abandon the lunatic fringe to which it had for so long remained confined. This was exactly the political void that Wallace filled with his discourse – a mixture of racism and most of the old populist themes (he was even the first presidential candidate to present himself as a worker). He never really came close to winning the presidency – the vote he obtained, except in his enclaves in the South, was merely a protest vote

– but his intervention had a lasting effect: it helped decisively to cement the articulation between popular identities and right-wing radicalism. Once this articulation was solid enough, other political forces, closer to the mainstream of the political spectrum, could profit from it. This is exactly what took place in the process leading from Nixon to Reagan. Wallace's streetfighter's rhetoric was replaced by the appeal to a 'silent majority' of producers and consumers.

> As liberalism crumbled, astute minds in the [Republican] party recognized that the defense of middle-class *values* – diligent toil, moral piety, self-governing communities – could now bridge gaps of income and occupation that the GOP had been unable to cross since the Great Depression. This became possible only because, away from the workplace, millions of white wage earners now proudly identified themselves as consumers and home owners.... By the end of the 1960s, whether one earned a wage or owned a little business, carried a union card or chafed at the restrictions imposed by labor was often less important than a shared dislike of a governing and cultural elite and its perceived friends in the ghettos and on campus.[12]

Is it necessary to mention how this polarization is projected today (June 2004) on to the immediate American electoral alternatives? Either middle America deserts the populist right-wing camp because it no longer recognizes itself in the aggressive neo-conservative onslaught of the Bush regime, with the result that new equivalential chains are formed – that is, we move to a new hegemonic formation – or the Republicans will be re-elected. What is pure illusion is to think that their long-term defeat could take place without some kind of drastic rearticulation of the political imaginary (the situation is too polarized for small changes in one direction or the other to be able to make any material difference). Even if Bush marginally loses the election, his successor will find his movements limited by the straitjacket of a hegemonic formation whose parameters remain substantially unchanged.

Heterogeneity enters the scene

We must now move on to the second simplifying assumption implicit in our model of empty signifiers – one which we must now eliminate. We have assumed so far that *every* unfulfilled demand can incorporate itself in the equivalential chain that is constitutive of the popular camp. Is this, however, a justified assumption? Two minutes of reflection are enough to conclude that it is not. Let us consider, in our initial diagram (p. 130), the lower semicircles in the circles representing the individual demands. While the upper semicircle points to the strictly equivalential moment (what the various demands share in their common opposition to the oppressive regime), the lower one represents the irreducible particularism of each individual demand. The important thing to realize is that the equivalential relation does not do away with this particularism, for the simple reason that without it there would be no possibility of an equivalential relation to start with. It is because all individual demands, in their very individuality, are opposed to the same oppressive regime, that an equivalential community between them can be established. I have already pointed out at the beginning of this chapter that between the upper and the lower semicircles in the diagram there is not only complementarity but also tension – while individual demands get reinforced through their equivalential inscription, the chain as a whole develops a logic of its own which can lead to a sacrifice or betrayal of the aims of its individual links.

I now want to point out another possibility implicit in the logic of our model: that a demand cannot be incorporated into the equivalential chain because it clashes with the particularistic aims of demands which are already links in that chain. If the particularism of the individual demands were totally neutralized by their equivalential inscription, this possibility could be ruled out, but we know that this is not the case. So an equivalential chain is not opposed only to an antagonistic force or power, but also to something which does not have access to a general space of representation. But 'opposed' means something different in each case: an *antagonistic* camp is fully represented as the negative reverse of a popular identity which would not exist without that negative reference; but in the case of an outside which is opposed to the inside just because it does not have access to the space of representation, 'opposition' means simply 'leaving aside' and, as such, it does not in any sense shape the identity of what is inside. We find a good example of this distinction in Hegel's philosophy of history: it is punctuated by dialectical reverses operating through processes of negation/supersession, but, apart from them, there is the presence of the 'peoples without history', entirely outside historicity. They are equivalent to what Lacan called *caput mortuum*, the residue left in a tube after a chemical experiment. The break involved in this kind of exclusion is more radical than the one that is inherent in the antagonistic one: while antagonism still presupposes some sort of discursive inscription, the kind of outside that I am now discussing presupposes exteriority not just to something within a space of representation, but to the space of representation as such. I will call this type of exteriority *social heterogeneity*. Heterogeneity, conceived in this way, does not mean *difference*; two entities, in order to be different, need a space within which that difference is representable, while what I am now calling heterogeneity presupposes the absence of that common space. So our next step is to reinscribe our discussion on popular identities within this complex articulation between homogeneity and heterogeneity.

Let us start by considering a situation from which heterogeneity, in the sense in which we understand it, is radically absent, so that we can see more clearly later the effects of its presence. Such a situation would be the one depicted in our first diagram: a strict frontier separating two antagonistic camps, and a saturated space within which all social entities can be located. We have, it is true, an antagonistic frontier, but one which cannot include, within its own logic, its own displacement in any direction. The reason for this is clear: if the excluded other is the condition of my own identity, persisting in my identity also requires the positing of the antagonistic other. On a terrain dominated by pure homogeneity (that is, full representability), this ambiguity in relation to the enemy cannot be superseded. This, to some extent, corresponds to the well-known fact that forces which have constructed their antagonism on a certain terrain show their secret solidarity when it is that very terrain which is put into question. It is like the reaction of two chess players to somebody who kicks the board. Let us think, as an example, of the European social-democratic parties' *Union sacrée* in 1914. The consequence of this argument, however, is that the structure described by the first diagram would reproduce itself *sine die*. There can be neither frontier displacements nor unrepresentable elements within a saturated space. But we know very well that those displacements occur all the time, and that the field of representation is a broken and murky mirror, constantly interrupted by a heterogeneous 'Real' which it cannot symbolically master. How can we make these phenomena compatible with our diagram? There are only two possible solutions: one is compatible with the notion of a saturated space; the other – the one which we will accept – renounces the idea of a saturated space, and of full representability.

Let us start with the first solution. Marx presents History as a coherent story unified by a single logic: the development of the productive forces, to which corresponds, at each of its stages, a certain system of relations of production. It has been asserted that the notion of productive forces is purely quantitative, but this is not true. One has to take into consideration that the logic of Marx's account is profoundly Hegelian, and corresponds not to the category of quantity but to that of measure – more precisely, to the infinite of measure[13] once the measureless has been superseded. In Hegel's own words: 'But this infinity of the specification of measure *posits* both the qualitative and the quantitative as *sublating* themselves in each other, and hence posits their first, immediate *unity*, which is measure as such, as returned into itself and therefore as itself *posited*.'[14] Thus quantity and quality come together, and this corresponds precisely to the type of unity existing between forces and relations of production. This point is important, because without this logical imbrication between the quantitative and the qualitative, History would not be a coherent story – the space of its representation would not be saturated. This clarifies the explanation of the displacements of the antagonistic frontier within this theoretical narrative. There are displacements of the frontier because, through them, a different drama is enacted: the compatibility/incompatibility between forces and relations of production at each of its stages. Our diagram would simply be a snapshot – and a static one – of an appariential form taken by that deeper movement at a certain point in time. As a result, the validity of this type of explanation stands or falls completely according to the ability of its narrative to reabsorb within itself any heterogeneous 'outside'.

We will approach this question by locating the problem of heterogeneity in a historical perspective. When I discussed the Hegelian notion of 'peoples without history', I was already indicating the treatment that the 'heterogeneous' receives when it is approached via a totalizing logic: its dismissal through the denial of its historicity. Since about the 1830s, however, the heterogeneous excess comes from a new source which was identified as 'the social question'. Traditional European thought had distinguished various social strata which, put together, composed a harmonious image of society: the nobility, the clergy, the peasants, the burghers of the city, and so on. There were also, of course, the poor, who were in excess of that classification, but could be dealt with through *ad hoc* procedures – the Poor Laws in England, for example. In Germany after the 1830s, however, this heterogeneous excess started to increase in alarming proportions, for reasons not so much related to incipient industrialization but, rather, to its opposite:[15] an inadequate industrial development which was unable to replace an economic structure dislocated by a plurality of factors – rapid population growth, emancipation from serfdom, enclosures, suppression of feudal distinctions in the towns, and so forth. These were the parameters of the social question as it presented itself in Germany at the time. Hegel was well aware of the problem, but the closest he came to proposing a solution was his suggestion that the excess population should be encouraged to emigrate to the overseas colonies.

Warren Breckman has pointed out that '[c]ontemporary observers registered these social changes [the transition to an industrial society] in the growing use of the term "proletariat" to designate this new class. The gradual abandonment of the old term *Pöbel* (rabble) signified an important shift in the analysis of poverty and the onset of the modern German discussion of industrial classes.'[16] But the association of the term 'proletariat' with the industrial working class took a long time to be established. As has been pointed out: 'Before Marx, *proletarian* [*prolétaire*] was one of the central signifiers of the passive spectacle of poverty. In England, Dr Johnson had defined *proletarian* in his *Dictionary* (1755) as "mean; wretched; vile; vulgar", and the word seems to have had a similar meaning in France in the early nineteenth century, where it was used virtually interchangeably with *nomade*'.[17] In this sense, the term 'proletariat' is part of a whole terminological universe which designates the poor, but a poor outside any stable social ascription. As Peter Stallybrass points out:

> Hence the curious way in which Marx ransacks French, Latin, and Italian to conjure up the nameless. They are *rovés, maquereaus* (pimps), what 'the French term *la bohème*'; they are literati; they are *lazzaroni*.... The OED defines the *lazzaroni* as 'the lowest class in Naples, living by odd jobs or begging'. In the seventeenth century, the *lazzari* had been defined as 'the scum of the Neapolitan people', and in the late eighteenth century *lazzaroni* was being used as a more extended term of social abuse.[18]

So the terms of the alternative are clear: if the heterogeneous excess can be contained within certain limits, reduced to a marginal presence, the dialectic vision of a unified history can be maintained. If, on the contrary, heterogeneity prevails, social logics will have to be conceived in a fundamentally different way. It is at the heart of this alternative that we can locate the masterly move of Marx, which consisted in isolating, from within the world of poverty that the transition to industrialism was generating, a differentiated sector which did not belong to the interstices of history – to the non-historical – but was destined to be a major historical protagonist. Within a history conceived as a history of production, the working class would be the agent of a new stage in the development of productive forces, and the term 'proletarian' was used to designate this new agent. In order to maintain its credentials as an 'insider' of the main line of historical development, however, the proletariat had to be strictly differentiated from the absolute 'outsider': the *lumpenproletariat*. Marx and Engels do not spare their invectives with respect to the latter. To quote just two of the texts studied by Stallybrass: in referring to the Mobile Guards in Paris after the February Revolution, Marx asserts that they 'belonged for the most part to the *lumpenproletariat*, which in all big towns form a mass sharply differentiated from the industrial proletariat, a recruiting ground for thieves and criminals of all kinds, living on the crumbs of society, people without a definite trade, vagabonds, *gens sans feu et sans aveu*, varying according to the degree of civilization of the nation to which they belong, but never renouncing their *lazzaroni* character'.[19] And Engels: 'The *lumpenproletariat*, in the big cities, is the worst of all possible allies. This rabble is absolutely venal and absolutely brazen .... Every leader of the workers who uses these scoundrels as guards or relies on them for support proves himself by this action alone a traitor to the movement.'[20]

So the character of pure outsider of the *lumpenproletariat*, its expulsion from the field of historicity, is the very condition of possibility of a pure interiority, of a history with a coherent structure. There is, however, a problem. The term *lumpenproletariat* has an intended referent: those lower sectors of society which have no clear insertion in the social order (although the terminological imprecision I have just mentioned should already alert us to the possibility that such reference is perhaps less unequivocal than intended). But apart from this reference, there is a clear attempt to give conceptual content to the category. Given that the 'inside' of history is conceived as a history of production ('the anatomy of civil society is Political Economy'), its distance from the productive process becomes the trademark of the *lumpenproletariat*. And the question arises: is that distance to be found only in the rabble of the big cities? For if that feature applies to sectors wider than the *lazzaroni*, its global effects would also be wider, and would threaten the internal coherence of the 'historical' world. The penetrating essay by Peter Stallybrass from which I have been quoting attempts to do precisely that: to show in Marx's texts – especially in *The Eighteenth Brumaire* – those crucial points in which the category of *lumpenproletariat* is destabilized and extends its social effects far beyond what Marx intended. It is to Stallybrass's analysis that I now turn.

There is in the first place the fact, pointed out by Marx himself in *The Class Struggles in France*, that the parasitism of the *lumpenproletariat*, the scum of society, is reproduced by the finance aristocracy at the highest levels of social organization – people who earn their income not through productive activities but 'by pocketing the already available wealth of others'. So the finance aristocracy 'is nothing but the *rebirth of the lumpenproletariat on the heights of bourgeois society*'. Moreover, for Marx this extension of the category is not a marginal one, limited to a small group of speculators, for it refers to the whole question of the relation between productive and unproductive labour, which political economists had discussed since Adam Smith, and which is central to the structuration of the capitalist system.[21] Once the 'outside' of production is conceived at this level of generality, it is difficult to exclude it from the field of historicity. But Stallybrass also discusses another aspect which blurs the line separating the 'inside' from the 'outside' even more. As he points out, the difficulty that Marx faces in his early analysis of Bonapartism in *The Eighteenth Brumaire* is to determine the social nature of the regime – given that all political regimes should be the expression of some kind of class interests. Marx's answer is that the social base of Louis Bonaparte's regime is the smallholding peasants. Almost immediately, however, he has to qualify his judgement by asserting that the peasants, given their dispersion, do not constitute a class but a simple aggregation, 'much as potatoes in a sack form a sack of potatoes'. This gives the Bonapartist state a higher degree of autonomy than that enjoyed by other regimes which depend on a more structured social base. Later, however, Marx rejected this solution, and saw Bonapartism as depending on a heterogeneous social basis which made it possible for the state to move in between different classes. This, according to Stallybrass, is the beginning of a crisis in Marxist theory. This crisis is synonymous with the emergence of political articulation as absolutely constitutive of the social link:

For Marx, in other words, as for Bataille, heterogeneity is not the *antithesis* of political unification but the very condition of possibility of that unification. I suspect that that is the real scandal of the lumpenproletariat in Marxist theory: namely, that it figures the political itself.... For the lumpen seems to figure less a class in any sense that one usually understands that term in Marxism than a group that is amenable to political articulation. And what group is not? ... But if the lumpenproletariat can as easily be exalted as base, its identity cannot be given in advance of the moment of political articulation.[22]

Once we have reached this point, it should be clear that we are abandoning the assumptions that made possible the explanation of historical change within the dialectical model. History, after all, is not the terrain on which a unified and coherent story would unfold. If social forces are the aggregation of a series of heterogeneous elements brought together through political articulation, it is evident that the latter is constitutive and grounding, not the expression of any deeper underlying movement. So our next step should be to elaborate this notion of heterogeneity and to see how, if it is taken at face value, it modifies our original diagram. Before doing so, however, I would like to refer briefly to the notion of 'marginal mass' proposed by José Nun, which helps to project in a wider perspective some aspects which we have discussed in relation to Marx's *lumpenproletariat*.[23]

Nun's starting point is a discussion of the category of 'industrial reserve army' introduced by Marx to describe a kind of unemployment which is functional to capitalist reproduction. Marx's argument is that wages cannot be pushed down below subsistence level, so temporarily unemployed workers are functional to capitalist accumulation because the competition of the many workers for the few jobs pushes down the level of wages and, in that way, increases the rate of surplus-value. The impossibility of lowering wages below subsistence level obviously sets a limit to that functionality. In terms of our previous discussion: although the temporarily unemployed are not part of the capitalist relations of production, they are still functional to capitalism because they help to increase the rate of profit. Although they are formally outsiders, this is a different 'outside' from that of the *lumpenproletariat*, because it has a functionality within the system and, as a result, these people are still part of a 'history of production'. The temporary nature of their unemployment stresses the point even more. What happens, however, if unemployment rises beyond what is needed to keep wages at the subsistence level? It is from here that Nun's argument starts. Clearly, unemployment beyond a certain point ceases to be functional to capitalist accumulation. It is the ensemble of these unemployed, who are no longer an internal need of the system – they can even be dysfunctional in relation to it – that Nun calls 'marginal mass'. As he points out, there is in Marx a notion of 'relative surplus population' which authors like Paul Sweezy and Oskar Lange have wrongly assimilated to the category of 'industrial reserve army'. Marx actually distinguished three types of relative surplus population – the latent, the stagnant and the fluctuating – and it is only on the last type that most authors – Marx included – have concentrated. Nun tried to redress the balance, showing the various ways in which unemployment of various sorts has been related to capitalist accumulation: 'Whatever the case, industry has undeniably declined as employer of the labor force in favor of a generalized process of expansion of the tertiary sector, both public and private. This has led to occupational structures that are far more heterogeneous and unstable than the earlier analyses had ever imagined, fragmenting labor markets and adding enormous complexity to the effects of surplus population on the movements of capitalist accumulation.'[24]

A very rich analysis of this complexity follows, which I cannot elaborate in the context of this discussion. One important point, however, must be retained. If the marginal mass has to be defined 'outside' its functionality within capitalist accumulation, and if marginality does not imply only fluctuating unemployment in the factory system but, as Nun's recent work shows, a variety of situations covering the whole movement of the population within fragmented and weakly protected markets, we are faced with a heterogeneity which cannot be subsumed under any single 'inside' logic. The construction of any 'inside' is going to be only a partial attempt to master an 'outside' which will always exceed those attempts. In a globalized world, this is becoming ever more evident. In that case, however, this contamination between inside and outside starts to look uncannily similar to the notion of the *lumpenproletariat* once we have expanded it to cover the whole of unproductive labour and identity construction through political articulation. The 'peoples without history' have occupied centre stage to the point of shattering the very notion of a teleological historicity. So forget Hegel.

We now have all the elements needed to discuss heterogeneity in connection with our original diagram. It could be represented like this:

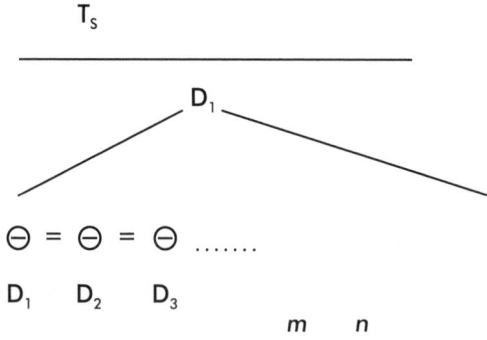

The demands *m* and *n* – which are not split – are heterogeneous in the sense that they cannot be represented in any structural location within the two antagonistic camps. As I said above, we are not dealing with a dialectical negation in which the negated element defines the identity of the negating one. The 'peoples without history' do not determine what the historical peoples are. That is why heterogeneity is constitutive: it cannot be transcended by any kind of dialectical reversal. We should ask ourselves, however: is it really true that the heterogeneous is to be found only at the margins of the diagram? Is it not already operating within it? Let us consider the matter carefully, starting with the frontier separating the two antagonistic camps. The dialectical explanation we have rejected presupposes that if there is an antagonistic (that is, contradictory) relation between A and B, I have within the concept of A everything we need to know that it will be negated by B and only by B. Negativity is there, but it is a mere sham, because it is present only in order to be superseded by a higher positivity. 'Determinate negation' is the name of that sham. Without a determinate negation itself inscribed in a process of further positings and reversals, however, there would be no history but the absolute positing of a binary opposition. So if we want to do away with both the dialectical solution and the static assertion of a binary opposition, we have to introduce something else within the schema. This is where heterogeneity comes into the picture. Let us consider the antagonism between workers and capitalists as presented in the Marxist tradition.[25] If the argument were truly dialectical it would have, on the one hand, to deduce the antagonism with the worker from the very logic of capital and, on the other, both worker and capitalist would have to be reduced to formal economic categories (if we were talking about purely *empirical* antagonisms, we would be outside the field of dialectical determination). But at the conceptual level, 'worker' means just 'seller of labour-power'. In that case, however, I am unable to define any kind of antagonism. To assert that there is an inherent antagonism because the capitalist extracts surplus-value from the worker is clearly insufficient, because in order to have antagonism it is necessary that the worker *resists* such extraction. But if the worker is conceptually defined as 'seller of labour-power', it is clear that I can analyse this category as much as I like, and I will still be unable to deduce from it logically the notion of resistance. That resistance will emerge – or not emerge – only in terms of the way the actual worker – not its pure conceptual determination – is constituted. This means that the antagonism is not inherent to the relations of production but it is established between the relations of production and an identity which is external to them. *Ergo*, in social antagonisms we are dealing with a *heterogeneity* which is not dialectically retrievable. The case of the heterogeneous other with which we started – the leaving aside which we exemplified with the Hegelian 'peoples without history' – is only one of the forms of the heterogeneous; we know now that, strictly speaking, without heterogeneity there would not be antagonism either.

We now have all the necessary elements to inscribe the notion of 'heterogeneity' within our argument concerning populism. How is this so? Let us start from the conclusion we reached in our last paragraph: antagonism presupposes heterogeneity because the resistance of the antagonized force cannot be logically derived from the form of the antagonizing one. This can only mean that the points of resistance to the antagonizing force are always going to be external to it. So there are no a priori privileged points of rupture and contestation; particularly intense antagonistic points can only be contextually established, never deduced from the internal logic of either of the two opposed forces taken in isolation. In practical terms – going back to the earlier example – there is no reason why struggles taking place within relations of production should be the privileged points of a global anti-capitalist struggle. A globalized capitalism creates myriad points of rupture and antagonisms – ecological crises, imbalance between different sectors of the economy, massive unemployment, and so on – and only an overdetermination of this antagonistic plurality can create global anti-capitalist subjects capable of carrying out a struggle worth the name. And, as all historical experience shows, it is impossible to determine a priori who the hegemonic actors in this struggle will be. It is by no means clear that they will be the workers. All we know is that they will be the outsiders of the system, the underdogs – those we have called the heterogeneous – who are decisive in the establishment of an antagonistic frontier. This means that the expansion of the category of *lumpenproletariat* – which, as we have seen, was already taking place in the work of the later Marx – at this point attains its full potential. Let us just look at the following passage from Frantz Fanon:

> The *lumpenproletariat*, once it is constituted, brings all its forces to endanger the 'security' of the town, and is the sign of the irrevocable decay, the gangrene ever present at the heart of colonial domination. So the pimps, the hooligans, the unemployed, and the petty criminals ... throw themselves into the struggle like stout working men. These classless idlers will by militant and decisive action discover the path that leads to nationhood .... The prostitutes too, and the maids who are paid two pounds a month, all who turn in circles between suicide and madness, will recover their

balance, once more go forward and march proudly in the great procession of the awakened nation.[26]

We are clearly at the antipodes of Marx and Engels's early references to the *lumpenproletariat*. From the perspective of our argument, what Fanon is doing in this passage is perfectly clear. First, he identifies the condition for the establishment of a radical frontier making possible the anti-colonialist revolution: a total exteriority of the revolutionary actors *vis-à-vis* the social categories of the existing status quo. Secondly, he asserts that since the outsiders are not linked to any particularistic interest, their confluence in a revolutionary will has to take place as a radical *political* equivalence (what Stallybrass calls political articulation). The subtext is that belonging to the established categories within colonial society would interfere with the formation of that revolutionary will. Here we are not far from the Maoist image of the revolutionary process as the surrounding of the cities by the countryside and the surrounding of the imperialist countries by a chain of anti-imperialist revolutions.

A note of caution, however, is necessary here. While Fanon is bringing the *lumpenproletariat* to the centre of the historical scene, he is not following the parallel line of thought which we have seen incipiently operating in Marx's later work: the extension of the notion of *lumpenproletariat* to the whole variety of those sectors which are not engaged in production. Thus he continues to identify the *lumpenproletariat* with its original referent – the rabble of the cities. The result is twofold: on the one hand, he has to overemphasize the degree of internal coherence of the order he wants to challenge; on the other, since he has identified the 'outsiders' with too rigid a referent, he cannot perceive the problem of heterogeneity in its true generality. In terms of our diagram: the total lack of identification of the bearers of the anti-colonial will with any particular demand within the existing system means that the circles representing the demands would not be internally split, for all particularity would have collapsed. We would have a *volonté générale* of such a kind that all individual wills would be materially identical. There is no possible political articulation here, because there is nothing to articulate.

Heterogeneity has simply disappeared as a result of the full return to a dialectical reversal. Jacobinism is just around the corner.

If we are to go beyond these simplifications, and see the problem of heterogeneity in its true generality, we must be aware that none of the differentiations of our two diagrams could have been established without the presence of the heterogeneous other. This is where my argument dovetails with the conclusions on populism reached at the end of Chapter 4. First, since the antagonistic frontier involves, as we have seen, a heterogeneous other which is dialectically irretrievable, there would always be a materiality of the signifier which resists conceptual absorption. In other words: the opposition A–B will never fully become A – not A. The 'B–ness' of the B will be ultimately non-dialectizable. The 'people' will always be something more than the pure opposite of power. There is a Real of the 'people' which resists symbolic integration. Secondly, in the diagram heterogeneity is also present in the particularism of the equivalential demands – a particularism which, as we know, cannot be eliminated because it is the very ground of the equivalential relation. Thirdly, as we have seen, particularism (heterogeneity) is also what prevents some of the demands from incorporating themselves in the equivalential chain.

The consequence of this multiple presence of the heterogeneous in the structuration of the popular camp is that the latter has an internal complexity which resists any kind of dialectical homogenization. Heterogeneity inhabits the very heart of a homogeneous space. History is not a self-determined process. The opaqueness of an irretrievable 'outside' will always tarnish the very categories that define the 'inside'. To return to our previous example: any kind of underdog, even in the extreme and purely hypothetical case in which it is exclusively a class defined by its location within the relations of production, has to have something of the nature of the *lumpenproletariat* if it is going to be an antagonistic subject. Once we have reached this point, however, the neatness of Fanon's distinction between the 'inside' and the 'outside' has to be replaced by a more complex game in which nothing is ever fully internal or fully external. Any internality will always be threatened by a heterogeneity which is never a pure outside, because it inhabits the very logic of the internal constitution. And, conversely, the possibility of an outside is always going to be short-circuited by the operation of homogenizing logics. My discussion of floating signifiers at the beginning of this chapter illustrates the point clearly. A pure inside/outside opposition would presuppose an immobile frontier – a hypothesis I have rejected as a description of any actual social process. On the contrary, it is as the essential undecidability between 'empty' and 'floating' – which we can now reformulate as the undecidability between the homogeneous and the heterogeneous or, in our example, between the proletariat and the *lumpenproletariat* – that the *political* game is going to take place. This game, which Gramsci called 'war of position', is, strictly speaking, a logic of displacement of political frontiers, in the sense I have defined.

To say that the political consists in an undecidable game between the 'empty' and the 'floating' is, however, the same as saying that the political operation *par excellence* is always going to be the construction of a 'people'. To some extent we had already reached this conclusion at the end of Chapter 4, but now, after the introduction of the notions of floating signifiers and heterogeneity, we can see more clearly the dimension of such a construction, which gives populism its true meaning. Firstly, there is the widening of the discursive–strategic operations that the construction of the 'people' requires. In our original model, only two of these operations were conceivable: the formation of the equivalential chain, and its crystallization in a unified entity through the production of empty signifiers. But the antagonistic frontier as such was taken as given, and was not an object of hegemonic construction. We know now that constructing a 'people' also involves constructing the frontier which the 'people' presupposes. Frontiers are unstable, and in a process of constant displacement. This is why I have talked about 'floating signifiers'. This entails a new hegemonic game: any new 'people' would require the reconstitution of the space of representation through the construction of a new frontier. The same happens with the 'outsiders' of the system: any political transformation implies not only a reconfiguration of already existing demands, but also the incorporation of new demands (that is, new historical actors) into the political scene – or its opposite: the exclusion of others who were previously present there.

This means that *all* struggles are, by definition, *political*. To talk about a 'political struggle' is, strictly speaking, a tautology. But this can be so only because the political has ceased to be a regional category. So there is no room for the distinction, as in classical socialism, between economic struggle and political struggle; economic struggles are as political as those taking place at the level of the state conceived in its restrictive sense.[27] The reason for this is clear. As I pointed out in Chapter 4, the political is, in some sense, the anatomy of the social world, because it is the moment of institution of the social. Not everything in society is political, because we have many sedimented social forms which have blurred the traces of their original political institution; but if heterogeneity is constitutive of the social bond, we are always going to have a political dimension by which society – and the 'people' – are constantly reinvented.

Does this mean that the political becomes synonymous with populism? Yes, in the sense in which I conceive this last notion. Since the construction of the 'people' is the political act *par excellence* – as opposed to pure administration within a stable institutional framework – the *sine qua non* requirements of the political are the constitution of antagonistic frontiers within the social and the appeal to new subjects of social change – which involves, as we know, the production of empty signifiers in order to unify a multiplicity of heterogeneous demands in equivalential chains. But these are also the defining features of populism. There is no political intervention which is not populistic to some extent. This does not mean, however, that all political projects are equally populistic; that depends on the extension of the equivalential chain unifying social demands. In more institutionalist types of discourse (dominated by the logic of difference), that chain is reduced to a minimum; while its extension will be maximal in rupturist discourses which tend to divide the social into two camps. But some kind of equivalence (some production of a 'people') is necessary for a discourse to be considered political. In any event, the important thing is that we are not dealing with two different types of politics: only the second type is political; the other simply involves the death of politics and its reabsorption by the sedimented forms of the social. This distinction coincides, to a large extent, with the one proposed by Rancière between *la police* and *le people*, which I shall discuss in my Concluding Remarks.

Let me say, in conclusion, that my analysis has many points of convergence with the one by Georges Bataille in his well-known essay on 'The Psychological Structure of Fascism'.[28] As he depicts it, the moment of homogeneity coincides almost point by point with what I have called 'logic of difference': '*Homogeneity* signifies the commensurability of elements and the awareness of this commensurability: human relations are sustained by a reduction to fixed rules based on the consciousness of the possible identity of delineable persons and situations; in principle, all violence is excluded from this course of existence' (p. 122). He also links the heterogeneous to what is in excess of a history of production: 'The *heterogeneous* world includes everything resulting from *unproductive* expenditure (sacred things themselves form part of this whole). This consists of everything rejected by *homogeneous* society as waste or as superior transcendent value ... the numerous elements or social forms that *homogeneous* society is powerless to assimilate: mobs, the warrior, aristocratic and impoverished classes, different types of violent individual or at least those who refuse the rule (madmen, leaders, poets, etc.) (p. 127). The affective element, which I have stressed in the constitution of popular identities, is equally present in Bataille's analysis: 'In heterogeneous reality, the symbols charged with affective value have the same importance as the fundamental elements, and the part has the same value as the whole. It is easy to note that, since the structure of knowledge for a homogeneous reality is that of science, the knowledge of a heterogeneous reality as such is to be found in the mystical thinking of primitives and in dreams: it is identical to the structure of the unconscious' (p. 128). Finally, he also stresses the homogenizing results of articulatory practices: 'Starting with formless and impoverished elements, the army, under the imperative impulse, becomes organized and internally achieves a *homogeneous* form on account of the negation directed at the disordered character of its elements: in fact, the mass that constitutes the army passes from a depleted and ruined existence to a purified geometrical order, from formlessness to aggressive rigidity' (p. 136).

Here our exploration comes to an end. The emergence of the 'people' depends on the three variables I have isolated: equivalential relations hegemonically represented through empty signifiers; displacements of the internal frontiers through the production of floating signifiers; and a constitutive heterogeneity which makes dialectical retrievals impossible[29] and gives its true centrality to political articulation. We have now reached a fully developed notion of populism.

6

Populism, Representation and Democracy

We have now reached a developed notion of populism. In this chapter I shall outline some of the consequences which follow from this for some of the central categories of political theory. Two of these categories are 'representation' and 'democracy', and it is on these that I shall concentrate my analysis.

The two faces of representation

Ernest Barker, discussing the large body of followers of Fascist dictators in connection with the notion of representation, asserts: 'The fundamental fact is that this following represents or reflects the will of the leader and not that the leader represents or reflects the will of the following. If there is representation, it is inverse representation, proceeding downwards from the leader. The party represents the leader: the people, so far as it takes its colour from the party, equally represents and reflects the direction of the leader'.[1] For Barker, representation is dominated by a sharp alternative: either the leader represents the will of his following, or the following represents the will of the leader. I must question Barker's alternative on two counts: (1) I have reason to doubt that the alternative is as exclusive as Barker thinks it is; (2) I also have reason to doubt that the second possibility – the following representing the will of the leader – is restricted to Fascist dictatorships.

Let us concentrate on what is involved in a process of representation under democratic conditions.[2] Democratic theory, starting with Rousseau, has always been highly suspicious of representation, and has accepted it only as a lesser evil, given the impossibility of direct democracy in large communities like modern nation-states. Given these premisses, democracy has to be as transparent as possible: the representative has to transmit as faithfully as possible the will of those he represents. Is this, however, a fair description of what is actually involved in a process of representation? There are good reasons to think that it is not. The function of the representative is not simply to transmit the will of those he represents, but to give credibility to that will in a milieu different from the one in which it was originally constituted. That will is always the will of a sectorial group, and the representative has to show that it is compatible with the interests of the community as a whole. It is in the nature of representation that the representative is not merely a passive agent, but has to add something to the interest he represents. This addition, in turn, is reflected in the identity of those represented, which changes as a result of the very process of representation. Thus, representation is a two-way process: a movement from represented to representative, and a correlative one from representative to represented. The represented depends on the representative for the constitution of his or her own identity. So the alternative that Barker describes is not one that corresponds to two different types of regime – it is, in fact, not an alternative at all: it simply points to two dimensions which are inherent in *any* process of representation.

It could be argued that although the two dimensions are inherent to representation, the latter would be more democratic whenever the first movement – from represented to representative – prevails over the second. This argument, however, does not take into account the nature of the will to be represented. If we had a fully constituted will – of a corporative group, for instance – the representative's room for manoeuvre would indeed be limited. This, however, is an extreme case within a wider range of possibilities. Let us take, at the opposite extreme, the case of marginal sectors with a weak degree of integration into the stable framework of a community. In this case we would be dealing not with a will to be represented but, rather, with the constitution of that will through the very process of representation. The task of the representative is, however, democratic, because without his intervention there would be no incorporation of those marginal sectors into the public sphere. But in that case, his task would consist less in transmitting a will than in providing a point of identification which would constitute as historical actors the sectors that he is addressing. As always, there will be some distance between a sectorial interest – even a fully constituted one – and the community at large; there will always be a space within which this process of identification will take place. It is on this moment of identification that we have now to concentrate our attention.

I will start by considering 'symbolic representation' as discussed by Hanna Fenichel Pitkin in a book which was published forty years ago but is still the best theoretical treatment of the notion of representation in the existing literature.[3] According to Pitkin, in symbolic representation:

> it does not really matter how the constituent is kept satisfied, whether by something the representative does, or how he looks, or because he succeeds in stimulating the constituent to identify with him.... But in that case a monarch or dictator may be a more successful and dramatic leader, and therefore a better representative, than an elected member of Parliament. Such a leader calls forth emotional loyalties and identification in his followers, the same irrational and effective elements produced by flag and hymns and marching bands. And, of course, representation seen in this light need have little or nothing to do with accurate reflection of the popular will, or with enacting laws desired by the people.[4]

Thus representation becomes the means of homogenizing what I called in Chapter 5 a heterogeneous mass: 'If the main goal to be achieved is the welding of the nation into a unified whole, the creation of a nation, then it is tempting to conclude that a single dramatic symbol can achieve this much more effectively than a whole legislature of representatives.... Real representation is charisma.'[5] The leader thus becomes a symbol-maker and his activity, no longer conceived as 'acting for' his constituents, becomes identified with effective leadership. The extreme form of symbolic representation is to be found in Fascism: 'At the extreme, this point of view becomes the fascist theory of representation (not the theory of the corporate state, but that of representation by a *Führer*).... But in fascist theory, this balance [the one between ruler and subject] is definitely shifted to the other side: the leader must force his followers to adjust themselves to what he does.'[6] Pitkin's critique of the limitations of a purely symbolic approach to representation concludes with a distinction between causes and reasons:

> It is important to ask what makes people believe in a symbol or accept a leader, but it is equally important to ask when they ought to accept, have good reason for accepting a leader. Only if we narrow our view of representation exclusively to the example of symbols are we tempted to overlook the latter question.... As one political scientist [Heinz Eulau] expressed it: 'Representation concerns not the mere fact' that the represented do accept the representative's decisions, 'but rather the reasons they have for doing so'; and reasons are different from causes.[7]

In my view, Pitkin has clouded the real issue. The question is not so much of distinguishing between causes and reasons – a distinction which I certainly accept – but of whether the sources of validity of reasons *precede* representation or are constituted *through* representation. Throughout her whole discussion she sidesteps the issue I raised at the beginning of this discussion: what happens if we have weakly consti-tuted identities whose constitution requires, precisely, representation in the first place? In my discussion in previous chapters, I addressed this issue in terms of the distinction between an ontic content and its onto-logical value. As I said, in a situation of radical disorder, *some* kind of order is needed, and the more generalized the disorder is, the less impor-tant the ontic content of that which restores order becomes. That ontic content is invested with the ontological value of representing order as such. In that case, identification will always proceed through this ontological investment and, as a result, it will always require the second movement that I have shown to be inherent to representation: the one from representative to represented. To go back to our discussion of psychoanalysis: investment in a partial object involves elevating that object to the dignity of the Thing. Once some basic political identifications have taken place, reasons can be given for particular decisions and choices, but the latter require as their starting point an identity which does not precede but results from the process of representation. We have seen in our discussion of Freud that the relationship with the leader depends on the degree of distance between the ego and the ego ideal. The shorter the distance, the more the leader becomes a *primus inter pares* and, as a result, the larger becomes the terrain where 'reasons', in Pitkin's sense, operate. But some distance between the two will always necessarily exist, so that identification through representation will also be to some extent present.

The difficulty with Pitkin's analysis is that, for her, the realm of reasons exists independently of any identification; reasons operate entirely outside representation. As a result, she can see only irrationality in any kind of symbolic representation. She cannot properly distinguish between manipulation and sheer contempt for the popular will, and constitution of that will through symbolic identification. It is true that she sees fascism as only an extreme case of symbolic representation but, given her premises, she does not have the theoretical tools to approach less extreme cases. For that reason, her entire discussion of this point revolves around the question of respect for or ignorance of the popular will, without considering how that popular will is constituted in the first place, and whether representation is not the very premiss of that constitution.

Once this conclusion has been reached, we start to glimpse the relevance of the problematic of representation for our discussion on populism, for the construction of a 'people' would be impossible without the operation of mechanisms of representation. As we have seen, identification with an empty signifier is the *sine qua non* for the emergence of a 'people'. But the empty signifier can operate as a point of identification only because it *represents* an equivalential chain. The double movement which we have detected in the process of representation is very much inscribed in the emergence of a 'people'. On the one hand, the representation of the equivalential chain by the empty signifier is not a purely passive one. The empty signifier is something more than the image of a pre-given totality: it is what *constitutes* that totality, thus adding a qualitatively new dimension. This corresponds to the second movement in the process of representation: from representative to represented. On the other hand, if the empty signifier is going to operate as a point of identification for all the links in the chain, it must actually represent them; it cannot become entirely autonomous from them. This corresponds to the first movement found in representation: from represented to representative. As we know, this double movement is the locus of a tension. Autonomization of the totalizing moment beyond a certain point destroys the 'people' by eliminating the representative character of that totality. But a radical autonomization of the various demands has the same effect, because it breaks the equivalential chain and renders the moment of representative totalization impossible. As we have seen, this is what happens when the differential logic prevails, beyond a certain point, over the equivalential one.

We could approach this question from a different angle which leads, however, to identical conclusions: through the combination between homogeneity and heterogeneity in which representation consists. The constitution of a 'people' requires an internal complexity which is given by the plurality of the demands that form the equivalential chain. This is the dimension of radical heterogeneity, because nothing in those demands, individually considered, announces a 'manifest destiny' by which they should tend to coalesce into any kind of unity – nothing in them anticipates that they should constitute a chain.[8] This is what makes the homogenizing moment of the empty signifier necessary. Without this moment, there would be no equivalential chain, so the homogenizing function of the empty signifier constitutes the chain and, at the same time, represents it. But this double function is none other than the two sides of the representative process that we have detected. The conclusion is clear: any popular identity has an inner structure which is essentially representative.

If representation illuminates something of the inner structure of populism, however, we could say that, conversely, populism throws some light on something that belongs to the essence of representation. For populism, as we have seen, is the terrain of a primary undecidability between the hegemonic function of the empty signifier and the equivalence of particularistic demands. There is a tension between the two, but this tension is none other than the space of constitution of a 'people'. And what is this but the tension we have found between the two opposite but necessary movements which constitute the inner structure of representation? Constructing a 'people' is not simply the application to a particular case of a general theory of representation which could be formalized at a more abstract level; it is, on the contrary, a *paradigmatic* case, because it is *the* one which reveals representation for what it is: the primary terrain of constitution of social objectivity.

Let us consider for a moment some of the other examples of symbolic representation discussed by Pitkin: a fish representing Christ, for instance. In all those cases – whether the symbol is purely arbitrary and, as a result, shades into a sign, or whether there is some kind of analogy which sustains and explains the symbolism – there is a common feature: what is being represented exists as a fully fledged object previous to and quite apart from the representation process. In psychoanalytic theory, this could be identified as a Jungian approach for which symbols are a priori attached to specific objects in the collective unconscious. It is only with the Freudian/Lacanian description of the working of the unconscious that representation becomes ontologically primary – as we have seen, names retrospectively constitute the unity of the object. And it is difficult to find a terrain which *reveals* this constitution better than the constant fluctuations in naming the 'people'. The main difficulty with classical theories of political representation is that most of them conceived the will of the 'people' as something that was constituted *before* representation. This is what happened with the aggregative model of democracy (Schumpeter, Downs) which reduced the 'people' to a pluralism of interests and values; and with the deliberative model (Rawls, Habermas), which found in either justice as fairness or in dialogical procedures the basis for a rational consensus which eliminated all opacity from the representation process.[9] Once that point has been reached, the only relevant question is how to *respect* the will of those represented, taking it for granted that such a will exists in the first place.

Democracy and popular identities

The transition from a discussion of symbolic representation to the political theory of Claude Lefort, with which I shall start our study of popular democracy, is easy, given that Lefort grounds his approach in the symbolic transformation which made possible the advent of modern democracy.[10] According to Lefort's well-known analysis, such a mutation involved a revolution in the political imaginary by which a hierarchical society centred on the king as point of unity of power, knowledge and law was replaced by a disincorporation materialized in the emergence of the place of power as essentially empty: 'Power was embodied in the prince, and therefore gave society a body. And because of this a latent but effective knowledge of what *one* meant to the *other* existed throughout the social. This model reveals the revolutionary and unprecedented feature of democracy. The locus of power becomes *an empty place.*... The exercise of power is subject to the procedures of periodical redistributions.... The phenomenon implies an institutionalisation of conflict' (p. 17). 'In my view, the important point is that democracy is institutionalized and sustained by the *dissolution of the markers of certainty*. It inaugurates a history in which people experience a fundamental indeterminacy as to the basis of power, law and knowledge, and so as to the basis of relations between *self* and *other*, at every level of social life' (p. 18).

What are we to think of this sequence? In some sense certain distinctions which, with a different terminology, I have introduced in this book are clearly present in Lefort's text. The notion of a hierarchical order

guaranteed and impersonated by the king, in which there is no institutionalization of social conflicts, looks very similar to what we have called
logic of difference. Since Lefort recognizes equality as a value as the
trademark of democracy, it would seem that we are not far away from
our equivalential logic. However, this is where Lefort's analysis takes a
very different route from the one I have chosen in my study of the formation of popular identities; for him, the democratic symbolic
framework has to be opposed to totalitarianism, which he describes in
the following terms:

> A condensation takes place between the sphere of power, the sphere of
> law and the sphere of knowledge. Knowledge of the ultimate goals of
> society and the norms which regulate social practices becomes the
> property of power, and at the same time power itself claims to be the
> organ of a discourse which articulates the real as such. Power is embodied
> in a group and, at its highest level, in a single individual, it merges with a
> knowledge which is also embodied, in such a way that nothing can split it
> apart. (p. 13)

Totalitarianism, however, although it is opposed to democracy, has
emerged within the terrain of the democratic revolution. This is how he
describes the mechanism of the transition from one to the other:

> When individuals are increasingly insecure as a result of an economic
> crisis or of the ravages of war, when conflicts between classes and groups
> is exacerbated and can no longer be symbolically resolved within the polit-
> ical sphere, when power appears to have sunk to the level of reality and to
> be no more than an instrument for the promotion of interests and
> appetites of vulgar ambition and when, in a word, it appears *in* society,
> and when at the same time society appears to be fragmented, then we see
> the development of the fantasy of the People-as-One, the beginnings of
> a quest for a substantial identity, for a social body which is welded to his
> head, for an embodying power, for a state free from division. (pp. 19–20)

At this point, readers of this book could start to feel that in this last description there is something which sounds vaguely familiar. For several of its features can be applied to populist movements described in this text, most of which, of course, are not in the least totalitarian. The construction of a chain of equivalences out of a dispersion of fragmented demands, and their unification around popular positions operating as empty signifiers, is not totalitarian but the very condition for the construction of a collective will which, in many cases, can be profoundly democratic. It is certainly true that some populist movements can be totalitarian, and present most or all of the features so accurately described by Lefort, but the spectrum of possible articulations is far more diversified than the simple opposition totalitarianism/democracy seems to suggest. The difficulty with Lefort's analysis of democracy is that it is concentrated exclusively on liberal-democratic *regimes*, and does not pay due attention to the construction of popular-democratic *subjects*. This has a series of consequences which limit the scope of the analysis. To give an example: for Lefort, the *place* of power in democracies is empty. For me, the question poses itself differently: it is a question of *producing* emptiness out of the operation of hegemonic logics. For me, emptiness is a type of identity, not a structural location. If, as Lefort thinks – and I agree with him on this point – the symbolic framework of a society is what sustains a certain regime, the place of power cannot be entirely empty. Even the most democratic of societies would have symbolic limits to determine who can occupy the place of power. Between total embodiment and total emptiness there is a gradation of situations involving partial embodiments. These partial embodiments are, precisely, the forms taken by hegemonic practices.

So how do we move from this point to discuss the relationship between populism and democracy more thoroughly? Here I would like to introduce into the argument a few distinctions contained in the recent work of Chantal Mouffe.[11] Mouffe starts by recognizing her intellectual debt to the work of Lefort, but she also adds a crucial qualification to that recognition which, in actual fact, changes the terrain of the debate:

instead of simply identifying the modern form of democracy with the empty place of power, I would also want to put emphasis on the distinction between two aspects: on one side, democracy as a form of rule, that is, the principle of sovereignty of the people; and on the other side, the symbolic framework within which this democratic rule is exercised. The novelty of modern democracy, what makes it properly 'modern', is that, with the advent of the 'democratic revolution', the old democratic principle that 'power should be exercised by the people' emerges again, but this time within a symbolic framework informed by the liberal discourse, with its strong emphasis on the value of individual liberties and human rights.[12]

So while Lefort sees the question of democracy only as linked to the liberal symbolic framework, implicitly identifying democracy with liberal democracy, Mouffe sees merely a contingent articulation between both traditions: 'On one side we have the liberal tradition constituted by the rule of law, the defence of human rights and the respect of individual liberty; on the other the democratic tradition whose main ideas are those of equality, identity between governing and governed and popular sovereignty. There is no necessary relation between those two distinct traditions but only a contingent historical articulation.'[13]

Once the articulation between liberalism and democracy is considered as merely contingent, two obvious conclusions do necessarily follow: (1) other contingent articulations are also possible, so that there are forms of democracy outside the liberal symbolic framework (the problem of democracy, seen in its true universality, becomes that of the plurality of frameworks which make the emergence of a 'people' possible); (2) since this emergence of a 'people' is no longer the direct effect of any particular framework, the question of the constitution of a popular subjectivity becomes an integral part of the question of democracy (this aspect is not taken sufficiently into account by Lefort). A corollary is that there is no political regime which is self-referential. We can, of course, enlarge the notion of a symbolic matrix to include within it the constitution of social and political subjects, but in that case we are blurring any sharp divide between state and civil society. Blurring the divide does not,

however, mean annihilating it in a totalitarian fashion – not all politiciza-
tion of civil society is equivalent to authoritarian unification. Gramsci's
vision of hegemony, for instance, cuts across the distinction state/civil
society, but is nevertheless profoundly democratic, because it involves
launching new collective subjects into the historical arena.

How do we conceive, however, this contingent articulation between
liberalism and democracy? Mouffe is highly critical of the so-called
'deliberative democracy' current, which tries precisely to eliminate the
contingent nature of the articulation, and to turn it into one of necessary implication (with Rawls leaning more to the side of liberalism, and
Habermas more to that of democracy). What is most revealing for our
purposes, however, is Mouffe's own attempt at explaining what should
be understood by contingent articulation. Her main effort, since she is
chiefly concerned with the question of democracy in societies where a
liberal symbolic framework dominates, is to propose what she calls an
agonistic model of democracy, but in the process of formulating it she
throws light on a multiplicity of aspects which are relevant to a general
theory of democracy – liberal or not:

> By privileging rationality, both the deliberative and aggregative perspec-
> tives leave aside a central element which is the crucial role played by
> passions and affects in securing allegiance to democratic values.... The
> failure of current democratic theory to tackle the question of citizenship
> is the consequence of their operating with a conception of the subject
> which sees individuals as prior to society, bearers of natural rights, and
> either utility-maximizing agents or rational subjects. In all cases they are
> abstracted from social and power relations, language, culture and the
> whole set of practices that make agency possible. What is precluded in
> these rationalistic approaches is the very question of what are the condi-
> tions of existence of a democratic subject.[14]

From this perspective, Mouffe makes several references to Wittgenstein:
to belief as anchored in a way of living, and to the need for a friction
which involves the need to give up the dream of a rationalistic consensus.

The main consequences of this analysis are that, on the one hand, we have to move from the formal structure of a politico-symbolic space to a wider 'way of living' where political subjectivity is constituted; and, on the other, that a vision of political subjectivity emerges in which a plurality of practices and passionate attachments enter into a picture where rationality – being individual or dialogical – is no longer the dominant component. But with this we reach a point at which this notion of democratic identity is practically indistinguishable from what I have called popular identity. All the components are there: the failure of a purely conceptual order to explain the unity of social agents; the need to articulate a plurality of positions or demands through nominal means, given that no a priori rationality pushes those demands to coalesce around a centre; and the primary role of affect in cementing this articulation. The consequence is unavoidable: the construction of a 'people' is the *sine qua non* of democratic functioning. Without production of emptiness there is no 'people', no populism, but no democracy either. If we add to this that the 'people', as we have seen, is not essentially attached to any particular symbolic matrix, we will have embraced the problem of contemporary populism in all its true dimensions.

We now have to ask ourselves about the points in which a discussion of democracy dovetails with a discussion of populism. The axis of our argument on democracy has been that it is necessary to transfer the notion of emptiness from the *place* of power in a democratic regime – as proposed by Lefort – to the very subjects occupying that place. My suggestion is as follows: it is not enough to pose the question as if emptiness meant simply the absence of any determination in the place of power, and that because of this absence, any particular force, without ceasing to be particular, could occupy that place. That could be true if we were dealing merely with the juridical, formal aspects of democracy, but as Lefort very well knows, the notion of *politeia* – of which he is extremely aware, and to which he refers – means a community's whole political way of life, where constitutional arrangements represent only a formal crystallization. So if the question of *politeia* is considered in its true generality – which also involves the formation of a political subjectivity, as discussed by Mouffe – the discussion of emptiness cannot remain at the level of a place unaffected by those who occupy it – and, conversely, the occupiers must also be affected by the nature of the place they occupy.

Let us consider the matter from both sides of this relation – in the first place, from the side of the occupiers of power. We know that there is an insurmountable abyss between the particularity of groups integrating a community – often in conflict with one another – and the community as a whole, conceived as a universalistic totality. We also know that such an abyss can only be hegemonically mediated, through a particularity which, at some point, assumes the representation of a totality which is incommensurable with it. But for this to be possible, the hegemonic force has to present its own particularity as the incarnation of an empty universality that transcends it. So it is not the case that there is a particularity which simply occupies an empty place, but a particularity which, because it has succeeded, through a hegemonic struggle, in becoming the empty signifier of the community, has a legitimate claim to occupy that place. Emptiness is not just a datum of constitutional law, it is a political construction. Let us now consider the matter from the other side: that of the place as empty. Emptiness, as far as that place is concerned, does not simply mean *void*; on the contrary, there is emptiness because that void points to the absent fullness of the community. Emptiness and fullness are, in fact, synonymous. But that fullness/emptiness can exist only embodied in a hegemonic force. This means that emptiness circulates between the place and its occupiers. They contaminate each other. So the logic of the King's two bodies has not disappeared in democratic society: it is simply not true that pure emptiness has replaced the immortal body of the King. This immortal body is revived by the hegemonic force. What has changed in democracy, as compared with the *anciens régimes*, is that in the latter that revival took place in only one body, while today it transmigrates through a variety of bodies. But the logic of embodiment continues to operate under democratic conditions and, under certain circumstances, it can acquire considerable stability. Think of a phenomenon such as Gaullism. One could say that one of the fundamental hegemonic defects of the French

Fourth Republic was its inability to provide relatively stable symbols to embody the empty place.

At this point, however, we have to move the argument one step forward. Empty signifiers can play their role only if they signify a chain of equivalences, and it is only if they do so that they constitute a 'people'. In other words: democracy is grounded only on the existence of a democratic subject, whose emergence depends on the horizontal articulation between equivalential demands. An ensemble of equivalential demands articulated by an empty signifier is what constitutes a 'people'. So the very possibility of democracy depends on the constitution of a democratic 'people'. We also know that if there is to be an articulation/combination between democracy and liberalism, demands of two different types have to be combined. Combination, however, can take place in two different ways: either one type of demands – liberalism, for instance, with its defence of human rights, civil liberties, and so on – belongs to the symbolic framework of a regime, in the sense that they are part of a system of rules accepted by all participants in the political game, or they are contested values, in which case they are part of the equivalential chain, and so part of the 'people'. In Latin America during the 1970s and 1980s, for instance, the defence of human rights was part of the popular demands and so part of the popular identity. It is a mistake to think that the democratic tradition, with its defence of the sovereignty of the 'people', excludes liberal claims as a matter of principle. That could only mean that the 'people'’s identity is fixed once and for all. If, on the contrary, the identity of the 'people' is established only through changing equivalential chains, there is no reason to think that a populism which includes human rights as one of its components is a priori excluded. At some points in time – as happens today quite frequently in the international scene – defence of human rights and civil liberties can become the most pressing popular demands. But popular demands can also crystallize in entirely different configurations, as Lefort's analysis of totalitarianism shows. It is on this variety in the constitution of popular identities that we must now focus our attention.

Part III

POPULIST VARIATIONS

7

The Saga of Populism

The fully fledged notion of populism which we have now developed amounts not to the determination of a rigid concept to which we could unequivocally assign certain objects, but to the establishment of an area of variations within which a plurality of phenomena could be inscribed. This inscription, however, should proceed not in terms of purely external comparisons or taxonomies, but by determining internal rules which make those variations intelligible. In this chapter I shall approach the variations as *trends*: that is to say, I shall locate apparently disparate phenomena within a continuum which makes comparison between them possible. In Chapter 8 I shall take a more *micro-analytical* approach: I will discuss three historical moments of the construction of the 'people', and show in them the full operation of some of the logics which we have theoretically analysed in the chapters above. Finally, I shall conclude Chapter 8 with a set of heuristic suggestions concerning what an empirical exploration of 'actually existing' populisms should aim at.

Let me start this discussion with the conceptual references contained in a recent article by Yves Surel.[1] Surel – quite correctly – rejects a series of identifications which impoverish the notion of populism by reducing it to the movements of the radical Right – as H. G. Betz does[2] – or to those trends which see in it an opposition to the constitutionalist logics operating in contemporary democracies. He sees in populism a phenomenon which relates more ambivalently to the institutional order. As he says – summarizing the thesis developed in *Par le peuple, pour le peuple*, for populism:

> (1) the 'people' is the sovereign of the political regime and the only legitimate referent to interpret social, economic and cultural dynamics; (2) power elites, especially political ones, have betrayed the 'people' by no longer fulfilling the functions for which they have been appointed; (3) it is necessary to restore the primacy of the 'people', which can lead to a valorization of a previous age, characterized by a recognition of the 'people'. This is the hard core of populism understood as an ideological schema, and it is an ensemble of discursive resources disseminated within the democratic regimes.[3]

So populism, in a way similar to the one I have described in this book, is not a fixed constellation but a series of discursive resources which can be put to very different uses (this approaches my notion of floating signifiers). Surel says: 'Against the idea according to which populism would represent a relatively stable and coherent trend, typical of the new radical Right, we want to defend the idea that it is less of a political family than a dimension of the discursive and normative register adopted by political actors. It is thus a set of resources available to a plurality of actors, in a more or less systematic way.'[4]

I can concur with everything in this analysis – I actually think the notion that populism is the democratic element in contemporary representative systems is one of the most insightful and original ideas in Mény's and Surel's work – except for one point: the limits they accept for the circulation of the resources available to populist construction – and thus for what can be characterized as 'populist' – are, in my view, too narrow. Surel is no doubt correct in criticizing those approaches which, by asserting a total exteriority of populism *vis-à-vis* the political system, assimilate it to the extreme Right (but, in actual fact, the same would equally apply to the extreme Left). Instead he shows sympathy for the model proposed by Andreas Schedler[5] according to which there would be: (1) democratic parties in power defining themselves by their support for those in charge of government; (2) the democratic opposition, attempting to seize power within the existing institutional framework; and (3) the anti-institutional parties, which reject the existing system of democratic rules. To this Schedler adds – and Surel concurs – the ambiguous situation of the populist movements: they exist on the margins of institutional regimes, oscillating between denouncing the systems as such, or just those occupying the places of power. The difficulty with this model is that it takes it for granted that there is something such as a well-established system of rules at any one time. This, in my view, does not sufficiently take into account the double face of populism to which I referred in my theoretical discussion: populism presents itself both as *subversive* of the existing state of things and as the starting point for a more or less radical *reconstruction* of a new order whenever the previous one has been shaken. The institutional system has to be (again, more or less) broken if the populist appeal is to be effective. In a situation of complete institutional stability (and 'complete', of course, implies a purely ideal situation) the only possible opposition to that system would emanate from a pure outside – that is, it would come from purely marginal and ineffectual strata.

This is because, as we have seen, populism never emerges from an absolute outside and advances in such a way that the previous state of affairs dissolves around it, but proceeds by articulating fragmented and dislocated demands around a new core. So some degree of crisis in the old structure is a necessary precondition of populism for, as we have seen, popular identities require equivalential chains of unfulfilled demands. Without the slump of the 1930s, Hitler would have remained a vociferous fringe ringleader. Without the crisis of the Fourth Republic around the Algerian war, De Gaulle's appeal would have remained as unheard as it had been in 1946. And without the progressive erosion of the oligarchical system in the Argentina of the 1930s, the rise of Perón would have been unthinkable.

If this is so, we have, rather than a populist movement with one foot inside and one foot outside the institutional system, a fluid situation whose main possibilities are:

1. A largely self-structured institutional system which relegates to a marginal position any anti-institutional challenge – that is to say, the latter's ability to constitute equivalential chains is minimal (this would correspond to the first two situations within Schedler's model).
2. The system is less well structured, and requires some kind of periodical recomposition. Here the possibility of populism in the Schedler/Surel's sense arises: the system can be challenged, but since its ability for self-structuration is still considerable, the populist forces have to operate both as 'insiders' and as 'outsiders'.
3. The system has entered a period of 'organic crisis' in the Gramscian sense. In that case, the populist forces challenging it have to do more than engage themselves in the ambiguous position of subverting the system and, at the same time, being integrated into it: they have to reconstruct the nation around a new popular core. Here, the reconstructive task prevails over that of subversion.

As we can see, the movement from the second possibility to the third is a matter of degree, of various historical alternatives emerging within a theoretical continuum. My only quarrel with Surel's approach is that, by limiting populism to the third option within Schelder's model, he has restricted it too much to what is possible today within the Western European horizon, while I want to inscribe populism within a wider system of alternatives.

In order to elucidate this system of alternatives, I will discuss some examples. The first is Boulangism.[6] If we are to understand the political emergence of General Boulanger, we have to remember the situation of France in the 1880s. Politically, the Republic – largely established as a result of internal disagreements between the monarchist forces – was by no means consolidated. A plurality of different ideological groups – from both the Right and the Left – were not really integrated into the parliamentary system, and dreamed of alternative constitutional formulas. Economically, France, apart from the ensemble of dislocations linked to the transition to an industrial society, since 1873 had experienced the effects of the world depression, to which must be added the financial crash of 1882 and the succession of financial scandals, especially the Wilson affair, which had discredited the republican government. We also have to take into account the high level of unemployment and the disarray of the labour movement after the repression following the Commune, which left the workers exposed to a variety of political influences. In these conditions, the political system was clearly vulnerable to any kind of extra-parliamentary initiative.

Who was General Boulanger? There is no room here to narrate the whole episode of his flagrant rise and fall – relevant to our purposes as it is – but I can at least sketch out the main events. Boulanger was a brilliant officer with a clear republican orientation (although his republicanism was somewhat opportunistic, for he had previously been Bonapartist and Orleanist). He became War Minister in 1886, and both his army reforms and his republican image soon gave him immense popularity. This worried the government, which forced him to resign and sent him out of Paris, to Clermont-Ferrand, despite public protests. Later, in 1888, he went into retirement. This allowed him to intervene openly in politics. He won a series of landslide electoral victories which culminated on 27 January 1889 when, after a resounding electoral triumph, the multitude demanded that he march on the Élysée and seize power – something he could well have done, for he had the support of a considerable section of the Army and the police. Boulanger, however, hesitated, and finally decided not to do it. That was the turning point in his career. The government, reassured, took a series of measures curtailing his activities, which culminated in taking him to court. He escaped to Brussels and for two years went between Belgium and London, before committing suicide in 1891.

Many aspects of the Boulanger episode are important for our theoretical purposes. First, the heterogeneity and marginality *vis-à-vis* the established system of the forces which supported him:

He enjoyed … the trust of the most diverse political sectors, both on the Right and on the Left … Boulanger assembles … around him all the disappointed democrats … irritated by the ministerial instability of the

French Third Republic and supporters of a state that is strong, albeit based on universal suffrage, Bonapartists nostalgic for the imperial power of Napoleon III, moderate monarchists attached to the dynastic branch of Orleans represented by the count of Paris – not forgetting the multiple left-wing currents, from what remained of the Commune's movement to a fraction of the radicals. That was the case, for instance, of the current represented by the newspaper *La Démocratie du Midi*, which demanded a direct democracy capable of reaching a 'really representative' government, denounced the corruption of the parliamentary regime, and waited for 'some virile act from a chief'.[7]

Secondly, Boulanger's support was concentrated mainly in the urban centres – unlike that of Napoleon III, who relied on a solid peasant base. Within these urban centres, Boulanger's social support had a strong proletarian component, but in actual fact it cut across most social strata: 'However, this substantial presence of a proletarian element did not mean that his following was not equally characterized by the fact that, encompassing every social milieu, it was equally recruited from the ensemble of the middle and even upper classes of the cities.'[8] Thirdly, the idea of an extra-parliamentary intervention was equally appealing to the radical Left, which saw in it a way of achieving a combination of strong state and direct democracy, and to the Right, for which it was the road to a conservative and militaristic nationalism. Fourthly, the only thing that kept all these heterogeneous forces together was a common devotion to Boulanger and his undeniable charisma. The proof is that, when he disappeared from the political scene, the coalition of his supporters quickly disintegrated. That was the anticlimax which led to the consolidation of the Third Republic.

Now, if we consider these four politico-ideological features, we will immediately see that they reproduce, almost point by point, the defining dimensions of populism which we have established in the theoretical part of this book. First, there is an aggregation of heterogeneous forces and demands which cannot be organically integrated within the existing differential/institutional system. Secondly, since the links between these demands are not differential, they can only be equivalential: there is an *air de famille* between them all, because they all have the same enemy: the existing corrupt parliamentary system. Thirdly, this chain of equivalences reaches its point of crystallization only around the figure of Boulanger, which functions as an empty signifier. Fourthly, however, in order to play this role 'Boulanger' has to be reduced to his name (and to a few other equally imprecise concomitant signifiers). This shows another of our theses in operation: the Lacanian thesis, according to which the name grounds the unity of the object. Fifthly, in order for the name to play this role, it has to be highly cathected – that is to say, it has to be an *objet petit a* (it has to constitute a hegemonic subject). So the role of affect is essential.

Going back now to our previous discussion: there is no doubt that the Boulangist experiment was populist; however, the alternative that Surel describes was not open to him as it was to Berlusconi – to be between the institutional order and the populist language, and to use the latter as a political tool. Boulanger was increasingly pushed outside the institutional choice, so that his only possible way forward was to become a constructor of a new order; he could not merely *play* at being a subversive. This meant, in his case, seizing the Élysée. This was the step, however, which he did not dare to take, and his hesitation led to his downfall. We can only speculate about what kind of institutional order would have resulted from a successful Boulanger coup, but one thing is certain: it could not have satisfied *all* the heterogeneous forces that made up his coalition. The empty signifiers could not have remained entirely empty; they would have had to be associated with more precise contents in order to construct a new differential/institutional order. But, although this transition does not interrupt the hegemonic game – the days of a regime which becomes unpopular beyond a certain point are numbered – it is infinitely easier to make choices when one is in power than when one is merely trying to seize it.

In the Boulanger example, however, the point of condensation of the equivalential chain – the empty signifier – is too weak. The whole Boulangist experience was a very short and conjunctural one, and there was no time for the 'Boulanger' signifier to mean much more than the personal whims of the General. So let us move on to a case in which the attempt to create the anchoring point of an equivalential chain was related to a deeper and more protracted political experience: the system of political alternatives open to the Italian Communist Party at the end of the Second World War. I have already briefly referred to this matter, and we will now go back to it in terms of the main issues discussed in this chapter. The alternative was as follows: either the Communist Party, as the party of the working class, had to reduce itself to being the representative of the latter's interests – in which case it would have been an essentially workerist party, a mere enclave in the industrial North – or it had to become the rallying point of a largely heterogeneous mass, so that 'working class' would operate as the metaphorical centre of a variety of struggles which would constantly go beyond a strict working-class provenance. A not dissimilar alternative emerged in South Africa in the years preceding the end of apartheid, when the political stage was occupied by a dispute whose two poles were called – interestingly enough – 'workerist' and 'populist'. The Italian debate was deeply rooted in a wider question: how to constitute an Italian nation. That was the task in which all social sectors in the country, including those involved in the Risorgimento and Fascism, had failed since the Middle Ages, and it was the task that the party of the working class – the modern Prince – was destined, according to Gramsci, to achieve.

What did this task involve? Creating hegemonically a unity – a homogeneity – out of an irreducible heterogeneity. When Palmiro Togliatti chose the populist alternative in the years following the war, he described it unequivocally: the *'partito nuovo'* had to carry out the 'national tasks of the working class': it had to be the rallying point of a multitude of disparate struggles and demands. What the person of Boulanger had represented for a fleeting moment in French history was now to be embodied by a party eager to be organically anchored in the whole Italian tradition. The task of the party was to constitute a 'people'.

At this point, I can address the question of the Italian alternative from the viewpoint of our distinction between names and concepts.

To say that the Communist Party, as the party of the working class, had to concentrate its activity in the industrial North, because that is where the working class was to be found, is to say that there was a conceptual content of the category 'working class' through which we recognize some objects in the world. In that case, our naming them does not have any performative function; it merely recognizes what they are. The name is the transparent medium through which something which is conceptually fully apprehensible shows itself. To name a series of *heterogeneous* elements as 'working class', instead, does something different: this hegemonic operation performatively brings about the unity of those elements, whose coalescence into a single entity is nothing other than the result of the operation of naming. The name, the signifier which has – to go back to Copjec's expression – the 'breast value of the milk', constitutes an *absolute historical singularity*, because there is no conceptual correlate of what it refers to.

This, of course, always happens to some extent, because there is no concept so pure that it is not exceeded by some meanings only connotatively associated with it. It is inevitable that for the peoples of two different countries, the term 'working class' will evoke different types of association. The crucial problem, however, is whether these associated meanings will be only peripheral to a core which will remain conceptually identical, and thus 'universal', or whether they will contaminate the moment of conceptual determination – will penetrate its substance, so that in the end, step by step, the core will cease to be a concept, and will become a name (an empty signifier, in our terminology). Only when this last transformation has taken place can we speak of a historical singularity. And when this happens, we no longer have a sectorial agent such as a 'class': we have a 'people'.

This, undoubtedly, was the real meaning of the Togliattian project in the 1940s. The Party, in his view, had to intervene in a plurality of democratic fronts (advocating a plurality of particular demands, in our terms) and to bring them into some kind of unity (conceived, as we know, as an equivalential unification). In that way, each of those isolated demands would become stronger through the links that it would establish with other demands and, most importantly, they would all have a new access to the public sphere. Through the presence of this new constellation of demands, the public sphere would become more democratic and, because of the geographical dispersion of that constellation, truly *national*. This would make it possible to transcend the management of Italian politics by a 'gentlemen's agreement' between the local cliques of the North and the South. That is, it was a matter of constructing the 'people' as a historical singularity.

Mao's Long March – which, politically, was obviously very different from the Togliattian project – can, nevertheless, be seen, as far as the construction of the 'people' is concerned, from the same perspective. The same can be said of the emergence of Tito's regime after the Partisans' war, and of a few other political experiences within the Communist tradition. The important thing to bear in mind, however, is that all the trends in that tradition militated in the opposite direction. That is, they tended to subordinate all national specificities to an inter-national centre and to a universal task, in which the various Communist parties were mere footsoldiers. The Komintern was the worst expression of this sterilizing politics. As a result of it, there was no chance for these parties to become populistic. Far from being encouraged to constitute historical singularities through the articulation of heterogeneous demands, they were conceived as mere branches which had automatically to apply policies planned from a centre. Let us remember the Komintern decision concerning the 'Bolshevization' of the Communist parties in the 1920s. Irrespective of national characteristics, they all had to have the same structure and the same rules of functioning. In these conditions, the constitution of a 'people' was impossible. If leaders like Togliatti, Mao and Tito, each in his own way, managed to achieve this, it was by constantly twisting the international directives, while being regarded with deep suspicion by the 'centre'. If the constitution of a 'people' meant moving from concept to name, here we have the opposite movement from name to concept: each Communist Party had to be as identical as possible to all the others, and they all had to be subsumable under the same, unequivocally defined, label. The small sects which, even today, consider themselves local sections of imaginary 'Internationals' are nothing but the *reductio ad absurdum* of this anti-populist trend of the Communist tradition.

If the Italian Communist Party (PCI) came up against structural limits to becoming a fully fledged populist movement as the result of belonging to the international Communist movement, those limits were also reinforced by other influences. First, there was the Cold War, which set definite limits on what could be achieved in Western Europe under Communist banners. The frontier through which the ruling coalition led by the Christian Democrats (DC) split the political spectrum was based precisely on the 'Communism' issue. In these conditions, 'Communism' in its Italian guise could not move beyond a certain point in the direction of constituting itself as the empty signifier unifying a historical singularity; the ideological issue denied the PCI access to a plurality of sectors whose incorporation was nevertheless vital to the success of the Togliattian project. And the limits were not only external: the PCI was, finally, a party of Communist militants, for whom a total break with the USSR would have been unthinkable. (In 1956 the PCI defended the Soviet invasion of Hungary; this cost it a great deal of national support.) So the situation came to a stalemate between the unification of the Christian electorate by the DC and the impossibility of the only truly national project, that of the PCI, transcending either its internal or its external limits.

> The price that the nation paid for this 'state confessionalism' was high, and led to the Constitution paying only lip-service to liberal democracy and its more advanced social democratic principles, and the rejection of 'antifascism as the constituent ideology'. Even though the Resistance … had partially provided the values on which a democratic identity could be based, the first years of the Italian Republic emphatically rejected the transformation of the 'founding myth' (even if only partial) into a 'vehicle for a renewed national identity'.[9]

So the same failure that the Risorgimento and Fascism experienced in trying to constitute a national consciousness was reproduced in the postwar period by a combination of a corrupt localistic power and confessionalism, on the side of the DC, and the inability of the only truly national project – that of the PCI – to advance beyond a certain point in its war of position with the existing system. Here we see the clear difference with the Boulangist movement. Its brevity as a political event allowed its unifying signifiers to operate as almost entirely empty – in actual fact the symbols of the Resistance in Italy functioned in a not dissimilar way in the few months following the Liberation. But the construction of a long-term hegemony is a very different matter: the process of emptying a few central signifiers in the creation of a historical singularity will always be subject to the structural pressure of forces that will try to reattach them to their original signifieds, so that any 'expanding' hegemony does not go too far. Limiting the scope of the movement from concept to name is the very essence of a counter-hegemonic practice.

The end of the cycle of postwar hegemonic confrontation in Italy is well known. After the economic crisis of the 1970s, which hit long-term political arrangements badly, the 1980s brought about a new scenario within which old political forces could survive only by becoming new historical actors. None was able to do so. Working-class centrality was seriously eroded by an advance of a tertiary sector whose values and aspirations exceeded both what the PCI could conceive in terms of its old strategy, and what the ruling DC coalition could absorb through its own clientelistic methods. So there was a crisis of representation which led to the demise of the entire dominant elite. The ruling coalition was wiped out after the *mani pulite* operation, and the PCI, which had been largely untainted by the anti-corruption crusade, was unable to take advantage of the new situation – it was still too much dominated by the ghosts of the past. In that situation, a set of wild new forces erupted.

The 'people' that the PCI had tried to constitute was resolutely 'national'. It was conceived as synonymous with the process of construction of a national state worth the name. The collapse of the Communist project did not lead to a simple relapse into traditional DC local clientelism, because of a variety of new elements – a general transition towards a more secular society in which the Catholic Church's power declined; the development of the media, especially TV, which created a wider national public; and, finally, the anti-corruption crusade which affected all the main political players,[10] but virtually wiped out the totality of the DC elite. In these circumstances, various attempts were made to construct the 'people' around the region as the limit of what equivalential chains could articulate. The 1980s saw the emergence of several 'leagues': the Sardinian Action Party, the Union Valdotaine, the South Tyrol People's Party, which had been active since 1945, and especially the *Liga Venetta* of Franco Rocchetta, which initially achieved considerable electoral success.

The most characteristic phenomena of the 1990s, however, were the various attempts by Umberto Bossi to extend the league's appeal from local to regional level first, and to national level later.[11] The Lombard League started in 1982 as one more case of ethnic politics. An imaginary Lombard *ethnic* identity was invented, and opposed to the centralizing forces of first Piedmont and later Rome. Very quickly, however, Bossi realized that confining himself to mere localism would not allow him to become a major player in national politics, so the next step was to proclaim what he called 'ethnic federalism' [*etnofederalismo*]: the attempt to extend the equivalential chain to the whole North of Italy, embracing in a single movement all the local organizations of the Po valley. This culminated in 1989 in the foundation of the Northern League, which absorbed most autonomist movements of Northern Italy under the leadership of Bossi and the hegemony of the Lombard League. The high point of that stage was the proclamation of a new 'nation', *Padania*. Very soon, however, the limits of this strategy became obvious. On the one hand, the aggressive anti-Mezzogiorno and anti-central state discourse limited the ideological impact of the League in both Central and Southern Italy, and also among Southerners living in the North. On the other hand, the League could not count on firm support even in its Northern base: Berlusconi's *Forza Italia* and Fini's *Alleanza Nazionale*[12] became competitors on the same terrain. So when Bossi joined the ruling coalition during the first Berlusconi government in 1984, the League had reached its limits as far as populist-aggressive anti-institutionalism was concerned. It no longer called for the demise of the national state, and started seeing the Padania adventure as a sin of youth. The effects of this ambivalence could only weaken the League – caught as it was between institutional participation and anti-institutional rhetoric.

All this becomes even clearer if we move to the actual discourses through which the League tried to build up a popular identity. As we know, any political frontier derives its meaning from the way in which what is beyond that frontier is identified. And here, the League, far from having the long-term political commitments that we can find in the Togliattian project, showed an extreme lability: everything changed according to its immediate political tactics.

> This collective identity is non-ideological, non-class, but purely territorial. But often more important were the negative components: the enemy, bearer of the 'negative identity', a negative concept which is often anthropomorphised. In the beginning, this enemy was simply called 'the centralist state', but it gradually became more specific, manifesting itself from time to time as: the party political system (*partitocrazia*), welfare state and the parasitic south, immigration, crime and drugs; any individuals and groups who were in any sense different or marginal; the press, the judiciary and all other groups who somehow or other were seen as part of the dying system. The League was thus building up a clear 'theory of the enemy'.[13]

The League did in fact have a 'theory of the enemy'; its problem was that it was unable to identify that enemy in any precise way. Its members had the idea that, if a radical change was to take place, the social field had to be split into two confrontational camps, but they did not know on what basis that division would take place. Abstract opposition to the status quo was the ground of their radical discourse, but they were at a loss to determine the limits of that status quo. The last stage in this indeterminacy in designating enemies was the translation of all territorial values into intersectorial ones: 'the public versus private, collective versus individual values, conservatism versus renewal, state intervention versus free enterprise'.[14] So the abandonment of territorial attachments took place in terms of a right-wing discourse whose lack of concrete reference meant that it was definitely more universal, but this was a vacuous universality: there was no production of empty signifiers but a purely shadowy emptiness, in which uncertainty concerning the anchoring points generated an indeterminancy which was anything but hegemonic. The entire history of the League after this point can be seen as the linking of every object, every resource, every political discourse, to material interests which are continuously transformed into values. The interests produced by capitalist society (the League's natural form of social organization) are values in themselves, and they are also values to the extent that other people want to destroy them: the state and the treasury. The adoption of economic liberalism and the unchallenged supremacy of the private sector as the locus of production and efficiency became the necessary step.[15]

The League's failure to transform itself into a national force is at the root of its lack of success in becoming a truly populist party. Bouillaud[16] has pointed out that all its attempts to become the hegemonic force of the anti-institutional trend of the 1990s failed, because it had to accept the protagonistic role of the other two forces that constituted the Berlusconi alliance. Biorcio and Diamanti,[17] who have insisted on the League's populistic character, have nevertheless restricted that character to the early, regionalist phase. Later attempts to address the whole country through a series of crusades against the central state, fiscal pressure, the *partitocrazia* and, finally, immigrants – Muslims in particular – were remarkably unsuccessful. The reasons are relatively clear: on the one hand, although the League never became a purely single-issue party,[18] its campaigns were too virulent, and moved kaleidoscopically without transition from one focus to the next; on the other, after the institutional crisis of the 1990s, the Italian political system managed to reconstruct a certain equilibrium – in our terms: the logic of differences became partially operative again, and limited the possibilities of equivalentially dividing the social field into two antagonistic camps. This left less scope for a pure politics of construction of a total enemy. From this viewpoint, the political evolution of Silvio Berlusconi is characteristic.[19] As Surel points out, there is in his career a movement away from populism and a progressive 'normalization' and co-option of his forces by a partially reconstituted political system. In 1994 his political discourse was highly heterogeneous: populism was certainly there – stressing his exteriority *vis-à-vis* the discredited political class – but there were also other components such as anti-Communism (which was partially invested with populist connotations) and the affirmation of economic liberalism and social conservatism. In the series of tensions which led to the fall of his first government, however, populism remains as the progressively central component. On the one hand, anti-Communism loses its meaning after the PCI is transformed into the *Partito Democratico della Sinistra*; on the other, economic liberalism clashes with the economic and social programme of Bossi, and with the statism of the *Alleanza Nazionale*. This leaves Berlusconi without solid roots within the system. 'Berlusconi, once dispossessed of his anti-communist, liberal and conservative adornments, can only find support in a simplistic discourse, with a strong populistic connotation which denounces the judicial institutions and the traditional political actors, described as grave-diggers of the regime and traitors to the popular will.'[20] In subsequent years, however, the movement towards 'normalization' (our differential logic) starts. Surel enumerates three basic changes: first, economic liberalism plays an increasingly central role in Berlusconi's picture of himself (he compares himself with Thatcher, Blair and Aznar); secondly, *Forza Italia* becomes more of a normal party as far as its internal functioning is concerned – it ceases to be a purely *ad hoc* formation controlled from the Fininvest; thirdly, the alliance between the three components of the coalition becomes more solid and more integrated into the party system. From this point onwards the populistic elements – albeit partially retained in the electoral campaigns – tend to fade away. Wild equivalential logics cease to be the ideological cement of the coalition.

Let us draw some more general theoretical conclusions from our analysis. The interest of the Italian case lies in the fact that Italy was the least integrated political system in Western Europe, the one in which the national state was less able to hegemonize the various aspects of social life. In such a situation, the community could not be taken for granted, and social demands could be absorbed only imperfectly by the central state apparatus. In those circumstances, the construction of a 'people' had a cardinal importance; the populist temptation was never far away. The 'nation' and the 'region' as limits of the community were two successive projects grounded in the expansion of equivalential logics. Neither, however, succeeded in becoming the principle of community reconstruction. At the present moment, in the unstable balance between differential and equivalential logics, it is the former which seems to be imposing itself in Italy. That confirms Surel's description of populism as an arsenal of rhetorical tools (floating signifiers) which can be put to the most disparate ideological uses. But at this point, a crucial distinction must be made. The fact that the political meaning of those floating signifiers depends entirely on conjunctural articulations does not necessarily mean that their use involves a purely cynical or instrumental manipulation by politicians. That could be a good description of Berlusconi's *cosa nostra*, but it is not a defining characteristic of populism as such. People like Mao, De Gaulle or Vargas (who paid for his convictions with his life) believed deeply in their own interpellations. What we could say as a general rule is that the more populist interpellations truly play the role of empty signifiers – the more they manage equivalentially to unify the community – the more they are also the object of a radical investment. And, obviously, there is nothing playful or superficial about the latter. Conversely, when we have a highly institutionalized society, equivalential logics have less terrain on which to operate; as a result, populist rhetoric becomes a kind of commodity lacking any sort of hegemonic depth. In that case, populism does indeed become almost synonymous with petty demagogy.

One further point should be addressed. It follows from our analysis that the rallying point in the constitution of a 'people' remains largely open. We can have a populism of the national state, following the Jacobin model, a regional populism, an ethnopopulism, and so on. In all cases the equivalential logic will be equally operative, but the central signifiers unifying the equivalential chain, those which constitute the historical singularity, will be fundamentally different. In Latin America, for instance, populist movements were essentially state populisms, trying to reinforce the role of the central state against landowning oligarchies. For that reason they were mainly urban movements, associated with the rising middle and popular classes in the period 1910–50. The emergence of this populism took place in two stages. At the beginning, the distance between democratic demands and the forms of the liberal state was not too great. Liberalism had been the typical regime established by the ruling oligarchies in most Latin American countries following the period of anarchy and civil wars after independence. An electoral system controlled by local landowners in the rural districts, to which one has to add the incipient urban sectors equally controlled through clientelistic networks, was the political formula which presided over the economic development and integration of Latin America into the world market during the second half of the nineteenth century. Economic development, however, brought about a rapid urbanization and the expansion of the middle and lower classes which, towards the turn of the nineteenth century and beginning of the twentieth (the period varies from country to country), started to demand redistributive policies and increasing political participation. Thus a typical political populist scenario emerged: the accumulation of unfulfilled demands which crystallized around the names of popular leaders, and an old clientelistic system which resisted any major political enlargement. At the beginning, however, democratic demands and liberalism were not opposed to each other: the demands were for an internal democratization of the liberal systems. Various generations of democratic political reformers emerged within this context: Irigoyen in Argentina, Battle y Ordoñez in Uruguay, Madero in Mexico, Alessandri in Chile, Ruy Barbosa in Brazil. In some cases the reforms could take place within the framework of the liberal state: this happened with the governments of the Radical Party in Argentina between 1916 and 1930, and in Uruguay with the reshaping of the state by the Colorado Party under the leadership of Battle. In other cases, however, the resistance of the oligarchical groups was too strong, and the process of democratic reforms required a drastic change of regime. This is what happened in Chile with the government of Arturo Alessandri Palma in the 1920s: impeded by conservative forces, his democratic programme was implemented by the populist dictatorship of General Ibañez.

It was after the slump of the early 1930s, however, that Latin American populism became more radical. The redistributive potential of the liberal–oligarchical states was drastically curtailed by the crisis, and the political systems became increasing less able to absorb democratic demands. This led to a sharp chasm between liberalism and democracy which would dominate Latin American politics for the next twenty-five years. Vargas and the *Estado Novo* in Brazil, Peronism in Argentina, the governments of the Movimiento Nacional Revolucionario in Bolivia, would implement redistributive programmes and democratic reforms under political regimes which were clearly anti-liberal, and in some cases overtly dictatorial. The important thing to stress is that in all cases the 'people' constituted through the mobilizations associated with these regimes had a strong *statist* component. The construction of a strong *national* state in opposition to local oligarchical power was the trademark of this populism.

If we move now to Eastern European populisms, we find a situation which was, to a large extent, the opposite of that of Latin America.[21] We have seen that in Latin American populisms a statist discourse of citizens' rights predominates,[22] while what we find in Eastern Europe is an *ethnic* populism trying to enhance the particularism of the national values of specific communities. The statist dimension is not, of course, entirely absent, because there are clear attempts to constitute national states, but such a construction starts, in most cases, from the assertion of the specificity of a locally defined cultural group, which tends to exclude or drastically diminish the rights of other ethnic minorities. In the Hungarian parliament in 1914, for instance, 407 out of 413 seats were occupied by Magyars, while the Croats or Slovakians were hardly represented.[23] Although the revolutionary statement of 1849 concerning Hungary's right to become an independent state did not recognize national distinctions between ethnic collectivities, in practice it involved subjecting all other collectivities to the Magyar hegemony. In the same way, the Kemalist 'people' – Atatürk asserted that his principle was 'populism' – was supposed to be a homogeneous entity without internal divisions, but in actual fact it was increasingly identified with Turkish nationalism, without any particular consideration for the situation of Armenians, Greeks, or Oriental Christians.

> The Kemalist 'people' was, in these conditions, transformed into a homogeneous cultural community constituted, according to Atatürk, 'by those peasants, merchants and workers who are listening to me'. It is not for nothing that he was called the 'Father of the Turks', even if he concealed his being torn by attaching himself at the level of words to a civic populism, which he perhaps believed would compensate for the ethnic populism that his actions made transparent.[24]

The existence of huge minorities in most Eastern European countries meant that a purely universalistic discourse was in most cases entirely farcical, and simply concealed the *de facto* concentration of power in the dominant ethnic group.

It is important to see how this process of formation of an ethnic cultural identity started. The decisive fact is that, in these societies, state frontiers have always been particularly unstable and, also, that for most of their history they had been subject to occupying powers. In these circumstances, state identification was weak, and cultural communitarian belonging tended to become decisive.

> In all cases, the secular maintenance of the identity of the peoples of Central and Oriental Europe *vis-à-vis* masters who, more than lords, were foreign occupiers, hardly needed any intellectual support, for it was grounded in the direct, spontaneous and quasi-instinctive evidence of an absolute opposition to them. From this feeling of a strong difference was born a self-consciousness which could only be 'demotic' because it could appeal neither to the state of the oppressors nor to the – nonexistent – one of the oppressed. So it was a consciousness based in their common

language, in the ancestral religion, in the attachment to their land, in shared sufferings and rough treatment, as well as in the common conditions of life, which went beyond the limits of the village or the neighbourhood to spread in a confusing way over an entire ethnic group.[25]

The intellectual elaboration of a communal consciousness – the invention of a mythical past – took place over several centuries. In the beginning it was the province of priests, well connected to local conditions, whose ecclesiastical network was the only type of institution people could identify with. Over the last two centuries, however, the contribution of secular intellectuals has become pivotal. Hermet recognizes three moments in this process. In a first stage we have elites unconnected with politics trying to rescue the values of local artistic and literary production within the context of the Austro-Hungarian Empire. In a second stage the movement spread to wider bourgeois circles which became less and less attached to Austria's cultural hegemony, and attempted to defend their native language. Finally, the influence of these nationalistic ethnic tendencies is extended to more modest sectors; it is then that it acquires political connotations, and is associated with a nationalistic and populistic programme.

This last transition involved the signifiers of communitarian belonging submitting to all the pressures inherent in a hegemonic contest – that, on the one hand, they were linked in a series of antagonistic ways to a process of state-building; and, on the other, that their equivalential impact depended heavily on the way they constructed the enemy, and the ideological aims of their appeal. In some cases populism was linked to the project of building up liberal Western-type states, but in most cases its ideological presence was associated with xenophobic attempts to oppose immediate neighbours and exclude internal minorities. It also constantly oscillated between the Left and the Right. In Romania, for instance, we witness a zigzag ideological movement by which the populist signifiers were articulated in the most contradictory ways after the establishment of the country as an autonomous entity in 1858. There was the agrarian populism of Prince Alexander Cuza, opposing the power of the big landowners; Prince Charles of Hohenzollern–Sigmaringen's attempt to establish, instead, a regime favouring those landowners but equally populist in its symbology; the governments of Marshal Alexander Averescu in 1920–21 and 1926–27, which tried to bring together the most disparate social strata; the monarchic populism of King Carol II; and, finally, the seizure of power by Marshal Antonescu and his Iron Guard, which had a definite pro-Fascist orientation. In all cases, the same set of central signifiers migrated from one political project to another. Their very emptiness made this process of migration possible. Let us just remember that the Communist regime of Ceausescu made use, with relatively few alterations, of these populist signifiers. Their very autonomy made possible a broad oscillation between ideological constellations. (To give one further example: think of the ideological reversals of a leader such as Joseph Pilsudski in Poland.) But populist signifiers can equally be associated with a left-wing orientation: it is enough to remember the attempts at agrarian reform of the governments of Alexander Stambolijski in 1920s Bulgaria.

The real interest of the Eastern European experience is that it shows, almost in *status nascens*, a feature of the emergence of a 'people' which I have not fully discussed. All the cases to which I have referred concerned the construction of an *internal* frontier in a *given* society. In the case of 'ethno-populism' we have an attempt to establish, rather, the limits of the community. This involves a series of consequences. The first is that the emptiness of the signifiers constituting the 'people' is drastically limited from the very beginning. The signifiers unifying the communitarian space are rigidly attached to precise signifieds. The condition of emptiness is, as we know, the indefinite expansion of an equivalential chain. This presupposes the internal division of the social field. But here this division has been cancelled: there is no *plebs* claiming to be a *populus*, because *plebs* and *populus* precisely overlap. The 'other' opposed is external, not internal, to the community. The ethnic principle establishes from the very outset which elements can enter into the equivalential chain. There is no possibility of pluralism for ethno-populism. Minorities can exist within the territory thus defined, but marginality has to be their permanent condition once the ethnic principle has defined the limits of the communitarian space. Cleansing of entire populations is always a latent possibility once the discursive construction of the community proceeds along purely ethnic lines. And the authoritarian propensities of this political logic are evident: since the other side of the equivalential chain is outside the community, the community can rely only on a differential logic as its own principle of organization. A tendency towards political uniformity is the necessary consequence.

A good example is the disintegration of contemporary Yugoslavia.[26] Tito's project after the Second World War had been to reinforce a Yugoslavian identity while giving the various republics a considerable degree of autonomy – an autonomy which was reinforced in a succession of constitutional revisions. Had this double operation succeeded, we would have had an equivalential relation between various national identities and a strong attachment to a federal state. But in fact the process went the other way, with the centrifugal tendencies progressively prevailing. This trend was accelerated after Tito's death, and led to the emergence of what Spyros Sofos has called 'populist nationalisms'. In Serbia, the rise of Milošević took place in the context of a nationalist groundswell around the dream of a 'great Serbia' and the uprising against the Albanian presence in Kosovo,[27] which put Serbia on a collision course with the other republics. In Croatia also, the possibility of a multi-ethnic society was undermined from the very beginning, and replaced by an attempt – largely successful – to create an ethnically unified society.

> Since independence, Croatian nationalism has been a central feature of social and political life in Croatian society .... The fusion of nationalism with the ideology of conservative circles within the Catholic Church has also led to the emergence of a powerful *nationalist social majority* movement which, in the name of the nation, has been systematically pursuing the establishment of a 'morally healthy' society, in which the national interest would prevail over sectional and individual interests and rights. By relying

primarily on this social and political constituency, the ruling political élite has managed to maintain its control over the state, the economy and the mass media and to suppress demands for democratisation.[28]

In Bosnia-Herzegovina the problem was particularly complex given that, according to the 1991 census, the population of the country consisted of 43.7 per cent Muslims, 31.4 per cent Serbs, 17.3 per cent Croats and 5.5 per cent Yugoslavs. As a result, the political spectrum was divided along ethnic lines, and war was inevitable. The Serbian nationalists, led by Vojslav Šešelj, were engaged in terrorist activities in the rural districts; the HOS – a Croatian ultranationalist party – demanded the annexation of Bosnia to Croatia; while the Muslim Party of Democratic Action, led by Aliji Izetbegović, showed an equally intransigent attitude towards non-Muslim ethnic groups.

A final conclusion must be added to our previous analyses. It is important to realize that an abstract universalism does not have as its only obverse the kind of ethnic populism I have just described. Everything depends on the links composing the equivalential chain, and there is no reason to suppose that they all have to belong to a homogeneous ethnic group. It is perfectly possible to constitute a 'people' in such a way that many of the demands of a more global identity are 'universal' in their content, and cut across a plurality of ethnic identities. When this happens, the signifiers unifying the equivalential chain will necessarily be more truly empty and less attached to particular communities – ethnic, or of any other type. I think it is to this problem that Jürgen Habermas is referring when he talks about 'constitutional patriotism'. Thus:

> the ethical substance of a constitutional patriotism cannot detract from the legal system's neutrality *vis-à-vis* communities that are ethically integrated at a subpolitical level. Rather, it has to sharpen sensitivity to the diversity and integrity of the different forms of life coexisting within a multicultural society. It is crucial to maintain that distinction between the two levels of integration. If they are collapsed into one level, the majority culture will usurp state prerogatives at the expense of the equal rights of

other cultural forms of life and violate their claim to mutual recognition. The neutrality of the law *vis-à-vis* internal ethnical differentiations stems from the fact that in complex societies the citizenry as a whole can no longer be held together by a substantial consensus on values but only by a consensus on the procedures for the legitimate enactment of laws and the legitimate exercise of power.[29]

While I agree with Habermas on the need to separate the two levels to which he refers, I do not believe that the distinction can be expressed in terms of an opposition between substantive and procedural values – if for no other reason than the fact that, in order to accept some procedures as legitimate, I have to share some substantial values with other people. The real question should be: what substantive values should people share for the distinction between Habermas's two levels to be possible? I have already begun to answer this question: in contemporary societies we do not have simply a juxtaposition of separate cultural ethnic groups; we also have multiple selves, people constituting their identities in a plurality of subject positions. In this way, demands of varying degrees of universality can enter into the same equivalential chain, and some kind of hegemonic universality can emerge. But this universalization is composed of *both* substantive and procedural claims.

8

Obstacles and Limits to the Construction of the 'People'

One conclusion to be drawn from the whole of our previous analysis is that there is nothing automatic about the emergence of a 'people'. On the contrary, it is the result of a complex construction process which can, among other possibilities, fail to achieve its aim. The reasons for this are clear: political identities are the result of the articulation (that is, tension) of the opposed logics of equivalence and difference, and the mere fact that the balance between these logics is broken by one of the two poles prevailing beyond a certain point over the other, is enough to cause the 'people' as a political actor to disintegrate. If institutional differentiation is too dominant, the equivalential homogenization that popular identities require as the precondition of their constitution becomes impossible. If social heterogeneity (which, as we have seen, is another form of differentiation) prevails, there is no possibility of establishing an equivalential chain in the first place. But it is also important to realize that *total* equivalence would also make the emergence of the 'people' as a collective actor impossible. An equivalence which was total would cease to be equivalence and collapse into mere identity: there would no longer be a chain but a homogeneous, undifferentiated mass. This is the only situation contemplated by early mass psychologists, to which they wrongly assimilated all forms of popular mobilization.

The conclusion to be drawn from all this is that the construction of a 'people' can easily misfire. I shall now discuss three experiences which illustrate some of the possibilities I have just referred to.

From the Omaha platform to the 1896 electoral defeat[1]

The People's Party of America was launched early in 1892 in St Louis. Its platform, which was later reproduced almost verbatim by the Omaha platform in July of the same year, attempted to describe the malaise of American society and the broad lines of the coalition that would remedy it:

We meet in the midst of a nation brought to the verge of moral, political and material ruin. Corruption dominates the ballot box, the legislatures, the Congress, and touches even the ermine of the bench. The people are demoralized. Many of the States have been compelled to isolate the voters at the polling places in order to prevent universal intimidation or bribery. The newspapers are subsidized or muzzled; public opinion silenced; business prostrated, our homes covered with mortgages, labor impover-ished, and the land concentrated in the hands of capitalists. The urban workmen are denied the right of organization for self-protection; imported pauperized labor beats down their wages; a hireling standing army, unrecognized by our laws, is established to shoot them down, and they are rapidly degenerating to European conditions. The fruit of the toils of millions are boldly stolen to build up colossal fortunes, unprece-dented in the history of the world, while their possessors despise the republic and endanger liberty. From the same prolific womb of govern-mental injustice we breed two great classes – paupers and millionaires. The national power to create money is appropriated to enrich bondholders; silver, which has been accepted as coin since the dawn of history, has been demonetized to add to the purchasing power of gold by decreasing the value of all forms of property as well as human labor; and the supply of currency is purposely abridged to fatten usurers, bankrupt enterprise and enslave industry. A vast conspiracy against mankind has been organized on two continents and is taking possession of the world. If not met and

overthrown at once it forbodes terrible social convulsions, the destruction
of civilization or the establishment of an absolute despotism.[2]

A series of demands followed; these included the democratization of
currency, the redistribution of land, the nationalization of the transport
system, the unlimited coinage of silver, control of the ways in which
taxation was used, and that the telegraph and telephone, as well as the
postal system, should be in the hands of the government.

So the intention was a populist dichotomization of the social space
into two antagonistic camps. This aim would be achieved by creation of
a third party which would break the bipartisan model of American
politics. From the point of view of the farmers, the backbone of the
populist movement, the idea of a People's Party was the culmination of
a long process going back to the Farmers' Alliance of the 1870s, in
which several mobilizations and co-operative projects had been initiated
without any lasting success. It became increasingly clear to the farmers
that any step forward in the promotion of their cause required direct
political involvement (a course of action whose possibility dawned only
slowly in their minds, and which many of them took only half-heartedly).
This, however, involved entering uncharted territory. It required that the
sectorialism of their demands should be played down, and that a much
larger and complex chain of equivalences had to be constructed, if the
'people' as a new collective actor was to emerge on the terrain of
national politics. Of course, there had been attempts to form third
parties in American politics before. 'For two decades, critics of the
Democrats and Republicans had been contesting national, state, and
local elections under a diversity of banners: Prohibition, Greenback,
Anti-Monopoly, Labor Reform, Union Labor, Working Men, and
hundreds of local and state Independent parties whose very name
denoted repudiation of the rules of the electoral game. Established
politicians had grown accustomed to deploying whatever linguistic and
legal weapons were needed – ridicule, repression, co-optation – to swat
down these disjointed but persistently fractious challengers' (Kazin,
p. 27). But the People's Party aspired to go beyond the sectorial, local or

issue-related character of these early attempts, and to constitute a truly national political language.

Although the terrain of a new global confrontation with the powers that be was, for the populists, uncharted, it was definitely not virgin. Since the antebellum period, a whole tradition of populist defence of the small man against a corrupt financial oligarchy was available, mainly as part of the Jeffersonian and Jacksonian ideological heritage. The separation of ordinary men from those in the heights of power was the constant leitmotiv of this tradition, although the characterization of the despised elite varied from one version to another. 'For Jeffersonians, it lay in a pro-British cabal or merchants, landholders, and conservative clerics; for Jacksonians, a "money power" directed by well-born cosmopolitans. For activists in the new Republican Party of the 1850s, it was the "slave power" of the South that throttled the civil liberties and drove down the earnings of Northern whites' (Kazin, p. 16). So the task of the populists of the 1890s was to delve into this tradition and to reformulate it in terms of the new context in which they were operating.

The situation that the People's Party faced had all the components I have enumerated as typical of the populist turn of politics: widespread disaffection with the existing status quo, incipient constitution of an equivalential chain of demands centred on a few cathected symbols, increasing challenge to the political system as a whole. An equivalential chain, however, is made up – as we have seen – of links which are split between the particularism of the demands they represent and the more 'universal' meaning imparted by their common opposition to the status quo. The whole success of the populist operation depends on making the universalistic moment prevail over the particularistic one. This, however, was far from plain sailing:

> The nascent producer coalition upon which the Populists based their hopes was an unstable amalgam of social groups and political organizations with clashing priorities. Small farmers anxious about their debts wanted to inflate the money supply; white urban workers feared a hike in the prices they paid for food and rent. Prohibitionists and currency

reformers both opposed the big money but differed over which of its sins were primary – the peddling of drink or the constriction of credit. And socialist voices in all their variety – Christian, Marxian, and Bellamyite – were at odds with the most unionist and agrarian rebels, who affirmed their faith in private property and the malleability of the class structure. Factionalism was a perennial feature of reform politics in these years; not until 1892 did most groups cease pitching their panaceas long enough to unite behind the same third-party ticket. (Kazin, p. 30)

Superseding this factionalism entailed both elaborating a common language and neutralizing the centrifugal tendencies towards particularism. These tendencies could be of two kinds. In the first place, there were those sectors which were heterogeneous *vis-à-vis* the main space of political representation (in the sense that we have attributed to the category of heterogeneity in Chapter 5). Prominent among these was the black population. Most populists did not question the dogma of Caucasian supremacy. The pragmatic way of dealing with the issue was to eliminate any idea of a biracial order, and to appeal to blacks only in matters of shared economic interests. Not surprisingly, the black people's reception of those overtures was not enthusiastic: 'the Populists continued to assume, as had their Jeffersonian and Jacksonian forebears, that "the plain people" meant those with white skin and a tradition of owning property on the land or in a craft. Not surprisingly, most blacks did not accept the Populists' circumscribed offer and instead cast their ballots, where they were still allowed to do so, either for the party of Lincoln or for that of their ancestral landlords' (Kazin, p. 41). We should add that this ambiguity towards black people did not exist in relation to Asiatic immigrants: they were fully and uncompromisingly excluded. The literature of the Knights of Labor and the Farmers' Alliance is full of derogatory references to 'Asiatics' and 'Mongolians'.

Apart from these sectors, which come into the general category of 'heterogeneous', there were also those which populist discourse attempted actually to interpellate, but whose differential particularism resisted integration into the populist crusade. The relation between the

People's Party and the Knights of Labor, for instance, was always tense, with many craft and industrial workers ignoring the populist appeal. The Christian evangelical discourse of the rural areas did not find a proper audience in the immigrant working-class population which, in many cases, did not have Protestant origins (Kazin, p. 43).

The attempt to establish an equivalential inscription which would prevail over such a differential particularism centred on a definition of the 'producers' (as opposed to the 'idlers' or the 'parasitic') which was so vague and abstract as to embrace most sectors of the population. This, however, as Kazin points out, was a double-edged weapon: if 'producers' became an empty signifier by loosening its links with particular referents, it could also be appropriated by sectors different from the populist ones, and reinscribed in an alternative equivalential chain – that is to say, it could become a floating signifier. This multiple reference to which populist discourse tended was reflected in the platform of the movement.

> For debt-ridden agrarians they promised an increase in the money supply, a ban on alien land ownership, and a state takeover of the railroads that so often made small farmers pay whatever they could bear. For wage earners, they endorsed the ongoing push for a shorter working day, called for the abolition of the Pinkerton Agency, and declared that 'the interests of rural and civil labor are the same'. For currency reformers and residents of Western mining states, they demanded the unlimited coinage of both silver and gold. Appended to the platform were such 'supplementary resolutions' as a 'pledge' to continue the healthy pensions already being granted to Union veterans and support for a boycott of a Rochester clothing manufacturer being struck by the Knights of Labor. (Kazin, p. 38)

So we have a typical 'war of position' between a populist attempt at equivalential inscription and a differential logic resisting it. The limits to the constitution of the 'people' were reflected in the electoral results of 1892 and 1894: although the overall number of votes obtained by the People's Party was impressive, these votes were almost entirely concentrated in the Deep South and the trans-Mississippi West. It was clear that, if the Party was going to become a truly national alternative, some kind of bold new step had to be taken. That led to the populist support, in 1896, for the Democratic candidate William Jennings Bryan, whose platform had many populist overtones (although it overemphasized the silver issue).

The American elections of 1896 have an almost paradigmatic value for our subject, because the two sides of the confrontation illustrate, in their purest form, what I have called logics of equivalence and of difference. The sucess of Bryan's campaign depended entirely on constituting the 'people' as a historical actor – that is, on having universal-equivalential identifications prevail over sectorial ones. The commonality of his political constituency had thus to be asserted at any price. This passage is typical of his discourse:

> As I look into the faces of these people and remember that our enemies call them a mob, and say they are a menace to free government, I ask: Who shall have the people from themselves? I am proud to have on my side in this campaign the support of those who call themselves the common people. If I had behind me the great trusts and combinations, I know that I would no sooner take my seat than they would demand that I use my power to rob the people in their behalf. (Quoted by Goodwyn, p. 523)

Against the 'people', McKinley's campaign – led by his adviser, Mark Hanna – coined the slogan of 'the progressive society'. Here there is no longer any appeal to a homogeneous, undifferentiated mass, but to the organic, orderly development of a society, each of whose members had a precisely differentiated place, and whose centre was an elite identified with American values.

> Given the ballot box potentiality of 'the people' as against 'the great trusts and combinations', Republicans obviously could not afford to have the campaign decided on that basis. The countervailing idea of the 'progressive society' materialized slowly out of the symbolic values embedded in

the gold standard.... But, gradually ... broader themes of 'peace, progress, patriotism, and prosperity' came to characterize the campaign for William McKinley. The 'progressive society' advanced by Mark Hanna in the name of the corporate community was inherently a well-dressed, churchgoing society. The various slogans employed were not mere expression of a cynical politics, but rather the authentic assertions of an emerging American world view. (Goodwyn, p. 534)

As Goodwyn asserts, the party of Lincoln had become the party of business and the political incarnation of corporative America.

It was white, Protestant and Yankee. It solicited the votes of all non-white, non-Protestant and non-Yankee voters who willingly acquiesced in the new cultural norms that described gentility within the emerging progressive society. The word 'patriotic' had come to suggest those things that Protestant Yankees possessed.... The wall erected by the progressive society against 'the people' signalled more than McKinley's victory over Bryan, more even than the sanctioning of massive corporate concentration; it marked out the permissible limits of the democratic culture itself. The bloody shirt could at last be laid away: the party of business had created in the larger society the cultural values that were to sustain it in the twentieth century. (Goodwyn, pp. 532–3)

Thus the defeat of the 'democratic promise' implicit in American populism adopted the pattern we have seen throughout this book: the dissolution of equivalential links and the differential incorporation of sectors within a wider organic society – 'transformism', to use Gramsci's term. And this differential incorporation was not, of course, equalitarian but hierarchical. To quote Goodwyn once more:

For increasing numbers of Americans, the triumph of the business credo was matched, if not exceeded, by a conscious or unconscious internalization of white supremacist presumptions. Coupled with the new sense of prerogative encased in the idea of progress, the new ethos meant that

Republican businessmen could intimidate Democratic employees in the North, Democratic businessmen could intimidate Populists and Republicans in the South, businessmen everywhere could buy state legislators, and whites everywhere could intimidate blacks and Indians. (Goodwyn, p. 535)

Atatürk's six arrows

In the case of America, we have seen a grass-roots populism whose limits were found in the impossibility of reinscribing differences within an equivalential chain. Institutional differentiations prevailed, ultimately, over dichotomic rearticulations. The whole populist political movement consisted in spontaneous equivalences searching for a dissolution of differential limits. The victory of the 'progressive society' over the 'people' amounted to the failure of that attempt at dissolution. But the terrain within which populism operated was one of spontaneous equivalences. What happens, however, if the 'people' is conceived as an a priori homogeneous entity postulated from a centre of power which, instead of being the social precipitate of an equivalential interaction of democratic demands, is seen as determining an identical substance that any demand expresses? In that case, the internal split inherent in any democratic demand within the equivalential chain collapses; the 'people' loses its internal differentiations, and is reduced to a substantial unity. The 'people' can still be conceived as a radical force opposed to the existing status quo, but it is no longer an underdog: the essential heterogeneity which is the basis of any populist identity has been surrendered and replaced by a homogeneous unity. That is what happened in Turkey, and it explains why Kemalism might have been a radical, ruptural discourse, but it was never populist.

Let us consider the six key words of the programme of the Turkish Republic which were represented as six arrows on the emblem of the Republican People's Party at the beginning of the 1930s: republicanism, nationalism, populism, revolutionism, secularism and etatism.[3] These were supposed to be the pillars of Kemalist ideology. Let us start with populism. The meaning given to this term in this book – the underdog, a *plebs* claiming to be the *populus* – is not the one we find in the notion of *halkçilik* (populism): the latter excludes any notion of antagonism or internal division. As Paul Dumont points out: '[populism] implied an attachment to the idea of democracy and militant intellectual activity aimed at leading the people on the road to progress. But it also had a much more specific meaning: a vision of a Turkish nation constituted not of classes but of solidary, closely interdependent occupational groups. It was a Turkish version of the solidarist ideas outlined by the French radical politician Léon Bourgeois and the sociologist Emile Durkheim.'[4] In the same vein, the ideologist Ziya Gökalp defined populism as follows: 'If a society comprises a certain number of strata or classes, this means that it is not egalitarian. The aim of populism is to suppress the class or strata differences and to replace them with a social structure composed of occupational groups solidary with each other. In other words, we can summarize populism by saying: there are no classes, there are occupations.'[5] And a theoretician of Kemalism, Mahmut Esat Bozkurt, wrote in 1938: 'No party in the civilized world has ever represented the whole nation as completely and as sincerely as the Republican People's Party. Other parties defend the interests of various social classes and strata. For our part, we do not recognize the existence of these classes and strata. For us, all are united. There are no gentlemen, no masters, no slaves. There is but one whole set and this set is the Turkish nation.'[6] We are, apparently, at the antipodes of our notion of populism: while the latter involves the dichotomic division of the communitarian space, Atatürk's populism presupposes a seamless community without internal fissures. We cannot, however, avoid the impression that there is something radically ruptural in Atatürk's notion of the 'people'. How is this possible? The answer to this riddle is to be found in the way Kemalist populism is articulated to the other five arrows.

Let us now consider 'revolutionism'. There was some hesitation at the time between the use of two Turkish words, *inkilab* and *ihtilâl*. 'The Ottoman word which comes closest [to express the meaning of 'revolutionalism'] is *ihtilâl*, which conveys the idea of a sudden and violent change in the political and social order. *Inkilab* implies radical change executed with order and method. Unlike *islâhat*, "reform", it does not apply to partial improvements in certain limited sectors of social life, but rather to attempts at social metamorphosis.'[7] This is crucial: piecemeal engineering as a method of social change is radically excluded. The constitution of the 'people' has to be a sudden and total event. The same goes for 'republicanism'. Its content – its ruptural connotations which associated it closely with 'revolutionism' – was given by the radical chasm it opened up with the caliphate and the sultanate. Although the idea of this chasm took a long time to mature in the minds of the revolutionary officers, once it was firmly adopted by Atatürk it acquired the value of a non-reversible change. As for 'nationalism', it also emphasized a homogeneous identity and the elimination of all differential particularism. This is how it was explained in 1931 by the Party secretary, Recep Peker:

> We consider as ours all those of our citizens who live among us, who belong politically and socially to the Turkish nation and among whom ideas and feelings such as 'Kurdism', 'Circassianism' and even 'Lazism' and 'Pomakism' have been implanted. We deem it our duty to banish, by sincere efforts, those false conceptions, which are the legacy of an absolutist regime and the product of long-standing historical oppression. The scientific truth of today does not allow an independent existence for a nation of several hundred thousand, or even of a million individuals.... We want to state as sincerely our opinion regarding our Jewish or Christian compatriots. Our party considers these compatriots as absolutely Turkish insofar as they belong to our community of language and ideal.[8]

The notions of religion and race, which had been closely associated with that of nation during the Ottoman period, were progressively eliminated from it within the first years of the Republic. 'Secularism', the word by which Turkish *layiklik* has been translated, does not fully express its meaning. As Dumont has asserted: 'The basic conflict in secularism [in the Turkish sense of the term] is not necessarily between religion and the world, as was the case in Christian experience. The conflict is often between the forces of tradition, which tend to promote the domination of religion and sacred law, and the forces of change. Laicism refers more narrowly to a specific process of separating church from state.[9] In other words, secularism could not limit itself to preserving a public sphere uncontaminated by religious values; it also had to push the struggle against traditional religious forces on to the very terrain of civil society. As my discussion of the other arrows abundantly shows, the Kemalist revolution did not conceive of itself as just a political revolution, but as an attempt drastically to reshape society through political means. And it is well known how ruthlessly its secularist aims were pursued: in 1924 the caliphate was abolished; later on came the dissolution of religious courts and Islamic schools, pious foundations and ministries of religion; religious brotherhoods, convents and sacred tombs were closed; the Gregorian calendar was introduced and pilgrimages to Mecca were forbidden. This strong political intervention within civil society allows us to understand the sixth arrow, 'etatism'. The state had to intervene in all spheres, and this obviously included the regulation of economic life.

A considerable amount of recent literature on Kemalism has tended to question the radical character of Atatürk's break with the tradition, and to stress the continuities, as far as basic moulds of thought are concerned, between the early Republic and the Ottoman past.[10] There is, of course, a good deal of truth in these claims in so far as all revolution has to work with attitudes and raw materials which do not emerge through spontaneous generation, but there can be no doubt that the articulation of these elements into a discourse of radical rupture with the past was a specific and original Kemalist contribution. What Atatürk did, however, inherit from the Ottoman tradition was the idea of the nation as something to be created anew, not simply handed down from the past; a vision of historical change as resulting from an act of will, not as an organic and spontaneous development of forces already shaping the contours of the social. This vision resulted from the way in which modernization took place in Turkey: in a reactive way *vis-à-vis* the most developed European nations. The need to catch up was the main stimulus for reform. The centrifugal forces which were undermining the

Ottoman Empire, however, created increasing doubts about who could be the viable subject of a rejuvenated nation. For a long time, the forces around the sultan thought that the Empire, if internal centralizing reforms managed to balance widespread diversity and localism, could become a viable political entity. During the Tanzimat period, some critical moments of reform – the suppression of the Janissaries' rebellion in 1826 and the reforms which followed; the administrative, military and educational reforms of the end of the 1830s and, again, during the period starting in 1856 – created the illusion that such an outcome was possible, but in the long term the centrifugal forces always prevailed. It is against this background that we can understand the intervention of the so-called Young Ottomans, a group of intellectuals whose ideas aimed at a radical refounding of the nation. Such a refounding should be based on a constitutional order grounded on Islamic principles; on a centralization of state power as against local, decentralized dispersion; and on a political identity based on loyalty to the *vatan*, the fatherland, which is beyond any kind of division (regional, ethnic or religious).[11] This last point is crucial: traditional allegiance to the *millet* (the religious community) had to be replaced by allegiance to a purely national entity. The Kemalian notion of nationalism is contained *in nuce* in this ideological turn. A constitution inspired by the Young Ottomans' ideas was established in 1876, but suppressed by the Sultan two years later. It was, however, re-established by the Young Turks' revolution of 1908, whose ideological arsenal continued, in several respects, the tradition of the Young Ottomans.

So if the moment of anti-status quo, which is an essential component of any populist rupture, was so present in Kemalism, why was Kemalism unable to follow a populist route? The reason is clear: because its homogenization of the 'nation' proceeded not through the construction of equivalential chains between actual democratic demands, but through authoritarian imposition. It was only during the War of Independence which followed the First World War that Kemalism relied, to some extent, on mass mobilization. During most of his rule – and this applies also to his immediate successors – Atatürk was confronted with the paradox of having to construct a 'people' without popular support.[12] He himself understood his role in those terms. In 1918 he wrote in his diary:

> If I obtain great authority and power, I think I will bring about by a coup – suddenly in one moment – the desired revolution in our social life. Because, unlike others, I don't believe that this deed can be achieved by raising the intelligence of others slowly to the level of my own. My soul rebels against such a course. Why, after my years of education, after studying civilization and the socialization processes, after spending my life and my time to gain pleasure from freedom, should I descend to the level of common people? I will make them rise to my level. Let me not resemble them: they should resemble me.[13]

The main vehicle of this programme of forced modernization was, of course, the Army, which has remained the ultimate arbiter of Turkish politics since Atatürk's time. The problem is that there is no alternative to equivalential mobilization except differential integration, and even the Army was not strong enough to create a totally new society shaped according to Kemalist designs. The result was that very soon the new Republic, orphan of mass support, could only rely at the local level on traditional forces which had little sympathy for the most ambitious aspirations of the 'Father of the Turks'.

> Whereas Ankara displayed all the formal requirements of modern legal authority, large parts of the country were still deeply rooted in traditional life. From the very beginning, the Kemalists compromised with traditional forms of domination and had to rely on traditional leaders as intermediaries between centre and periphery. Like the Unionist before, the Kemalist movement was organized around traditional notables in the countryside, and their influence 'was amply felt in parliamentary politics and party activities' (Sayari 1977: 106). Under the umbrella of the nation-state, the Republican regimes sustained major patterns of Anatolia's traditional society.[14]

The failure of the Kemalist experiment in constituting a 'people' was evident whenever there was an opening in the political system. When President Inönü decided to hold democratic elections in 1950, the oppositional Democratic Party won 408 seats in Parliament against 69 for the official Republican Party (RPP).[15] Equivalences spread wildly, but in directions which had little to do with Atatürk's six arrows: first, the neo-populism of Adnan Menderes; later the renaissance of Islamism. The result was a tortuous process, in which periods of democratic opening were interrupted by successive military interventions.

The return of Perón

American populism met its limits in the impossibility of expanding the equivalential chain beyond a certain point, as a result of resistance from well-entrenched systems of differences to the populist appeal; Atatürk met his in his attempt to construct the 'people' as an organic unity not mediated by any equivalential logic. The case of the Peronism of the 1960s and 1970s was different: it was its very success in constructing an almost unlimited chain of equivalences that led to the subversion of the principle of equivalence as such. How is this so?

The popular Peronist government was overthrown in September 1955. The last years of the regime had been dominated by a characteristic development: the attempt to overcome the dichotomic division of the political spectrum through the creation of a fully integrated differential space. The symbolic changes in the regime's discourse bear witness to this mutation: the figure of the *descamisado* (literally 'shirtless', the Argentinian equivalent of the *sans-culotte*) tended to disappear, to be replaced by the image of the 'organized community'. The need to stabilize the revolutionary process became a leitmotiv of Peronist discourse – not only in the years before 1955, but also in the years thereafter. I remember that in 1967 Perón sent a letter to a left-wing organization to which I belonged, in which he asserted that any revolution goes through three stages: first, the ideological preparation – that is, Lenin; second, the seizure of power – that is, Trotsky; third, the institutionalization of the revolution – that is, Stalin. He added that the Peronist revolution had to move from the second stage to the third.

The coup of 1955, however, changed the terms of the political debate. Despite the aggressive anti-Peronist rhetoric of the new authorities – which was actually far more than rhetoric, because they dissolved the Peronist Party, intervened in the trade unions and made it a crime to mention the name of Perón – very soon there were conversations with groups of Peronist politicians to discuss ways of integrating them into the new political system. This integration, of course, excluded Perón himself; he had to be permanently proscribed, and his exile was supposed to be *sine die*. The idea of a 'Peronism without Perón' circulated widely. From his exile, Perón strongly resisted these attempts – from both inside and outside Peronism – to marginalize him. The more repressive the new regime became, and the more its economic programme was seen as a sellout to international finance capital, the more the figure of Perón became identified with an anti-system popular and national identity. A duel between Perón (from exile) and successive anti-Peronist governments was starting; this would go on for seventeen years, and come to an end only with Perón's triumphant return to Argentina and to government.

It was around this duel that the new Argentinian populism started to take shape. If we are to understand its pattern a few circumstances have to be taken into account. In the first place, Argentina is an ethnically homogeneous country whose dominant urban population is concentrated in the triangle constituted by the three industrial cities of Buenos Aires, Rosario and Córdoba. Any major ideological event therefore had an immediate equivalential impact over this whole area, and its effects spread quickly through the rest of the country. Without this type of impact, Perón's moves during the 1960s would have been unsuccessful – the new regime would have been able to deal in a piecemeal way with a fragmented Peronist opposition. In the second place, however, the very conditions of enunciation of Perón's discourse from exile determined the peculiar nature of its success. The condition that the host countries imposed on Perón as an exiled politician was that he had to abstain from political statements, and in Argentina the circulation of any statement from him was, of course, strictly forbidden. Thus he was restricted to sending private letters, cassettes and verbal instructions, which were, however, of the utmost importance for the Peronist resistance which was slowly organizing itself in the factories and working-class districts of the industrial cities. So, as recent studies have shown,[16] there was a permanent chasm between Perón's acts of enunciation (which were invisible) and the contents of those enunciations. As a result of this chasm, those contents – in the absence of any authorized interpreter – could be given a multiplicity of meanings. At the same time, many apocryphal messages were also circulating, as well as others whose authenticity was dubious, or at the very least questioned by those who opposed their contents. This complicated situation, however, had a paradoxical effect: the multilayered nature of the messages – resulting from the chasm between acts and contents of the enunciation – could be consciously cultivated so that they became deliberately ambiguous. As a result, Perón's word lost none of its centrality, but the *content* of that word could allow for endless interpretations and reinterpretations. As Perón wrote to his first personal representative in Argentina, John William Cook: 'I always follow the rule of greeting everybody because, and you must not forget it, I am now something like the Pope.... Taking into account this concept, I cannot deny anything [because of] my infallibility ... which, as it is the case of all infallibility, is precisely based on not saying or doing anything, [which is the] only way of assuring such infallibility.'[17]

Of course, a cynical reading of this passage is possible: one could understand it as if Perón were trying to be all things to all men, but such a reading is short-sighted. Perón, from exile, could not have given precise directives to the actions of a proliferation of local groups engaged in resistance; even less could he have intervened in the disputes that arose among those groups. On the other hand, his word was indispensable in giving symbolic unity to all those disparate struggles. Thus his word had to operate as a signifier with only weak links to particular signifieds. This is no major surprise: it is exactly what I have called empty signifiers. Perón won the duel with successive anti-Peronist regimes because these regimes lost the struggle to integrate the neo-Peronist groups – those postulating a 'Peronism without Perón' – into an enlarged political system, while the demand for Perón's return to Argentina became an empty signifier unifying an expanding popular camp.

At this point, however, it is necessary to introduce some distinctions. The role of Pope that Perón attributed to himself (which so neatly evokes Lacan's notion of 'master-signifier') could be conceived in various ways. In the first place, it could be seen as a centre of equivalential irradiation which, however, does not entirely lose the particularity of its original content. To go back to a previous example: the demands of *Solidarność* became the rallying point of equivalential associations vaster than themselves, but they were still linked to a certain programmatic content – it was precisely that contact which made it possible to maintain a certain coherence between the particularities integrating the chain (the lower semi-circles in our first diagram; see p. 130 above). But there is another possibility: that the tendentially empty signifier becomes *entirely* empty, in which case the links in the equivalential chain do not need to cohere with each other at all: the most contradictory contents can be assembled, as long as the subordination of them all to the empty signifier remains. To go back to Freud: this would be the extreme situation in which love for the father is the *only* link between the brothers. The political consequence is that the unity of a 'people' constituted this way is extremely fragile. On the one hand, the potential antagonism between contradictory demands can break out at any moment; on the other, a love for the leader which does not crystallize in any form of institutional regularity – in psychoanalytic terms: an ego ideal which is not partially internalized by ordinary egos – can result only in fleeting popular identities. The more we advance into the 1960s, the more we see that Peronism was dangerously bordering on this second possibility. Perón's reflection (mentioned above) about the need for the Peronist revolution to move to a third stage of institutionalization shows that he was not entirely unaware of this potential threat.

In the early 1960s, however, that danger lay somewhere in the future. The immediate task was to fight those political forces within Peronism which were pushing in the direction of a 'Peronism without Perón'. The main threat came from the conditions in which the trade-union movement was normalized after the return to constitutional rule in 1958 and Arturo Frondizi's accession to the presidency. (His election had been ensured by Perón's decision to ask his followers – whose Party had been proscribed – to vote for him and against Ricardo Balbín, the quasi-official candidate.) In 1959, trade-union activity was legalized under Law 14.445.

The new labour law gave the State exceptional power *vis-à-vis* the union movement. A union's very ability to bargain collectively with employers was dependent on its *personería* (an official recognition exclusively conceded by the government). Therefore, the institutional future of any trade union (the future satisfaction of its needs) was intrinsically bound up with its relations with the State. Consequently, the provisions of the Law 14.455 contained a powerful inducement to the adoption of pragmatic realism for union leaders, despite their own ideological profile, individual views and personal advantages that they took from their posts.[18]

In actual fact, the trade-union movement was in a complicated situation. On the one hand, members had to act cautiously *vis-à-vis* the government, because their legal status was a precondition for their defence of the interests and demands of the workers, who would have withdrawn their support in case the union leadership was not successful; on the other, since their social base was solidly Peronist, they could not afford an open break with Perón. It was in these circumstances that an intensifying conflict took place in the first half of the 1960s between trade-union officials led by the general secretary of the metalworkers, Augusto Vandor, and, on the opposite side, Perón and the most radical-ized sectors within Peronism. The trade-union project – never explicitly formulated, for nobody within Peronism could have had an open con-frontation with Perón – was to obtain a progressive integration of Peronism within existing political system, with Perón becoming a purely ceremonial figure, and the actual power within the movement being transferred to the union leadership. The conflict went through various vicissitudes and culminated in the provincial elections of April 1966 in Mendoza, where two Peronist lists – one supported by Perón, the other by Vandor – competed with each other, the landslide victory going to the orthodox Peronist list.

Once again, however, this developing conflict was complicated by the arrival of a player who kicked the board. In 1966 the armed forces deposed President Illia and started a military dictatorship under the rule of General Onganía. This was not the most repressive regime the country was to experience – for that we have to wait until the 1970s – but it was definitely the most stupid and inefficient. In a matter of months it had alienated all relevant forces in the country – except a small sector of big business. It dissolved all political organizations, savagely repressed the union movement, and intervened in the universities. After a few months in office, it was clear to everybody that no institutional channels for the expression of social demands existed any longer, and that some kind of violent reaction entirely outside the institutional order would be the only possible response to this political blind alley.

Social protest erupted in 1969 with the so-called *Cordobazo*, the violent seizure of the city of Córdoba by armed groups, which later expanded to other cities in the interior of the country. Other developments also contributed to a violent confrontation with the regime. First, there was the emergence of new left-wing Peronist guerrilla groups – Perón called them his 'special formations'. But, secondly, the very repression unleashed by the government against the trade-union movement considerably reduced the room for manoeuvre of Vandor and the neo-Peronist groups, who could no longer deliver the goods. This situation finally led to the assassination of Vandor by left-wing Peronist guerrillas, and to the division of the trade-union movement between a right-wing and a left-wing faction. In any case, the consequences of these developments were clear: the reinforcement of the central role of Perón, who was presented, depending on the political orientation of those supporting him, either as the leader of an anti-imperialist coalition which was going to be the first step in the advance towards a socialist Argentina, or as the only guarantee that the popular movement would be contained within manageable limits, and would not degenerate into left-wing chaos.

> Therefore, and even though his relationship with Peronist guerrilla groups was wrapped into a political ambiguity similar to the one present in his relation with Peronist left union leaders, Perón needed to endorse these organizations to create the political conditions to prompt his return. By the end of 1971, Perón was in a position to employ what he called 'his two hands'. He had his 'right hand' mainly located in Peronist unions.... Perón's 'left hand' was mainly represented by left-wing youth organizations and what he called his 'special formations': the guerrilla groups which proclaimed their loyalty to the conductor and which made of his return to Argentina the initial moment of a revolutionary transformation of the country. The exiled leader employed both hands with great mastery, indeed. Between 1971 and 1972 Perón deployed all his political talent in an amazing manner.[19]

From then on, events unfolded quickly. The kidnapping and execution of former president Aramburu by the Peronist Montoneros guerrillas led to the fall of General Onganía, who was replaced by General Roberto Mario Levingston and later by General Alejandro Lanusse, who finally, in 1973, called general elections in which Peronism won a landslide victory. It was then, however, that the above-mentioned dangers inherent in the way in which Peronist equivalences had been constructed started to reveal their deadly potential. Once in Argentina, Perón could no longer be an empty signifier: he was the President of the Republic and, as such, he had to take decisions and opt between alternatives. The game of the years of exile – by which each group reinterpreted his word according to his own political orientation, while Perón himself maintained a cautious distance from all interpretation – could not be pursued once he was in power. The consequences unfolded rapidly. The right-wing trade-union bureaucracy, on the one hand, and the Peronist youth and the 'special formations', on the other, had nothing in common – they saw each other as deadly enemies. No equivalence between them had been internalized, and the only thing which kept them within the same political camp was the common identification with Perón as leader. This amounted to very little, for Perón embodied for each faction totally incompatible political principles. For a while he tried to hegemonize the totality of his movement in a coherent way, but he failed: the process of antagonistic differentiation had gone too far. After Perón's death in 1974, the struggle between the various Peronist factions accelerated, and the country again entered into a process of rapid de-institutionalization whose consequence was the military takeover of 1976 and the establishment of one of the most brutally repressive regimes of the twentieth century.

I have presented three cases of populist mobilization, considered both their achievements and their failures, and claimed that there is an essential comparability among them, both in their differences – they come from far-distant geographical areas and political cultures – and in the logics which underlie their discourse. Let us say, to start with, that they do not exhaust the possible alternatives within the combinations of the variables which have been brought into the analysis – there are always different combinations and possibilities. The advance towards a wider typological description should obviously be the aim and ambition of a fully developed theory of populism. In the advance towards this diversified typology, however, there are some preconditions that I must emphasize as basic requirements of any establishment of a bridge between theoretical reflection and empirical analysis.

The first is that the different theoretical traditions interrogated in this exploration have shown, with remarkable regularity, the recurrence of a distinction which is crucial in any discursive approach to the question of social identities. In linguistics, this is the distinction between syntagms and paradigms (identities created on the basis of either relations of substitution or relations of combination); in rhetoric, it is the distinction between metonymy and metaphor; in politics, that between equivalence and difference. This constant reproduction of the same distinction in different theoretical registers clearly points to a problem – perhaps *the* problem – with which a social ontology has to deal today as its most urgent task: how to make this distinction – which involves a new relation between entities – become accessible to thought?

In the second place, however, if that distinction is actually going to inform concrete analysis, it cannot be considered as a transcendentally fixed entelechy whose presence in concrete situations we simply have to *trace*, but as a fertile terrain on which concrete analysis and transcendental exploration have to feed each other endlessly. There is no concrete analysis which can be downgraded to the status of empirical research without theoretical impact; conversely, there is no transcendental exploration which is absolutely 'pure', without the presence of an excess of what its categories can master – an excess which contaminates the transcendental horizon with an impure empiricism. Populism, for political analysis, is one of the privileged places of emergence of this contamination. In an article full of interest, Margaret Canovan has used Michael Oakshott's distinction between redemptive and pragmatic politics to characterize the 'no-terrain' within which populist politics is constructed.[20] I fully agree with that view; and for reasons that I hope have been made clear enough in the preceding pages, I see this grey area of contamination not as some kind of marginal political phenomenon, but as the very essence of the political.

Perhaps what is dawning as a possibility in our political experience is something radically different from what postmodern prophets of the 'end of politics' are announcing: the arrival at a fully political era, because the dissolution of the marks of certainty does not give the political game any aprioristic necessary terrain but, rather, the possibility of constantly redefining the terrain itself.

Concluding Remarks

Let us now draw the main conclusions of our analysis. Thinking the 'people' as a social category requires a series of theoretical decisions that we have made in the course of our exploration. The most crucial is, perhaps, the *constitutive* role that we have attributed to social *heterogeneity*. If we do not assign the heterogeneous this role, it could be conceived, in its opacity, as merely the apparent form of an ultimate core which, in itself, would be entirely homogeneous and transparent. That is, it would be the terrain on which the philosophies of history could flourish. If, on the contrary, heterogeneity is primordial and irreducible, it will show itself, in the first place, as *excess*. This excess, as we have seen, cannot be mastered by any sleight of hand, whether by a dialectical reversal or some other means. Heterogeneity, however, does not mean pure plurality or multiplicity, as the latter is compatible with the full positivity of its aggregated elements. Heterogeneity, in the sense in which I conceive it, has as one of its defining features a dimension of *deficient being* or *failed unicity*. If heterogeneity is, on the one hand, ultimately irreducible to a deeper homogeneity, it is, on the other, not simply absent but *present as that which is absent*. Unicity shows itself through its very absence. As we have seen, the result of this presence/absence is that the various elements of the heterogeneous ensemble are differentially cathected or overdetermined. We have, however, partial objects that, through their very partiality embody an ever-receding totality. The latter requires a contingent social construction, as it does not result from the positive, ontic nature of the objects themselves. This is what we have called *articulation* and *hegemony*. We find in this construction – which is far from being a merely intellectual operation – the starting point for the emergence of the 'people'. Let us recapitulate the main conditions for this emergence. First, I will enumerate the set of *theoretical* decisions necessary for something like a 'people' to become intelligible, then the historical conditions that make its emergence possible.

1. A first theoretical decision is to conceive of the 'people' as a *political* category, not as a *datum* of the social structure. This designates not a *given* group, but an act of institution that creates a new agency out of a plurality of heterogeneous elements. For this reason, I have insisted from the very beginning that my minimal unit of analysis would not be the *group*, as a referent, but the socio-political *demand*. This explains why questions such as 'Of what social group are these demands the *expression*?' do not make sense in my analysis, given that, for me, the unity of the group is simply the result of an aggregation of social demands – which can, of course, be crystallized in sedimented social practices. This aggregation presupposes an essential asymmetry between the community as a whole (the *populus*) and the underdog (the *plebs*). I have also explained why the latter is always a partiality that identifies itself with the community at large.

2. It is in this contamination of the universality of the *populus* by the partiality of the *plebs* that the peculiarity of the 'people' as a historical actor lies. The logic of its construction is what I have called 'populist reason'. We can approach its specificity from two angles: the universality of the partial and the partiality of the universal. Let us deal with them successively. In what sense is the partial universal? We already have all the elements to answer this question properly. Partiality, it should be clear, is used here almost as an oxymoron: it has lost its merely partitive meaning

and become one of the names of the totality. A popular demand is one that embodies the absent fullness of the community through a potentially endless chain of equivalences. That is why populist reason – which amounts, as we have seen, to *political* reason *tout court* – breaks with two forms of rationality which herald the end of politics: a total revolutionary event that, bringing about the full reconciliation of society with itself, would make the political moment superfluous, or a mere gradualist practice that reduces politics to administration. Not for nothing was the gradualist motto of Saint-Simon – 'from the government of men to the administration of things' – adopted by Marxism to describe the future condition of a classless society. But a partial object, as we have seen, can also have a non-partitive meaning: not a part *of* a whole, but a part that *is* the whole. Once this reversal of the relation part/whole is achieved – a reversal that is inherent to the Lacanian *objet petit a*, and to the hegemonic relation – the relation *populus/plebs* becomes the locus of an ineradicable tension in which each term at once absorbs and expels the other. This *sine die* tension is what ensures the political character of society, the plurality of embodiments of the *populus* that does not lead to any ultimate reconciliation (that is, overlapping) of the two poles. This is why there is no partiality that does not show within itself the traces of the universal.

3. Let us move now to the other angle: the partiality of the universal. This is where the true ontological option underlying our analysis is to be found. Whatever ontic content we decide to privilege in an ontological investment, the *traces* of that investment cannot be entirely concealed. The partiality we privilege will also be the point that universality necessarily inhabits. The key question is: does this 'inhabiting' do away with the specificity of the particular, such that universality becomes the true medium for an unlimited *logical* mediation, and particularity the merely apparent field of *expressive* mediation? Or, rather: does the latter oppose a non-transparent medium to an otherwise transparent experience, so that an irreducibly opaque (non-)representative moment becomes constitutive? If we adopt this last alternative, we see immediately that the 'people' (as constituted through a nomination that does not conceptually

subsume it) is not a kind of 'superstructural' effect of an underlying infrastructural logic, but a primary terrain in the construction of a political subjectivity.

Some of the main effects of the mutual contamination of universality and particularity are to be found here. The particular has transformed its very partiality in the name of a transcendent universality. That is why its ontological function can never be reduced to its ontic content. But because this ontological function can be present *only* when it is attached to an ontic content, the latter becomes the horizon of all there is – the point at which the ontic and the ontological fuse into a contingent but indivisible unity. To go back to a previous example: at some point, the symbols of *Solidarność* in Poland became the symbols of the absent fullness of society. Since society as fullness has no proper meaning beyond the ontic contents that embody it, those contents are, for the subjects attached to them, *all there is*. They are thus not an empirically achievable second best *vis-à-vis* an unattainable ultimate fullness for which we wait in vain. This, as we have seen, is the logic of hegemony. This moment of fusion between partial object and totality represents, at one point in time, the ultimate historical horizon, which cannot be split into its two dimensions, universal and particular. History cannot be conceived therefore as an infinite advance towards an ultimate aim. History is rather a discontinuous succession of hegemonic formations that cannot be ordered by a script transcending their contingent historicity. 'Peoples' are real social formations, but they resist inscription into any kind of Hegelian teleology. That is why Copjec is absolutely right to insist on the Lacanian distinction between desire and drive: while the first has no object and cannot be satisfied, the second involves a radical investment in a partial object and brings about satisfaction. This is also why, as we shall see later, political analyses which attempt to polarize politics in terms of the alternative between total revolution and gradualist reformism miss the point: what escapes them is the alternative logic of the *objet petit a* – that is to say, the possibility that a partiality can become the name of an impossible totality (in other words, the logic of hegemony).

4. Three brief points of clarification must be added here. The first is that the relationship between *naming* and *contingency* now becomes fully intelligible. If the unity of social actors were the result of a logical link subsuming various subject positions under a unified conceptual category, 'naming' would simply involve choosing an arbitrary label for an object whose unity was ensured by purely a priori means. If, however, the unity of the social agent is the result of a plurality of social demands coming together through equivalential (metonymic) relations of contiguity, the contingent moment of naming has an absolutely central and constitutive role. The psychoanalytic category of overdetermination points in the same direction. In this respect, naming is the key moment in the constitution of a 'people', whose boundaries and equivalential components permanently fluctuate. Whether nationalism, for instance, is going to become a central signifier in the constitution of popular identities depends on a contingent history impossible to determine through a priori means. As has been asserted of present-day Iraq, 'the sense of nationalism is tenuous at best and could easily be displaced by other forms of collective allegiance. The recent surge in feelings of kinship between Sunnis and Shiites actually shows the malleability of self-identity. The idea of a nation's existence – and one's belonging to it – are concepts that shift constantly.'[1] The same author quotes Professor Stephen D. Krasner of Stanford University: 'Individuals always have choices because they have multiple identities: Shia, Iraqi, Muslim, Arab. Which among this repertoire of identities they choose has to depend on the circumstances, on the pluses or minuses of invoking a particular identity.'[2] It is not only that 'nationalism' can be substituted by other terms in its role as empty signifier, but also that its own meaning will vary depending on the chain of equivalences associated with it.

A second point concerns the role of affect in the constitution of popular identities. The affective bond becomes more central whenever the combinatorial/symbolic dimension of language operates less automatically. From this perspective, affect is absolutely crucial in explaining the operation of the substitutive/paradigmatic pole of language, which is more freely associative in its workings (and thus more open to psychoanalytic exploration). As we have seen, equivalential logic is decisive in the formation of popular identities, and in these substitutive/equivalential operations the imbrication of signification and affect is most fully visible. This is the dimension that, as we recall, early theoreticians of mass society saw as most problematic, and involving a major threat to social rationality. And in contemporary rationalist reconstructions of social sciences, from structuralism to rational choice, this is also the pole that is systematically demoted at the expense of the combinatorial/symbolic one, which allows for a 'grammatical' or 'logical' calculation.

We need to make a final point. The passage from one hegemonic formation, or popular configuration, to another will always involve a radical break, a *creatio ex nihilo*. It is not that all the elements of an emerging configuration have to be entirely new, but rather that the articulating point, the partial object around which the hegemonic formation is reconstituted as a new totality, does not derive its central role from any logic already operating within the preceding situation. Here we are close to Lacan's *passage à l'acte*, which has been central in recent discussions concerning the ethics of the Real.[3] As Alenka Zupančič claims, 'the *Aktus der Freiheit*, the "act of freedom", the genuine ethical act, is always subversive; it is never simply the result of an "improvement" or a "reform"'.[4]

As the equivalential/articulating moment does not proceed from any logical need for each demand to move into the others, what is crucial for the emergence of the 'people' as a new historical actor is that the unification of a plurality of demands in a new configuration is constitutive and not derivative. In other words, it constitutes an *act* in the strict sense, for it does not have its source in anything external to itself. The emergence of the 'people' as a historical actor is thus always transgressive *vis-à-vis* the situation preceding it. This transgression is the emergence of a new order. As Zupančič asserts apropos of Oedipus: 'Oedipus' act, his utterance of a word, is not simply an outrage, a word of defiance launched at the Other, it is also an act of creation of the Other (a different Other). Oedipus is not so much a "transgressor" as the "founder" of a new order.'[5]

While I concur for the most part with Zupančič's description of the true act, my view diverges from hers with respect to the nature of the situation transgressed. Because her main emphasis is on the radicality of the break brought about by the act, she tends to stress its transgressive function, together with the newness of what it establishes. But this leads her, in my view, to present the situation preceding the *passage à l'acte* as more closed and monolithic than it really is. What if the situation were internally dislocated and the act did not simply *replace* an old order with a new one, but *introduced* order where there was, at least partially, chaos? In that case the order introduced would still be new, but it would also be the embodiment of order *tout court* as that which was missing. This is important for one key point in Zupančič's analysis: her assertion that in a true act there is no divided subject: 'If the division of the will or the division of the subject is the mark of freedom, it is not, however, the mark of the act. *In an act, there is no divided subject.* Antigone is whole or "all" in her act; she is not "divided" or "barred". This means that she passes over entirely to the side of the object, and that the place of the will wanting this object "remains empty".'[6] My quarrel with this formulation is not the assertion that in the act the subject passes entirely to the side of the object. I can concur with that. My difficulty is that – for reasons I have just given – *I see the object itself as divided.* Because the act, on the one hand, brings about a *new* (ontic) order, but, on the other, has an *ordering* (ontological) function, it is the *locus* of a complex game by which a concrete content actualizes, through its very concreteness, something that is entirely different from itself: what I have called the absent fullness of society. It is easy to see why, without the very complexity of this game, there would be no hegemony and no popular identities.

5. I shall now discuss the *historical* conditions that make the emergence and expansion of popular identities possible. The *structural* condition we already know: the multiplication of social demands, the heterogeneity of which can be brought to some form of unity only through equivalential political articulations. The question concerning historical conditions

should therefore be: are we living in societies that tend to increase social homogeneity through immanent infrastructural mechanisms or, on the contrary, do we inhabit a historical terrain where the proliferation of heterogeneous points of rupture and antagonisms require increasingly *political* forms of social reaggregation – that is to say, that the latter depend less on *underlying* social logics and more on *acts*, in the sense that I have described. This question hardly needs an answer. What requires some consideration, however, are the conditions causing the balance to tip increasingly towards heterogeneity. There are several interrelated conditions, but if I had to subsume them under one label, it would be: *globalized capitalism*. By capitalism, of course, we should no longer understand a self-enclosed totality governed by movements derived from the contradictions of commodity as an elementary form. We can no longer understand capitalism as a purely economic reality, but as a complex in which economic, political, military, technological and other determinations – each endowed with its own logic and a certain autonomy – enter into the determination of the movement of the whole. In other terms, heterogeneity belongs to the essence of capitalism, the partial stabilizations of which are hegemonic in nature.

I cannot enter into a discussion of the aforementioned problems here for this would require another book. I shall just mention briefly – almost telegraphically – some aspects that a consideration of populism in contemporary societies cannot afford to ignore.[7] First, there is the question of the unstable balance between *concept* and *name*, broached at various points of my discussion. In societies where the disparate subject positions of social actors have a limited range of horizontal variations, they could be conceived as expressing the identity of the *same* social actors. Workers, for instance, living in a certain neighbourhood, working in comparable jobs, having the same access to consumer goods, culture, recreation and so on, can have the illusion that in spite of their heterogeneity, all of their demands issue from the same group, and that there is a natural or essential link between them. When these demands become more heterogeneous in the living experience of people, it is their unity around a 'taken-for-granted' group that is questioned. At this point the logics constructing the 'people' as a contingent entity become more autonomous from social immanence but, for that very reason, more constitutive in their effects. This is the point at which the *name*, as a highly cathected rallying point, does not *express* the unity of the group, but becomes its *ground*.

Second, there is the question of the discursive construction of social division. I have presented a structural explanation of popular identity formation in which antagonistic frontiers are grounded in equivalential logics. Frontiers are the *sine qua non* of the emergence of the 'people': without them, the whole dialectic of partiality/universality would simply collapse. But the more extended the equivalential chain, the less 'natural' the articulation between its links, and the more unstable the identity of the enemy (located on the other side of the frontier). This is something I have encountered at various points in my analysis. In the case of a specific demand formulated within a localized context, it is relatively easy to determine who is the adversary; if, however, there is an equivalence between a multiplicity of heterogeneous demands, to determine what your goal is and whom you are fighting against becomes much more difficult. At this point, 'populist reason' becomes fully operative. This explains why what I have called 'globalized capitalism' represents a qualitatively new stage in capitalist history, and leads to a deepening of the logics of identity formation as I have described. There has been a multiplication of dislocatory effects and a proliferation of new antagonisms, which is why the anti-globalization movement has to operate in an entirely new way: it must advocate the creation of equivalential links between deeply heterogeneous social demands while, at the same time, elaborating a common language. A new internationalism is emerging that, at the same time, makes traditional institutionalized forms of political mediation obsolete. The universality of the 'party' form, for instance, is radically questioned.

Finally, there is the question of the status of the political. In my view, the political is linked to what could be called contingent articulation – another name for the dialectic between differential and equivalential logics. In this sense, all antagonism is essentially political. In that case,

however, the political is not linked to a regional type of conflict different from, for instance, the economic one. Why? For two main reasons.
The first is that demands that put a state of affairs into question do not
grow spontaneously out of the logic of the latter, but consist in a break
with it. A demand for higher wages does not derive from the logic of
capitalist relations, but interrupts that logic in terms that are alien to it
– those of a discourse concerning justice, for example. So any demand
presupposes a constitutive heterogeneity – it is an event that breaks with
the logic of a situation. This is what makes such a demand a political
one. In the second place, however, this heterogeneity of the demand *vis-
à-vis* the existing situation will rarely be confined to a specific content;
it will, from the very beginning, be highly overdetermined. The request
for a higher level of wages in terms of justice will be rooted in a wider
sense of justice linked to a variety of other situations. In other words,
there are no pure subjects of change; they are always overdetermined
through equivalential logics. This means that political subjects are
always, in one way or another, popular subjects. And under the conditions of globalized capitalism, the space of this overdetermination
clearly expands.

I have now presented the main features of my conception of the
logics that determine the formation of popular identities. The specificity
of my approach can be made clearer, however, if I compare it with alternative approaches that have been proposed in recent years. First, I shall
discuss two of them with which I fundamentally disagree – those
proposed by Slavoj Žižek, and Michael Hardt and Antonio Negri – then
move on to one that is closer to the vision presented in this book: that
of Jacques Rancière.

Žižek: waiting for the Martians

A first approach to the question of the unity of popular subjects is to be
found in new versions of traditional Marxism: popular unity is reduced
to class unity. I shall take the work of Žižek as a representative example
of this position.[8] He presents his own views on the subject in the course

of a critique of my work. His main points: (1) Behind my position lies an only slightly disguised Kantianism:

> [T]he main 'Kantian' dimension of Laclau lies in his acceptance of the unbridgeable gap between the enthusiasm for the impossible Goal of a political engagement and its more modest realizable content.... My claim is that if we accept such a gap as the ultimate horizon of political engagement, does it not leave us with a choice apropos of such an engagement: either we must blind ourselves to the necessary ultimate failure of our endeavour – regress to naivety, and let ourselves be caught up in the enthusiasm – or we must adopt a stance of cynical distance, participating in the game while being fully aware that the result will be disappointing? (pp. 316–17)

(2) After falsely assimilating my position to that of multicultural identity politics, Žižek concludes: 'However, this justified rejection of the fullness of post-revolutionary Society does *not* justify the conclusion that we have to renounce any project of a global social transformation, and limit ourselves to partial problems to be solved: the jump from a critique of the "metaphysics of presence" to anti-utopian "reformist" gradualist politics is an illegitimate short circuit' (p. 101). (3) Behind the historical narrative of the increasing disintegration of classical essentialist Marxism and the emergence of a plurality of new popular historical actors, Žižek argues, lies a certain 'resignation', an 'acceptance of capitalism as "the only game in town"', the renunciation of any real attempt to overcome the existing capitalist liberal regime' (p. 95). (4) '[A]gainst the proponents of the critique of global capitalism, of the "logic of Capital", Laclau argues that capitalism is an inconsistent composite of heterogeneous features which were combined as the result of a contingent historical constellation, not a homogeneous Totality obeying a common underlying Logic' (p. 225). (5) And, finally, the kernel of Žižek's argument, which would ground our different conceptions of social identities: 'my point of contention with Laclau here is that I do not accept that all elements which enter into hegemonic struggle are in

principle equal: in the series of struggles (economic, political, feminist, ecological, ethnic, etc.) there is always *one* [class struggle] which, while it is part of the chain, secretly overdetermines its very horizon. This contamination of the universal by the particular is stronger than the struggle for hegemony.... [I]t structures in advance *the very terrain* on which the multitude of particular contents fight for hegemony' (p. 320).

Let us explore this accumulation of misrepresentations. To start with, the reader of this book will have no difficulty in locating Žižek's basic misreading of my work.[9] In characterizing my approach, he opposes 'global social transformation' to partial changes, and assimilates the latter to gradualist reformism. This opposition makes no sense, and the assimilation is a purely arbitrary invention. I have never spoken of 'gradualism' – a term that, in my theoretical approach, could only mean a differential logic unimpeded by any kind of equivalence or: a world of punctual demands that would not enter into any kind of popular articulation. Popular identities, in my sense, always constitute totalities. It is true that I have spoken of partial struggles and demands, but this partiality has nothing to do with gradualism: as this book makes sufficiently clear, my notion of partiality converges with what in psychoanalysis is called a 'partial object' – that is, a partiality functioning as a totality. So what Žižek is ignoring is the whole logic of the *objet petit a*, which, as I argued above, is identical to the hegemonic logic. That the object is 'elevated to the dignity of the Thing' is what Žižek seems to exclude as a political possibility. The alternative he presents is: either we have access to the Thing as such, or we have pure partialities not linked by any totalizing effect. I think that a Lacanian such as Žižek should know better.

For the same reason, the partiality of a hegemonic horizon does not involve any kind of resignation. Copjec's argument regarding the object of the drive's being able to bring about satisfaction is quite relevant here. For a subject within a hegemonic configuration, that configuration is everything there is; it is not a moment within an endless approach towards an Ideal. For that reason, Žižek's references to Kant are entirely misplaced. For Kant the regulative role of the Idea does result in an infinite approach towards the noumenal world, but nothing of the kind happens in the case of a hegemonic identification. Infinite approach to what? The alternative Žižek presents – either naive expectations or cynicism – collapses once a radical investment has been made in a partial object (once the object 'has been elevated to the dignity of the Thing'). And this object, albeit always partial, could involve radical change or global social transformation, but even when this is the case, the moment of radical investment will necessarily be present. At no point will the Thing as such be touched directly without its representation through an object. In fact, there is no such 'Thing' other than as a retrospective assumption. But this partiality of the object does not involve any resignation or renunciation.

What is, however, the true root of this theoretical disagreement? It lies, I think, in the fact that Žižek's analysis is entirely eclectic, for it is grounded in two incompatible ontologies: one linked to psychoanalysis and the Freudian discovery of the unconscious, the other to the Hegelian/Marxian philosophy of history. Žižek performs all kinds of implausible contortions to put the two together, but he is clearly far from successful. His favourite method is to try to establish superficial homologies. At some point he asserts, for instance, that capitalism is the Real – in the Lacanian sense – of contemporary society, since it is what always returns. But if indefinite repetition were the only feature inherent to the Real, we could equally say that cold is the Real of capitalist society because it returns every winter. A true metaphorical analogy – one with an epistemological value – would have to show that capitalism is beyond social symbolization: something that Žižek would find impossible to prove.

According to Žižek, I maintain that capitalism is the conjunctural and incoherent combination of a multiplicity of heterogeneous features. Needless to say, I have never said such a stupid thing. What I *have* actually said – and this is entirely different – is that the coherence of capitalism as a social formation cannot be derived from the mere logical analysis of the contradictions implicit in the commodity form, for the social effectivity of capitalism depends on its relation to a heterogeneous outside that it can control through unstable power relations, but which cannot be derived from its own endogenous logic. In other words, capitalist domination is not self-determined, derivable from its own form, but the result of a hegemonic construction, so that its centrality derives, like anything else in society, from an overdetermination of heterogeneous elements. For that reason, something such as a relation of forces can exist in society – a 'war of position' in the Gramscian sense. If capitalist domination could be derived from the analysis of its mere form – if we were confronted with a homogeneous, self-developing logic – any kind of resistance would be utterly useless, at least until that logic developed its own internal contradictions (a conclusion with which the Marxism of the Second International was flirting, and Žižek is not in fact far from reaching).

Žižek says his disagreement with me stems from the fact that, for him, the elements entering the hegemonic struggle are not equal; there is always one that, while 'it is part of the chain, overdetermines its very horizon'. This means, according to him, that there is something more fundamental than the struggle for hegemony, something that structures the terrain on which the latter takes place. The assertion that there is an essential unevenness of the elements entering the hegemonic struggle is something with which I can certainly concur – the theory of hegemony is precisely the theory of this unevenness. Yet Žižek presents not a *historical* argument, but a *transcendental* one. For him, in every possible society this determining role corresponds necessarily to the economy (it seems, at this point, that we are going back to those naive 1960s distinctions between 'determination in the last instance', 'dominant role', 'relative autonomy', and so on). The first thing I can say about Žižek's empty gesture towards classical Marxism is that it misuses the Freudian category of overdetermination. For Freud, the overdetermining instance depends entirely on a personal history – there is no element that is overdetermining in and by itself. If Žižek, however, is now telling us that some elements are historical a priori, predestined to be overdetermining, he is entirely abandoning the Freudian camp – he is in fact closer to Jung. In his desperation to defend 'determination in the last instance by the economy', Žižek speaks at times of an ultimate redoubt of naturalism that should be maintained. This will not do. One cannot put together two incompatible ontologies. Either overdetermination is universal in its effects – in which case, as Copjec has recently written, the theory of the drives occupies the space of classical ontology – or it is a regional category surrounded by an area of full determination, which becomes the field of a fundamental ontology, while legislating the limits within which overdetermination is able to operate.

The irony is that Žižek did not need this clumsy eclectic discourse to show the centrality of economic processes in capitalist societies. Nobody seriously denies this centrality. The difficulties come when he transforms 'the economy' into a self-defined homogeneous instance operating as the ground of society – when, that is, he reduces it to a Hegelian explanatory model. The truth is that the economy is, like anything else in society, the locus of an overdetermination of social logics, and its centrality is the result of the obvious fact that the material reproduction of society has more repercussions for social processes than do other instances. This does not mean that capitalist reproduction can be reduced to a single, self-defining mechanism.

Here we reach the crux of the difficulties in Žižek's approach. On the one hand, he is committed to a theory of the full revolutionary act that would operate in its own name, without being invested in any object outside itself. On the other hand, the capitalist system, as the dominating, underlying mechanism, is the reality with which the emancipatory act has to break. The conclusion from both premises is that there is no valid emancipatory struggle except one that is fully and directly anti-capitalist. In his words: 'I believe in the central structuring role of the anti-capitalist struggle.'[10] The problem, however, is this: he gives no indication of what an anti-capitalist struggle might be. Žižek quickly dismisses multicultural, anti-sexist and anti-racist struggles as not being directly anti-capitalist. Nor does he sanction the traditional aims of the Left, linked more directly to the economy: the demands for higher wages, for industrial democracy, for control of the labour process, for a progressive distribution of income, are not proposed as anti-capitalist either. Does he imagine that the Luddites' proposal to destroy all the machines would bring an end to capitalism? Not a single line in Žižek's work gives an example of what he considers an anti-capitalist struggle. One is left wondering whether he is anticipating an invasion of beings from another planet, or as he once suggested, some kind of ecological catastrophe that would not transform the world but cause it to fall apart.

So where has the whole argument gone wrong? In its very premises. Since Žižek refuses to apply the hegemonic logic to strategico-political thought, he is stranded in a blind alley. He has to dismiss all 'partial' struggles as internal to the 'system' (whatever that means); and since the 'Thing' is unattainable, he is left without any concrete historical actor for his anti-capitalist struggle. Conclusion: Žižek cannot provide any theory of the emancipatory subject.[11] Since, at the same time, his systemic totality, being a ground, is regulated exclusively by its own internal laws, the only option is to wait for these laws to produce the totality of its effects. *Ergo*: political nihilism.

If, however, we put into question both of Žižek's premises we produce a scenario in which there is more room for hope. First, let us address the partiality of the struggles. As we have seen, there is no struggle or demand without an area of equivalential irradiation. Žižek is wrong to present struggles such as the multicultural ones as secondary and totally integrable within the existing system. To present the problem as a question of which term is more fundamental is wholly inappropriate. As we have seen, centrality is always linked to the formation of popular identities that are nothing more than an overdetermination of democratic demands. The centrality of each will therefore depend not on its location within an abstract geometry of social effects, as Žižek imagines, but on its concrete articulation with other demands in a popular ensemble. Obviously, this does not guarantee the 'progressive' character of that whole, but it does create a terrain within which various hegemonic attempts can take place. Secondly, we can see clearly why there is not something like an anti-capitalist struggle *per se*, but anti-capitalist effects that can derive, at a certain ruptural point, from the articulation of a plurality of struggles. To mention only revolutionary movements, none of the major upheavals of the past century – not the Russian, the Chinese, the Cuban or the Vietnamese revolutions –

declared themselves mainly anti-capitalist. What I have said in my psychoanalytic argument about the 'breast value' of milk can be referred to here as the 'anti-capitalist' value of a political investment. A problem remains, however: What is the semantic content of 'anti-capitalism'? Is anti-capitalism an empty signifier – one of the names of the lack, mentioned above – in which case 'capitalism' would be a construction of the anti-capitalist movement, the 'other side' of a frontier constituting the unity of the camp of anti-capitalist equivalences? Or is capitalism, rather, the underlying logic of the whole system, in which case anti-capitalism would only be an internal effect of the very logic of capitalism itself? Here we can see exactly what separates Žižek from me. He remains within the field of total immanence – which, in Hegelian terms, can only be a logical immanence – while, for me, the moment of negativity (radical investment, opaqueness of representation, division of the object) is irreducible. This is why, for me, the central historical actor – which at some point could empirically be a 'class' – will always be a 'people' of sorts, while for Žižek it will always be a 'class' *tout court*. Although he is closer in this respect to Hegel than to Lacan, I think I am closer to Lacan than to Hegel.

Hardt and Negri: God will provide

While Žižek tries to ground the identity of social actors in the 'historical a priori' of a determination in the last instance, Hardt and Negri avoid any such attribution of a transcendental ontological privilege.[12] For them, all social struggles, though unconnected, converge in the constitution of an emancipatory subject that they call 'the multitude.' Now, apparently there would be some analogy between their 'multitude' and what, throughout this book, I have called the 'people', but this analogy is purely superficial. Let us briefly consider the main features of their approach in so far as it is related to the subject of our research. Their starting point is the Deleuzian/Nietzschean notion of immanence, which Hardt and Negri connect to the secularizing process of modern times. A secular immanentism, however, requires the operation of a universal mechanism and the emergence, at some point, of a universal historical actor. Yet everything depends on the way this universality is conceived: whether as a partial, politically constructed universality, or as an underlying and spontaneous one. Radical immanentism is, obviously, only compatible with the latter position, and Hardt and Negri resolutely adopt it. The former position – which is mine – requires a negativity that fragments the social ground and is irreducible to pure immanence. Radical immanence, for Hardt and Negri, reaches its highest point of visibility with the constitution of Empire, an entity without boundaries and – in opposition to old imperialism – without a centre. The features of this formless but self-defined totality are transmitted to the multitude as Empire's grave-digger – in a way reminiscent of Marx's description of the universalization brought about by capitalism as a prelude to the emergence of the proletariat as the universal class. Sovereignty in modern times would have been a historical defeat for the multitude, as it would have entailed the re-establishment of the absolute power of the kings, and mechanisms of representation that would have fettered that spontaneous convergence that is the only mechanism making possible the creation of the unity of the multitude. How does this unifying mechanism operate? According to *Empire*, it does not involve any kind of political mediation. Because it is only natural, according to the authors, that the oppressed revolt, their unity is simply the expression of a spontaneous tendency to converge. Unity, as a gift from Heaven, occupies in their theory the same place we attribute to hegemonic articulation. Since vertically separated struggles do not need to be horizontally linked, every political construction disappears. The only principle ensuring the union of the multitude around a common goal is what Hardt and Negri call 'being against': it is a matter of being against everything, everywhere. The aim is universal *desertion*. This process is already taking place through the nomadic, rhizomatic movements of people across frontiers.

What should we think of this theoretical sequence? One cannot avoid being struck by the superficiality of the whole analysis. Rather than point out its only too obvious weaknesses, let us unveil their sources, for they are not simply errors, but the results of mistaken ways of dealing with real and important issues. Let us first take up the category of 'being against'. At face value, it does not make any sense: people are not against everything, everywhere. If, however, we try – paraphrasing Marx – 'to extract the rational kernel from the mystical shell', we will see that an important problem lies behind this clumsy formulation: the problem that, in this book, I have tried to tackle in terms of 'social heterogeneity'. While for Marx the unity of the revolutionary subject – the proletariat – was the expression of an essential homogeneity resulting from the simplification of social structure under capitalism, Hardt and Negri's multitude does not deny the heterogeneity of social actors, neither does it ground unity, *à la* Žižek, in the transcendentally established priority of one struggle over all others. I have also, in my notion of the 'people', recognized the basic heterogeneity of social demands, and their convergence in collective entities, which are not the expression of any underlying mechanism separate from the forms of their articulation. Even the notion of 'being against', without concrete referent, evokes, in a faint way, what I have called 'empty signifiers'. Where, in that case, does the difference lie? Quite simply, in our different approaches to the question of political articulation. For me, the emergence of unity out of heterogeneity presupposes the establishment of equivalential logics and the production of empty signifiers. In *Empire*, it results from people's natural tendency to fight against oppression. It does not matter if one calls this tendency a gift from Heaven or a consequence of immanence. *Deus sive Natura*. What is important is that Hardt and Negri's approach to this question leads them to oversimplify the political process. If there is a natural tendency to revolt, no political construction of the subject of the revolt is needed. But society is far more complicated than this simplistic formulation allows. People are never just 'against', but against some particular things and for others, and the construction of a wider 'against' – a more global popular identity – can only be the result of a protracted political war of position (which can, of course, fail). As for the picture of an imperial totality without a centre – a sort of Spinozan eternity – from which internal poles of power would have disappeared, this does not fare any better. We have only to look at what has happened on the international scene since 9/11.

Something similar can be said about another aspect of Hardt and Negri's argument. It absolutely privileges tactics over strategy. Again, there is in this something with which I can concur. The socialist tradition advocated a total subordination of tactics to strategy as a result of its vision of history as based in the operation of necessary laws that made long-term predictions possible and its notion of social agents as constituted around rigid class positions. Today, however, because the future is seen as open to contingent variations, and the heterogeneity of social actors is increasingly recognized, the relation of strategy and tactics is reversed: strategies are, necessarily, more short term, and the autonomy of tactical interventions has increased. This, however, has led Hardt and Negri to an extreme – and, in my view, mistaken – conclusion: strategy disappears totally, while unconnected tactical interventions become the only game in town. Again: only punctual vertical struggles are recognized as objects of a militant engagement, while their articulation is left to God (or to Nature). In other words, we have the complete eclipse of politics. The approach of Hardt and Negri evinces the worst limitations of the Italian *operaismo* of the 1960s.

If we now compare Žižek's approach with Hardt and Negri's, we find that, in both cases, their theoretical and political impasses derive from the same theoretical root: their ultimate dependence on one form of immanence or another – an immanence that is, admittedly, different in both cases. In the case of Žižek, as I have pointed out, we are dealing with a logical immanence of a Hegelian type. This is reflected in his attempt to transfer social unevenness to the transcendental level of a social a priori. In actual fact, Žižek's thought retreats from all the encouraging promises of his early work. His insightful approach to the question of naming, which I have discussed, loses most of its edge once naming finds conceptual limits in a previous transcendental constitution of the object – limits that no naming can transgress. Nor can he maintain the fundamental role of affect. There cannot be *radical* investment in an *objet petit a* if an a priori framework determines what entities will be the objects of such an investment. Finally, Žižek has changed his view as far as negativity is concerned. He had enthusiastically greeted my analysis of the irreducible negativity of antagonism, which he saw as the re-emergence, within the field of social theory, of the Lacanian Real. Now he argues against me, that the determination of the subjects of antagonism is dictated by an a priori morphology of history. This amounts to saying that the Symbolic is an ultimate framework establishing the limits within which the Real can operate. This is utterly un-Lacanian. Žižek's project collapses in an eclecticism that his usual army of jokes, puns and cross-references can hardly conceal.

The immanence with which Hardt and Negri operate is not Hegelian, but Spinozan-Deleuzian. They do not share Žižek's Lacanian scruples, so they manage in this respect to be more coherent and non-eclectic. But precisely for that reason, the limitations of a purely immanentist approach are shown more clearly in their work than in Žižek's. As I said above, the authors of *Empire* have no coherent explanation of the source of social antagonisms. The most they can do is postulate, as a sort of Spinozan *conatus*, people's natural and healthy propensity to revolt. But presenting this postulate as an ungrounded *fiat* has several serious consequences for their theory, some of which I have already indicated. First, they tend to oversimplify the tendencies towards unity operating within the multitude. They have a somewhat triumphalist and exaggeratedly optimistic vision of these tendencies, although one can never decide, on the basis of their account, whether they are virtual or actual. Secondly, and for the same reason, they tend to reduce the importance of the confrontations taking place within Empire. But thirdly, and most importantly, they are unable to give any coherent account of the nature of the break that would lead from Empire to the power of the multitude. I am not, of course, talking about a futurological description of the revolutionary break, but about something more basic: what does a revolutionary break consist of? I would argue that this explanatory failure – which has serious consequences for socio-political analysis – is not peculiar to *Empire*, but is inherent in any radical, immanentist approach, whose explanations are always uneasily suspended in an undecided terrain between *break* and *continuity*. Hegel's dialectics was a failed attempt to provide a synthesis capable of reintegrating these two polar moments into a unity. Most of the difficulties we found in Žižek's analysis can also be referred back to this issue.

These difficulties cannot be solved on the terrain of radical immanence. What we need therefore is a change of terrain. This change, however, cannot consist in a return to a fully fledged transcendence. The social terrain is structured, in my view, not as completely immanent or as the result of some transcendent structure, but through what we could call *failed transcendence*. Transcendence appears within the social as the presence of an absence. It is around a constitutive lack that the social is organized. It is easy to see how we can move from here to the main categories that have informed our analysis: absent fullness, radical investment, *objet petit a*, hegemony and so forth. This is the ultimate point at which *multitude* and *people* as theoretical categories part company. I will move now to another contemporary attempt – one of the most important, in my view – to think the specificity of the 'people'.

Rancière: the rediscovery of the people

How does Rancière construct his concept of the 'people'? He starts by pointing to a crucial disagreement between political philosophy and politics: the former is not a theoretical discussion of the latter but an attempt to neutralize its disruptive social effects. Where does the disagreement lie? Essentially, in the fact that, while the idea of a good, ordered community depends on subordinating its parts to a whole – on *counting* them as parts – there is a paradoxical part within this counting, a part that, without ceasing to be a part, presents itself as the whole. How does this happen? Rancière begins his analysis by reflecting on the concept of community in classical Greek philosophy. He finds there an opposition between relations among individuals based on a notion of *arithmetical* equality – which governs commercial exchanges and the assignment of penalties in criminal law – and those based on a notion of *geometrical* harmony – which ascribes to each part a specific function within the economy of the whole. A good, ordered community would be one in which the geometrical principle played the ultimate ruling role. This possibility, this distribution – or counting – of agents according to functions, is interrupted by an anomaly: the emergence of something that is essentially uncountable and that, as such, distorts the very principle of counting. This is the emergence of the *demos* – the 'people' – which, while being a part, also claims to be the whole.

In *Politics*, Aristotle tries to determine three *axiai* of the community: the wealth of a small number (the *oligoi*), the virtue or excellence of the *aristoi*, and the freedom belonging to all. The difficulty here, as Rancière points out, is that the three principles are not regional categories within a coherent ontological classification. While wealth is an objectively determinable category, virtue is less so, and when we arrive at the 'people's' freedom we enter into something that ceases to have a particular determinable location. Freedom, as an axiological principle, is at once an attribute of the members of the community at large and the *only* defining feature – the only communitarian function – of a particular group of people. We have therefore a particularity, the role of which is to be the embodiment of universality. This distorts the whole geometrical model of the good community. The ambiguity we have described between the 'people' as both *populus* and *plebs* has prepared the way for us to understand what Rancière is talking about. Once we reach this point, we can fully grasp his distinction between *police* and *politics*: while police involves the attempt to reduce all differences to partialities within the communitarian whole – to conceive any difference as mere particularity, and refer the moment of universality to a pure, uncontaminated instance (the philosopher-king in Plato, state bureaucracy in Hegel, the proletariat in Marx) – politics involves an ineradicable distortion, a part that functions simultaneously as the whole. While the task of political philosophy traditionally has been to reduce *politics* to *police*, truly political thought and practice would consist in liberating the political moment from its enthralment to policed societal frameworks.

There are two aspects in which Rancière's analysis comes very close to my own. First, the emphasis on a part that functions as a whole: what we have characterized as the unevenness inherent in the hegemonic operation is conceptualized by Rancière as an uncountable that disrupts the very principle of counting and, in that way, makes possible the emergence of the political as the set of operations taking place around that constitutive impossibility. Secondly, Rancière's notion of a class that is not a class, that has as a particular determination something in the nature of a universal exclusion – of the principle of exclusion as such – is not far from what I have called 'emptiness'. He perceives very acutely the universal function of particular struggles when they are invested with a symbolic meaning which transcends their own particularity. He refers, for example, to the case of Jeanne Deroin who, in trying to vote in a legislative election in 1849, exposed through her action the contradiction between universal suffrage and her gendered exclusion from the universal. Similarly, undocumented immigrant workers, stripped of their identity as workers and reduced to a purely ethnic identity, are dispossessed of those forms of political subjectivity that would have made them part of the counted.

Although in many respects my analysis is close to that of Rancière, there are two points on which they differ. First, the way of conceptualizing 'emptiness': Rancière rightly argues that political conflict differs from any conflict of 'interests' in so far as the latter is always dominated by the partiality of what is countable, while what is at stake in the former is the principle of countability as such. I fully endorse his argument up to that point. But this means that there is no a priori guarantee that the 'people' as a historical actor will be constituted around a progressive identity (from the point of view of the Left). Precisely because what is put into question is not the *ontic* content of what is being counted but the *ontological* principle of countability as such, the discursive forms that this putting into question will adopt will be largely indeterminate. Rancière identifies the possibility of politics too much, I believe, with the possibility of an emancipatory politics, without taking into account other alternatives – for example, that the uncounted might construct their uncountability in ways that are ideologically incompatible with what either Rancière or I would advocate politically (in a Fascist direction, for instance). It would be historically and theoretically wrong to think that a

Fascist alternative inhabits the area of the countable entirely. To explore the system of alternatives, we need a further step that Rancière has not taken so far: namely, an examination of the forms of representation to which uncountability can give rise. Objects that are impossible but necessary always find ways of gaining access – in a distorted way, no doubt – to the field of representation.

The second point on which my views differ slightly from those of Rancière is in the conceptualization of the 'people'. He asserts:

> It is in the name of the wrong done them by the other parties that the people identify with the whole of the community. Whoever has no part – the poor of ancient times, the third estate, the modern proletariat – cannot in fact have any part other than all or nothing. On top of this, it is through the existence of this part of those who have no part, of this nothing that is all, that the community exists as a political community – that is, as divided by a fundamental dispute, by a dispute to do with the counting of the community's parts even more than of their 'rights'. The people are not one class among others. They are the class of the wrong that harms the community and establishes it as a 'community' of the just and the unjust.[13]

I can endorse this analysis as far as the formation of popular subjectivity is concerned. The way Rancière enumerates the figures of the 'people' is most revealing: it is clear that we are not dealing with a sociological description, with social actors having a particular location, precisely because the presence of the 'people' ruins all geometrical differentiation of function and place. As we have seen, an equivalential logic can cut across very different groups in so far as they are all on the same side of an antagonistic frontier. The notion of the proletariat as described by Rancière stresses the non-sociological nature of the 'people's' identity. Thus:

> The proletariat are neither manual workers nor the labor classes. They are the class of the uncounted that only exists in the very declaration in which

they are counted as those of no account. The name *proletarian* defines neither a set of properties (manual labor, industrial labor, destitution, etc.) that would be shared equally by a multitude of individuals nor a collective body, embodying a principle of which those individuals would be members ... 'Proletarian' subjectification defines a subject of wrong. (p. 38)

There is in Rancière, however, an ambiguity that limits the important theoretical consequences that can be derived from his analysis. After neatly cutting any link between his notion of the proletariat and the sociological description of a group, he suddenly starts to make certain sociological concessions. For example, he identifies the institution of politics with the institution of class struggle. True, he immediately qualifies this statement: 'The proletariat is not so much a class as the dissolution of all classes; this is what constitutes its universality, as Marx would say.... Politics is the setting-up of a dispute between classes that are not really classes. "True" classes are, or should be, real parts of society, categories that correspond to functions' (p. 18). But this formulation will not do. The reference to Marx is not particularly helpful, because for Marx the centrality of the proletariat and its marking the dissolution of all classes was the result of a process described in very precise sociological terms: the simplification of social structure under capitalism. The relation between actual workers and proletarians is far more intimate than it is for Rancière. And, of course, while for Rancière class struggle and politics cannot be differentiated, for Marx the disappearance of politics and the withering away of the state are consubstantial with the establishment of a classless society. For Marx, increasing social homogeneity was the precondition of a proletarian victory, while for Rancière an irreducible heterogeneity is the very condition of popular struggles.

What conclusions can we draw from these reflections? Simply that it is necessary to go beyond the notion of 'class struggle' and its eclectic combination of political logics and sociological description. I do not see the point of talking about class struggle simply to add that it is the struggle of classes that are not classes. The incipient movement, in

Gramsci, from 'classes' to 'collective wills' needs to be completed. Only then can the potential consequences of Rancière's fruitful analysis be fully drawn.

It is time to conclude. A comparison of my project with the three approaches I have discussed, renders its specific nature and dimensions more visible. Against Žižek, I maintain that the overdetermined nature of all political identities is not established a priori in a transcendental horizon, but is always the result of concrete processes and practices. This is what gives naming and affect their constitutive roles. Against the authors of *Empire*, I would posit that the moment of articulation, although it is certainly more complex than simple formulas – such as party mediation – advocated in the past, has lost nothing of its relevance and centrality. When it comes to Rancière, the answer is more difficult, for I share some of the central presuppositions of his approach. The 'people' is, for him as for me, the central protagonist of politics, and politics is what prevents the social from crystallizing in a fully fledged society, an entity defined by its own clear-cut distinctions and functions. That is why, in my view, conceptualizing social antagonisms and collective identities is so important, and the need to go beyond stereotyped and almost meaningless formulas such as 'class struggle' is so pressing.

There is an ethical imperative in intellectual work, which Leonardo called 'obstinate rigour'. It means, in practical terms – and especially when one is dealing with political matters, which are always highly charged with emotion – that one has to resist several temptations. They can be condensed into a single formula: never succumb to the terrorism of words. As Freud wrote, one must avoid making concessions to faint-heartedness: 'One can never tell where that road may lead one; one gives way first in words, and then little by little in substance too.'[14] One of the main forms this faintheartedness takes in our time is the replacement of analysis with ethical condemnation. Some subjects, such as Fascism or the Holocaust, are particularly prone to this type of exercise. There is nothing wrong, of course, in condemning the Holocaust. The problem begins when condemnation replaces explanation, which is what happens when some phenomena are seen as aberrations dispossessed of any rationally graspable cause. We can only begin to understand Fascism if we see it as one of the internal possibilities inherent to contemporary societies, not as something beyond any rational explanation. The same happens with terms that have positive emotional connotations. On the Left, terms such as 'class struggle', 'determination in the last instance by the economy' or 'centrality of the working class' function – or functioned until recently – as emotionally charged fetishes, the meanings of which were increasingly less clear, although their discursive appeal could not be diminished.

The politico-intellectual task as I see it today – and to which I have tried to make a modest contribution here – is to go beyond the horizon drawn by this faintheartedness, in its praises and in its condemnations. The return of the 'people' as a political category can be seen as a contribution to this expansion of horizons, because it helps to present other categories – such as class – for what they are: contingent and particular forms of articulating demands, not an ultimate core from which the nature of the demands themselves could be explained. This widening of horizons is a precondition for thinking the forms of our political engagement in the era of what I have called globalized capitalism. The dislocations inherent to social relations in the world in which we live are deeper than in the past, so categories that synthesized past social experience are becoming increasingly obsolete. It is necessary to reconceptualize the autonomy of social demands, the logic of their articulation, and the nature of the collective entities resulting from them. This effort – which is necessarily collective – is the real task ahead. Let us hope that we will be equal to it.

Notes

1 Populism: Ambiguities and Paradoxes

1 Gino Germani, *Authoritarianism, Fascism and National Populism*, New Brunswick, NJ, Transaction Books, 1978, p. 88.

2 Margaret Canovan, *Populism*, London, Junction Books, 1981. At this point, I am referring only to this early comprehensive study. In the second part of this book I shall refer to Canovan's recent work, which opens a variety of new perspectives.

3 Ghita Ionescu and Ernest Gellner (eds), *Populism: Its Meaning and National Characteristics*, London, Macmillan, 1969.

4 Canovan, *Populism*, p. 4.

5 Ibid., p. 13.

6 Ibid., p. 58.

7 Ibid., p. 294.

8 Ibid., p. 294.

9 Ibid., pp. 295–6.

10 Donald MacRae, 'Populism as an Ideology', in Ionescu and Gellner (eds), *Populism*, p. 168.

11 Ibid., p. 164.

12 Peter Wiles, 'A Syndrome, not a Doctrine: Some Elementary Theses on Populism', in Ionescu and Gellner (eds), *Populism*, pp. 163–79.

13 Ibid., p. 178.

14   Kenneth Minogue, 'Populism as a Political Movement', in Ionescu and Gellner, *Populism*, pp. 197–211.

15   Ibid., p. 198.

16   Ibid., p. 208.

17   Ibid., p. 209.

18   Ibid., p. 199.

19   See especially pp. 204–8.

20   See Ernesto Laclau and Chantal Mouffe, *Hegemony and Socialist Strategy*, London and New York, Verso, 1985, Chapter 3.

21   Peter Worsley, 'The Concept of Populism', in Ionescu and Gellner (eds), *Populism*, pp. 212–50.

22   Ibid., p. 213.

23   Ibid., p. 245.

24   Ibid., p. 229.

25   Ibid., pp. 245–6.

2 Le Bon: Suggestion and Distorted Representations

1   Gustave Le Bon, *The Crowd*, New Brunswick and London, Transactions Publishers, 1995, with a new introduction by Robert A. Nye. [Originally published in French in 1895 as *Psychologies des foules*.]

2   Ibid., p. 124.

3   Ibid., pp. 124–5.

4   Ibid., p. 125.

5   Ibid., pp. 126 and 129.

6   Ibid., pp. 128–9.

7   Ibid., p. 132.

8   Ibid., p. 146.

9   Ibid., p. 147.

10   Ibid., p. 148.

11   Saussure's examples come from the *Cours de linguistique générale, édition critique* by Tullio de Mauro, Paris, Payot, pp. 224–5. For an analysis of this aspect of the Saussurean approach see Claudine Normand, *Métaphore et Concept*, Brussels, Edition Complexe, 1976, pp. 27–37.

12 I take the analysis of this aspect of Freud's study of the Rat Man from Bruce Fink, *The Lacanian Subject*, Princeton, NJ, Princeton University Press, 1995, p. 23. For a study of the question of the relationship between linguistic formalism and the elimination of the question of substance from the duality signifier/signified, see my essay 'Identity and Hegemony: The Role of Universality in the Constitution of Political Logics', in Judith Butler, Ernesto Laclau and Slavoj Žižek, *Contingency, Hegemony, Universality: Contemporary Dialogues on the Left*, London and New York, Verso, 2000, pp. 68–71.

13 *Benjamin Franklin's Autobiographical Writings*, selected and edited by Carl van Doren, New York, Viking Press, 1945, p. 625.

14 Le Bon, *The Crowd*, pp. 86–7.

15 Sigmund Freud, *Group Psychology and the Analysis of the Ego*, in James Strachey (ed.), *The Standard Edition of the Complete Psychological Works of Sigmund Freud*, London, 2001, vol. 18, p. 89.

16 Le Bon, *The Crowd*, p. 52.

17 Serge Moscovici, 'The Discovery of the Masses', in Carl F. Graumann and Serge Moscovici (eds), *Changing Conceptions of Crowd Mind and Behaviour*, New York – Berlin – Heidelberg – Tokyo, Springer-Verlag, 1986, p. 11.

3 Suggestion, Imitation, Identification

1 H. A. Taine, *The Revolution*, London, Daldy, Isbister & Co., 1878, vol. I, pp. 12–14.

2 Ibid., pp. 79–80.

3 For the information concerning Taine and his intellectual context I am particularly indebted to Susanna Barrows, *Distorting Mirrors: Visions of the Crowd in Late Nineteenth Century France*, New Haven, CT, Yale University Press, 1981, and Jaap van Ginneken, *Crowds, Psychology and Politics, 1871–1899*, Cambridge, Cambridge University Press, 1992.

4 Barrows, *Distorting Mirrors*, p. 43.

5 Ibid., p. 86.

6 Van Ginneken, *Crowds, Psychology and Politics*, p. 26.

7 As Barrows (*Distorting Mirrors*, p. 80), reminds us, George Rudé's studies on *The Crowd in the French Revolution* (Oxford, Oxford University Press, 1959)

show that alcoholism played only a minor role in the events of April and July 1789.

8   Van Ginneken, *Crowds, Psychology and Politics*, p. 43.

9   See 'Metaphors of Fear: Women and Alcoholics', in Barrows, *Distorting Mirrors*, pp. 43–71, from which I derive the information to be found below.

10 Barrows, *Distorting Mirrors*, p. 60.

11 My main sources of information for the early stages of hypnotism in France are Dominique Barrucand, *Histoire de l'hypnose en France*, Paris, Presses Universitaires de France, 1967; and Henri F. Ellenberger, *The Discovery of the Unconscious: The History and Evolution of Dynamic Psychiatry*, New York, Basic Books, 1970. On Italian criminology, see Barrows, *Distorting Mirrors*; Van Ginneken, *Crowds, Psychology and Politics*. On the reception of hypnotic theory by crowd theorists, see Erika Apfelbaum and Gregory R. McGuire, 'Models of Suggestive Influence and the Disqualification of the Social Crowd', in Carl F. Graumann and Serge Moscovici (eds), *Changing Conceptions of Crowd Mind and Behaviour*, New York – Berlin – Heidelberg – Tokyo, Springer-Verlag, 1986.

12 Apfelbaum and McGuire, *Models of Suggestive Influence*, p. 32.

13 Ibid., p. 44.

14 Ibid., p. 39.

15 Ibid., p. 45.

16 *L'Uomo deliquente*, Part I, Chapter 5, p. 137 (second edition, 1877). Quoted by Van Ginneken, *Crowds, Psychology and Politics*, pp. 61–2.

17 See Barrows, *Distorting Mirrors*, pp. 129–30.

18 See Van Ginneken, *Crowds, Psychology and Politics*, Chapter 5.

19 There is a recent edition published by Presses Universitaires de France, 1989.

20 Gabriel Tarde, 'Les foules et les sectes criminelles', in *L'Opinion et la foule*, Paris, Presses Universitaires de France, 1989, p. 145 (all quotations from Tarde have been translated by me).

21 Ibid., pp. 146–7.

22 Ibid., p. 148.

23 Ibid., p. 173.

24 Ibid., p. 175

25　Here, I follow the description of these changes given by Van Ginneken, *Crowds, Psychology and Politics*, pp. 217–19. It is worth stressing that Freud's references to Tarde are somewhat unfair, since they do not take this evolution into account. Freud asserts in *Group Psychology*: 'Tarde calls [suggestion] "imitation"; but we cannot help agreeing with a writer who protests that imitation comes under the concept of suggestion, and is in fact one of its results (brugeilles, 1913)' (Freud, Standard Edition, vol. XVIII, p. 88). This is certainly true of *Les Lois de l'imitation*, to which Freud refers, but much less so of Tarde's later writings, published well before the time at which Freud wrote his book.

26　Van Ginneken, *Crowds, Psychology and Politics*, pp. 217–19.

27　Tarde, 'Le public et la foule', in *L'Opinion et la foule*, p. 31.

28　Ibid., p. 38.

29　Ibid., p. 39.

30　Tarde uses the term 'race' in its nineteenth-century sense: 'the English race', 'the French race', 'the Italian race', and so on.

31　Tarde, 'Le public et la foule', p. 41.

32　Ibid., p. 46.

33　Ibid., p. 49.

34　Ibid., p. 70.

35　Ibid.

36　William McDougall, *The Group Mind*, Cambridge, Cambridge University Press, 1920, p. 23.

37　Ibid., p. 25.

38　Ibid., p. 40.

39　Ibid., p. 45.

40　Ibid., p. 48.

41　Ibid., pp. 49–50.

42　Ibid., pp. 52–3.

43　Ibid., p. 54.

44　Ibid., p. 87.

45　S. Freud, *Group Psychology and the Analysis of the Ego* (1921), in *The Standard Edition of the Psychological Works of Sigmund Freud*, Volume XVIII, p. 69, London, Vintage, 2001. All subsequent quotations are from this edition.

46　Ibid.

47   Thus: 'Further reflection will show us in what respect this statement [that group psychology is the oldest psychology] requires correction. Individual psychology must, on the contrary, be just as old as group psychology, for from the first there were two kinds of psychologies, that of the individual members of the group and that of the father, chief, or leader. The members of the group were subject to ties just as we see them to-day, but the father of the primal horde was free. … Consistency leads us to assume that his ego had few libidinal ties; he loved no one but himself, or other people only in so far as they served his needs. To objects his ego gave away no more than was barely necessary' (ibid., p. 123).

48   Ibid., pp. 90–1.

49   Ibid., p. 102.

50   Ibid., p. 105.

51   Ibid., p. 108.

52   Ibid.

53   Ibid., pp. 112–13.

54   Ibid., p. 113.

55   Ibid.

56   Ibid., pp. 113–14.

57   Ibid., p. 114.

58   Ibid., p. 116.

59   Ibid., p. 116.

60   Mikkel Borch-Jacobsen, 'La bande primitive', in *Le Lien affectif*, Paris, Aubier, 1991, pp. 13–31.

61   Freud., p. 86.

62   Ibid., p. 129.

63   Ibid., p. 134.

64   Ibid., p. 100.

65   Ibid.

4 The 'People' and the Discursive Production of Emptiness

1   Ernesto Laclau and Chantal Mouffe, *Hegemony and Socialist Strategy*, London, Verso, 1985, Chapter 3; Ernesto Laclau, 'New Reflections on the Revolution

of Our Time', in the book of the same title, London and New York, Verso, 1990; Ernesto Laclau, *Emancipation(s)*, London and New York, Verso, 1996, *passim*.

2   In Laclau, *Emancipation(s)*, pp. 36–46.

3   See Patricia Parker, 'Metaphor and Catachresis', in J. Bender and D. E. Wellberg (eds), *The Ends of Rhetoric: History, Theory, Practice*, Stanford, CA, Stanford University Press, 1990.

4   'Populism: What is in the Name?', in F. Panizza (ed.), *Populism and the Mirror of Democracy*, London and New York, Verso, 2005.

5   On the 'democratic' component of the notion of 'democratic demand', see the Appendix to this chapter.

6   George Rudé, *The Crowd in History: A Study of Popular Disturbances in France and England (1730–1848)*, New York – London – Sydney, John Wiley & Sons, 1964.

7   Ibid., p. 29.

8   Ibid., p. 31.

9   Ibid., p. 217.

10   Ibid., p. 224.

11   Ibid., pp. 224–5.

12   Ibid., Chapter 8.

13   Daniel Guérin, *La lutte de classes sous la première République (1793–1797)*, Paris, Gallimard, 1946, 2 vols.

14   See Laclau and Mouffe, *Hegemony and Socialist Strategy*, Chapter 3.

15   This argument is cogently developed by Joan Copjec in 'Sex and the Euthanasia of Reason', in *Read My Desire*, Cambridge (MA)/London, MIT Press, 1995, pp. 201–36.

16   Let me make myself clear: we are speaking only about a *positivation* of lack, which is possible at all because it is grounded in a more primary lack which precedes any kind of subjectivation.

17   See Georges Lavau, *À quoi sert le PCF*, Paris, Fayard, 1981.

18   Yves Mény and Yves Surel, *Par le peuple, pour le peuple. Le populisme et les démocraties*, Paris, Fayard, 2000, p. 230. The authors refer to the findings of Nonna Mayer (*Les Français qui votent FN*, Paris, Flammarion, 1999). While, in 1988 61% of the workers voted for Mitterrand in the first ballot and

70% in the second, in 1997 30% voted for Le Pen, as against 18% three years before.

19 See Chantal Mouffe, 'The End of Politics and the Challenge of Right-wing Populism', in Panizza (ed.), *Populism and Shadow of Democracy*.

20 In 'Why do empty signifiers'....

21 In S. Freud, *Group Psychology and the Analysis of the Ego* (1921), in James Strachey (ed.), *The Standard Edition of the Psychological Works of Sigmund Freud*, London, Vintage, 2001, vol. 18, p. 101.

22 Gareth Stedman Jones, 'Rethinking Chartism', *Languages of Class: Studies in Working Class History 1832–1902*, Cambridge, Cambridge University Press, 1983.

23 Ibid., p. 157.

24 Ibid., p. 169.

25 'There was no necessity for middle-class discontent to take a Chartist form. Some portion of middle-class opinion expressed its dissent from the doctrinaire policy of the Whigs in the 1830s by voting Conservative in the 1841 election. But fear and dislike of government extremism was counter-balanced by anxiety about the threatening and potentially insurrectionary character of Chartist discontent. The electorate therefore voted for a strong government promising to maintain and protect existing institutions' (*ibid*, p. 176).

26 Ibid., p. 177.

27 Jacques Rancière, *Disagreement: Politics and Philosophy*, trans. Julie Rose, Minneapolis, University of Minnesota Press, 1999, pp. 8–9.

28 Louis Althusser, 'Contradiction and Overdetermination', in *For Marx*, London, Penguin, 1969, pp. 49–86.

29 Slavoj Žižek, *The Sublime Object of Ideology*, London and New York, Verso, 1989, pp. 89–97.

30 Saul Kripke, *Naming and Necessity*, Cambridge, MA, Cambridge University Press, 1980.

31 Žižek, *The Sublime Object of Ideology*, pp. 94–5.

32 Ibid., p. 95.

33 Ibid., pp. 95–6.

34 Ibid., p. 97.

35 Paul de Man, 'The Politics of Rhetoric', in *Material Events: Paul de Man and the Afterlife of Theory*, ed. Tom Cohen, J. Hillis Miller, Andrzej Warminski and Barbara Cohen, Minneapolis, Minnesota University Press, 2001, pp. 229–53.

36 This does not mean that such a remainder of particularism belongs to the order of the signified: it is the complex of an articulated signifying ensemble which includes both signifiers and signifieds.

37 Joan Copjec, *Imagine there's no Woman: Ethics and Sublimation*, Cambridge, MA, MIT Press, 2003. All quotations from Copjec are from this edition. Page numbers are given in parentheses in text.

38 Ernesto Laclau, 'Constructing Universality', in Judith Butler, Ernesto Laclau and Slavoj Žižek, *Contingency, Hegemony, Universality: Contemporary Dialogues on the Left*, London and New York, Verso, 2000, pp. 282–4.

39 Walter Benjamin, *Reflections, Essays, Aphorisms, Autobiographical Writings*, New York, Schocken Books, p. 281.

5 Floating Signifiers and Social Heterogeneity

1 Ernesto Laclau, 'Constructing Universality', in Judith Butler, Ernesto Laclau and Slavoj Žižek, *Contingency, Hegemony, Universality. Contemporary Dialogues on the Left*, London and New York, Verso, 2000, pp. 302–5.

2 Michael Portillo, 'I'm Living Proof that Failure is Good for You', *The Sunday Times (News Review)*, 22 February 2004, p. 9.

3 Michael Kazin, *The Populist Persuasion: An American History*, Ithaca, NY, and London, Cornell University Press, 1995, p. 250. Most of my information concerning the conservative turn of populist politics in America comes from this useful book. The books by Kevin Phillips to which I refer are *The Emerging Republican Majority*, New Rochelle, NY, Arlington House, 1969; and *Mediacracy: American Parties and Politics in the Communications Age*, Garden City, NY, Doubleday, 1975.

4 Kazin, *The Populist Persuasion*, p. 251.

5 Ibid., pp. 192–3.

6 Ibid., p. 167.

7 Ibid., p. 168.

8   Ibid., p. 173.

9   See ibid., Chapter 9.

10   Ibid., pp. 222–3.

11   Ibid., p. 224.

12   Ibid., p. 246.

13   The name 'infinite of measure' does not appear either in the *Greater Logic* or in the *Encyclopaedia*, but has been proposed by W. T. Stace (*The Philosophy of Hegel*, New York, Dover, 1955). Since the category is strictly symmetrical to the qualitative and quantitative infinites, the name chosen is perfectly reasonable.

14   *Hegel's Science of Logic*, Atlantic Highlands, NJ, Humanities Press International, 1993, p. 372.

15   Warren Breckman, *Marx, the Young Hegelians and the Origins of Radical Social Theory*, Cambridge, Cambridge University Press, 1999, pp. 149–50.

16   Ibid., p. 150.

17   Peter Stallybrass, 'Marx and Heterogeneity: Thinking the Lumpenproletariat', in *Representations*, no. 31, Special Issue: The Margins of Identity in Nineteenth-Century England (Summer 1990), pp. 69–95 (p. 84).

18   Ibid., p. 83.

19   Karl Marx, *The Class Struggles in France, 1848 to 1950*, in Karl Marx and Frederick Engels, *Collected Works*, vol. 10, p. 62, London, Lawrence & Wishart, 1978.

20   Quoted by Stallybrass, 'Marx and Heterogeneity', p. 89.

21   Stallybrass quotes a passage from *The Wealth of Nations* which is quite revealing: having described the 'menial servants' as unproductive labourers, he adds: 'In the same class must be ranked some both of the gravest and most important and some of the most frivolous professions: churchmen, lawyers, physicians, men of letters of all kinds; players, buffoons, musicians, opera-singers, opera-dancers, etc. The labour of the meanest of these has a certain value, regulated by the very same principles which regulate that of every other sort of labour; and that of the noblest and most useful, produces nothing which could afterwards procure an equal quantity of labour. Like the declamation of the author, the harangue of the orator, or the tune of the musician, the work of all of them perishes in

the very instant of its production' (Stallybrass, 'Marx and Heterogeneity', p. 27. The Smith quotation comes from *The Wealth of Nations*, London, 1910, Book 2, Chapter 3, pp. 295–6.

22 Stallybrass, 'Marx and Heterogeneity', p. 88.

23 As far as I am aware, only one essay by Nun on this subject has been translated into English: 'The End of Work and the "Marginal Mass" Thesis', *Latin American Perspectives*, Issue 110, vol. 27, no. 1, January 2000, pp. 6–32. Many other essays developing this important theoretical approach exist, of course, in Spanish.

24 Ibid., p. 11.

25 For an earlier version of this argument see Ernesto Laclau, *New Reflections on the Revolution of Our Time*, London, Verso, 1990, pp. 9–10.

26 Frantz Fanon, *The Wretched of the Earth*, New York, 1968, p. 130. Quoted by Stallybrass, 'Marx and Heterogeneity', p. 89. As Stallybrass quite rightly points out, Fanon's position is quite close here to that of the early Bakunin in his defence of the revolutionary potential of the outlaw, the criminal and the bandit.

27 This is why Gramsci talked about the 'integral state' and the '*becoming* state' of the working class – not the *seizure* of state power. So far was he from conceiving of the economic struggle as different from the political one that he asserted that the construction of hegemony starts in the factory. For an opposite attempt – to regionalize the political struggle, and strictly separate it from the economic one – see this passage from Slavoj Žižek: 'The second form of leftist politics – which I also reject – could be characterized as a kind of pure politics which is associated mainly with Badiou and at least a certain version of Laclau and Mouffe. What Badiou formulates (and Balibar could also be included here) is a kind of a pure emancipatory, and although he would insist that he belongs to a Marxist lineage it is basically clear that there is no need for a Marxist critique of political economy in his work.... And although the French Jacobin orientation of pure radical politics and the more Anglo-Saxon orientation of multiculturalist struggle are opposed to each other, they nonetheless share something: the disappearance of economy as the fundamental site of the struggle' (Slavoj Žižek and Glyn Daly, *Conversations with Žižek*, London,

Polity, 2004, pp. 144–5). It is rather strange to assert so bluntly that the field of struggles in the economic sphere is totally absent from Badiou's work (and I must make it clear that Badiou's politics are very different from mine); everybody knows that *L'Organisation politique* – Badiou's movement – is almost exclusively centred in the radicalization of the workers' struggle. So where does the misunderstanding lie? The answer comes a few pages later: 'I don't mean economy in the vulgar sense of, yes we must do something for the workers' lot. I am aiming here at something more radical. I think that there is a central idea developed by Georg Lukács and The Frankfurt School which, in spite of all my criticism of the Western Marxist tradition, is today more actual than ever. The idea is that the economy is not simply one among the social spheres. The basic insight of the Marxist critique of political economy – of commodity fetishism and so on – is that the economy has a certain proto-transcendental social status.... Here again I disagree with the postmodern mantra: gender, ethnic struggle, gender, whatever, and then class. Class is not one in the series. For class, we read, of course, anti-capitalist economic struggle' (Žižek and Daly, *Conversations with Žižek*, pp. 146–7). It could hardly be clearer. The economy is a self-determined sphere endowed with 'a certain proto-transcendental status' (and the 'proto' is a mere euphemism). Needless to say, heterogeneity in the sense I have defined it has to be rigorously excluded. We know, however, that without heterogeneity there can be no antagonism and no struggle. Not surprisingly, Žižek has to exclude from an emancipatory politics in the economic sphere not only multicultural struggles but also those of the workers to improve their conditions. His quarrel, given his vision of the economy, is not with this or that kind of struggle, but with the notion of 'struggle' *tout court*. It is true that at the end of the passage he takes from his hat the rabbit of 'anti-capitalist economic struggle', but this is merely gestural: he cannot provide a single example of such a struggle. It is not surprising: once he has determined an *objective* regional territory as the necessary area of emergence of a 'fundamental' antagonism, he cannot maintain a notion of heterogeneity which, by definition, subverts territorial delimitations. I shall return to this issue in Concluding Remarks.

28 Georges Bataille, 'The Psychological Structure of Fascism', in Fred Botting and Scott Wilson (eds), *The Bataille Reader*, Oxford, Blackwell, 2000, pp. 122–46. Page numbers of the quotes are given in the text.

29 Jeffrey Mehlman (*Revolution and Repetition: Marx/Hugo/Balzac*, Berkeley, 1977) has convincingly argued that the element of heterogeneity, and its break with the notion of class representation, leads to the breakdown of the totalizing ambitions of the dialectics. Stallybrass ('Marx and Heterogeneity', pp. 80–2) has objected that starting from heterogeneity, Marx is able to reintroduce a homogenizing movement of a dialectical type. While I agree that the homogenizing moment is not perhaps given its true weight by Mehlman, I think he is right to assert that heterogeneity undoes dialectical totalization. Whatever the importance of the homogenizing tendencies, it is clear that, after the passage through heterogeneity, we will be dealing with a homogeneity which would be essentially non-dialectical.

6 Populism, Representation and Democracy

1 Ernest Barker, *Reflections on Government* (1942). Quoted by Hanna Fenichel Pitkin, *The Concept of Representation*, Berkeley – Los Angeles – London, University of California Press, 1967, p. 109.

2 What follows in this paragraph and the next is a summary of an argument that I have presented more thoroughly in 'Power and Representation', in *Emancipation(s)*, London and New York, Verso, 1996.

3 Pitkin, *The Concept of Representation*.

4 Ibid., p. 106.

5 Ibid., pp. 106–7.

6 Ibid., p. 107.

7 Ibid., p. 111.

8 This point is what separates my approach from that of Hardt and Negri, which I discuss below in Concluding Remarks.

9 These various models are extensively discussed in Chantal Mouffe, *The Democratic Paradox*, London and New York, Verso, 2000, *passim*.

10 I am quoting from Lefort's essay 'The Question of Democracy', in

Democracy and Political Theory, Minneapolis, University of Minnesota Press, 1988, pp. 9–20. Page numbers of our quotes are indicated in the text.

11 *The Democratic Paradox.*

12 Ibid., p. 2.

13 Ibid., pp. 2–3.

14 Ibid., pp. 95–6.

7 The Saga of Populism

1 Yves Surel, 'Berlusconi, leader populiste?', in *La Tentation populiste en Europe*, sous la direction de Oliver Ihl, Janine Chêne, Eric Vial, Ghislain Wartelot, Paris, La Découverte, 2003, pp. 113–29.

2 H. G. Betz, *Radical Right-Wing Populism in Western Europe*, New York, St. Martin's Press, 1994.

3 Surel, 'Berlusconi', p. 116. See also Yves Mény and Yves Surel, *Par le peuple, pour le peuple. Le Populisme et les démocraties*, Paris, Fayard, 2000.

4 Surel, 'Berlusconi', p. 127.

5 Andreas Schedler, 'Anti-Political Establishment Parties', *Party Politics*, vol. 2, no. 3, 1996, pp. 291–312.

6 See Guy Hermet, *Les populismes dans le monde. Une histoire sociologique XIXe–XXe siècles*, Paris, Fayard, 2001, pp. 181–92, where a similar thesis is defended.

7 Ibid., pp. 185–6.

8 Ibid., p. 190.

9 William Brierley and Luca Giacometti, 'Italian National Identity and the Failure of Regionalism', in Brian Jenkins and Spyros A. Sofos (eds), *Nation and Identity in Contemporary Europe*, London, Routledge, 1996, pp. 172–97.

10 Especially the Partito Socialista Italiano of Bettino Craxi.

11 On the League, I have consulted Brierley and Giacometti, 'Italian National Identity'; Christophe Bouilland, 'La Lega Nord, ou comment ne pas réussir à être populiste (1989–2002)', in Ihl, Chêne, Vial and Wartelot, *La Tentation populiste en Europe*, pp. 130–45; I. Diamanti, *La Lega. Geografia, storia e sociologia di un nuovo soggetto politico*, Rome, Donzelli, 1993; R. Mannehimer (ed.), *La Lega Lombarda*, Milan, Feltrinelli, 1991; R Borcio, *La Padania promessa.*

La storia, la idea e la logica d'azione della Lega Nord, Milan, Il Saggiatore, 1997.

12 The Alleanza Nazionale, led by Gianfranco Fini, is a descendant of the Movimento Soziale Italiano, the neo-Fascist organization founded at the end of the Second World War by Giorgio Almirante. Today it has broken most ties with its Fascist past. On the difference with the League, it has no strong regional leanings: since it corresponds to a force proceeding from the Fascist tradition, it favours a strong centralized state.

13 Brierley and Giacometti, 'Italian National Identity', p. 184.

14 Ibid., p. 186.

15 Ibid.

16 Bouillaud, 'La Lega Nord', *passim*.

17 See Borcio, *La Padania promessa*; Diamanti, *La Lega*.

18 Bouillaud, 'La Lega Nord', pp. 142–4.

19 Surel, 'Berlusconi', passim.

20 Ibid., p. 123.

21 See various chapters of Jenkins and Sofos, *Nation and Identity in Contemporary Europe*, and Hermet, *Les Populismes dans le monde*, Chapter VIII.

22 This assertion, however, requires some qualification. In countries with a sizeable Indian population, there was a nativism which at some moments approached ethnic populism.

23 See Hermet, *Les Populismes dans le monde*, pp. 253–4.

24 Ibid., p. 255.

25 Ibid., p. 268.

26 See Spyros A. Sofos, 'Culture, Politics and Identity in Former Yugoslavia', in Jenkins and Sofos, *National Identity in Contemporary Europe*, pp. 251–82.

27 'The regime encouraged revival of Serbian-Orthodox rituals such as the mass baptisms of Serbs and Montenegrins in Kosovo Polje, or the procession of the alleged remains of Prince Lazar through a series of sacred sites and monasteries en route to Kosovo Polje where they were reinterred. The return of the defeated prince to the place where the Serbs had been defeated by the Turks and he lost his life gave the impression of a complete circle, a "new beginning". Both rituals constituted a symbolic confirmation of the will of the Serb nation to restore and reclaim its dignity' (ibid., p. 279, n. 35).

28 Ibid., pp. 268–9.

29   Jürgen Habermas, *The Inclusion of the Other. Studies in Political Theory*, Cambridge, MA, MIT Press, 1998, p. 225.

8 Obstacles and Limits to the Construction of the 'People'

1   The literature on twentieth-century American Populism is almost inexhaustible, and has often been submitted to interpretative shifts governed by ideological biases. For a good summary of this discussion, see Margaret Canovan, *Populism*, London, Junction Books, 1981, pp. 46–51. My own reading of the period has been particularly influenced by Lawrence Goodwyn, *Democratic Promise: The Populist Movement in America*, New York, Oxford University Press, 1976; and Michael Kazin, *The Populist Persuasion*, Ithaca, NY, and London, Cornell University Press, 1998. Subsequent references to these two works will be given parenthetically in the text.

2   This document is reproduced in John D. Hicks, *The Populist Revolt. A History of the Farmers' Alliance and the People's Party*, Lincoln, University of Nebraska Press, 1970, pp. 435–9.

3   See Paul Dumont, 'The Origins of Kemalist Ideology', in Jacob M. Landau (ed.), *Atatürk and the Modernization of Turkey*, Boulder, CO, Westview Press, 1984, pp. 21–44.

4   Ibid., p. 31.

5   Quoted in ibid., p. 32.

6   Quoted in ibid., p. 33.

7   Ibid., p. 34.

8   Quoted in ibid., p. 29.

9   Ibid., p. 36.

10   For this thesis, as well as a good discussion of the relevant literature on the subject, see Dietrich Jung and Wolfango Piccoli, *Turkey at the Crossroads: Ottoman Legacies and a Greater Middle East*, London and New York, Zed Books, 2001.

11   See ibid., p. 44.

12   See S. Mardin, 'Ideology and Religion in the Turkish Revolution', *International Journal of Middle East Studies* (2), pp. 197–211.

13   Quoted in Jung and Piccoli, *Turkey at the Crossroads*, pp. 79–80.

14 Ibid., p. 79. The work by Sayari cited by the authors is 'Political Patronage in Turkey', in E. Gellner and J. Waterbury (eds), *Patrons and Clients in Mediterranean Societies*, London, Duckworth, 1977, pp. 103–14.

15 See Eric J. Zürcher, *Turkey: A Modern History*, London and New York, I. B. Tauris, 1998, p. 231.

16 On Peronist enunciation, see Silvia Sigal and Eliseo Verón, *Perón o muerte. Los fundamentos discursivos del fenómeno peronista*, Buenos Aires, Legasa, 1985. See also G. H. Castagnola, *Body of Evidence: Juan Domingo Perón's Discourse during His Political Exile (1955–1972)*, PhD thesis, Department of Government, University of Essex, October 2000.

17 Castagnola, *Body of Evidence*, p. 63.

18 Ibid., p. 79.

19 Ibid., pp. 138–9.

20 Margaret Canovan, 'Trust the People! Populism and the Two Faces of Democracy', *Political Studies*, XLVII, 1999, pp. 2–16.

Concluding Remarks

1 Edward Wong, 'Iraqi Nationalism Takes Root, Sort Of', *New York Times*, 25 April 2004, section 4, p. 1.

2 Ibid., p. 16.

3 Alenka Zupančič, *Ethics of the Real: Kant, Lacan*, London and New York, Verso, 2000.

4 Ibid., p. 11. Zupančič is referring to Kant here, but she assimilates the Kantian position on this point to Lacan's: 'Is not Lacan's own conception of the *passage à l'acte* itself founded on such a Kantian gesture?'

5 Ibid., p. 204.

6 Ibid., p. 255.

7 Such a discussion should move in the direction of a typology of situations and movements. The aim of *On Populist Reason* has been more limited: the determination of the basic operations of populist reason.

8 I will be referring mainly to Žižek's interventions in Judith Butler, Ernesto Laclau, and Slavoj Žižek, *Contingency, Hegemony, Universality: Contemporary Dialogues on the Left* (London and New York, Verso, 2000). Subsequent

references will appear parenthetically within the text. Given the procedures we established to write this book, I could read Žižek's last pieces only once I had already written mine, so there was no opportunity for me, within the context of that book, to answer his latest criticisms of my work. So what follows is, to some extent, my reply. It does not, however, cover the whole of Žižek's critique, only those aspects connected to the main subject of this book.

9 This misreading is, I must say, rather disingenuous, for in other works Žižek shows a perfect understanding of my arguments. Thus he says approvingly: 'It is the merit of Ernesto Laclau and Chantal Mouffe that they have, in *Hegemony and Socialist Strategy* ... developed a theory of the social field founded on such a notion of antagonism – on an acknowledge-ment of an original "trauma", an impossible kernel which resists symbolization, totalization, symbolic integration.... They emphasize that we must not be "radical" in the sense of aiming at a radical solution: we always live in an interspace and in borrowed time; every solution is provisional and temporary, a kind of postponing of a fundamental impos-sibility' (*The Sublime Object of Ideology*, London and New York, Verso, 1989, pp. 5–6).

10 Slavoj Žižek and Glyn Daly, *Conversations with Žižek*, Cambridge, Polity, 2004, p. 149.

11 During our discussion in *Contingency, Hegemony, Universality*, I asked Žižek repeatedly to specify who, for him, the emancipatory subject was and what the general strategic line was that he proposed in order that the debate might proceed on more political and less 'metaphysical' grounds. No reply was forthcoming.

12 Michael Hardt and Antonio Negri, *Empire*, Cambridge, MA, Harvard University Press, 2000.

13 Jacques Rancière, *Disagreement: Politics and Philosophy*, trans. Julie Rose, Minneapolis, University of Minnesota Press, 1999, p. 9. Subsequent refer-ences will appear parenthetically within the text.

14 Sigmund Freud, *Group Psychology and the Analysis of the Ego*, in *The Standard Edition of the Complete Psychological Works of Sigmund Freud*, ed. and trans. James Strachey *et al.*, London, Hogarth Press, 1953–1974, vol. 18, p. 91.

Index